Dark Laughter

WISCONSIN FILM STUDIES

Patrick McGilligan
Series Editor

Dark Laughter

*Spanish Film, Comedy,
and the Nation*

Juan F. Egea

The University of Wisconsin Press

Publication of this volume has been made possible, in part, through support from the
Anonymous Fund of the College of Letters and Science at the University of Wisconsin–Madison.

The University of Wisconsin Press
1930 Monroe Street, 3rd Floor
Madison, Wisconsin 53711-2059
uwpress.wisc.edu

3 Henrietta Street
London WC2E 8LU, England
eurospanbookstore.com

Library of Congress Cataloging-in-Publication Data

Egea, Juan F.
Dark laughter : Spanish film, comedy, and the nation / Juan F. Egea.
p.   cm. — (Wisconsin film studies)
Includes bibliographical references and index.
ISBN 978-0-299-29544-8 (pbk. : alk. paper) — ISBN 978-0-299-29543-1 (e-book)
1. Motion pictures, Spanish—History and criticism. 2. Comedy films—Spain—History
and criticism. 3. Black humor—Spain. I. Title. II. Series: Wisconsin film studies.
PN1993.5.S7E34   2013
791.430946—dc23
2013010413

To Sarli and Sofía, for all their love and laughter

Contents

Illustrations

Acknowledgments

Even though I dedicate this book to them, I also need to acknowledge my wife's and daughter's constant support and understanding. Writing on comedy can be fun, but it is still writing, and both Sarli and Sofia either forgave or pretended they did not notice the moodiness and the crankiness when things were not moving along smoothly. I think they do like me.

I would also like to thank my colleagues in the Department of Spanish and Portuguese at the University of Wisconsin–Madison. They have pushed my scholarship in great measure just by being solid and generous scholars themselves. It is peer pressure, and they do not even suspect it. I have a special debt of gratitude to those of them who actively participated in making my English and my thoughts clearer and sounder: Glen Close, Bill Cudlipp, David Hildner, Steve Hutchinson, Will Risley, and Kathryn Sanchez. John Burns, from Rockford College, also suffered my linguistic *sablazos* and provided me with much more than style recommendations. If my academic prose still has some awkward moments, it is solely due to the stubbornness of a nonnative demanding flexibility from rules he thinks should apply to him differently.

Earlier versions of two chapters in this book were published in scholarly journals, and I am grateful to the publishers for their permission to use that material here. Part of chapter 2 appeared in Spanish as "Paralítico o no: Comedia irónica, disidencia e identidad en *El cochecito*," *Anales de literatura española contemporánea* 28.1 (2003): 77–93. An earlier version of chapter 3, also in Spanish, was published with the title "Para una anatomía de la complicidad: *El verdugo* de Berlanga," *Letras peninsulares* 19.2/19.3 (Fall/Winter 2006–7): 211–26. A section of chapter 7 was published in the book *Contemporary Spanish Cinema and Genre*, edited by Jay Beck and Vicente Rodríguez Ortega (Manchester: Manchester University Press, 2008), 107–21, with the title "*Justino, un asesino de la tercera edad*: Spanishness, Dark Comedy and Horror." I thank the people at Manchester University Press for their kind permission to reprint that text here.

Finally, I also want to thank the two anonymous readers who helped me with their thorough comments, as well as all the individuals at the University of Wisconsin Press who have made the publication of this book possible. I am especially indebted to Raphael Kadushin, who believed in this project from day one and pushed me, as gently as any editor would ever do, to stop taking forever and to not forget Almodóvar.

While my family in Spain did not help me with any single word, I feel they are in each and every one of them. Their sacrifices for the one who left must be acknowledged at the onset of anything I would ever write.

Dark Laughter

Introduction

The early 1960s in Spain witnessed a series of dark cinematic comedies that all but constitute an autochthonous variation on that genre in the film medium. *El pisito* (Marco Ferreri, 1959), *El cochecito* (Marco Ferreri, 1960), *Viridiana* (Luis Buñuel, 1961), *Plácido* (Luis García Berlanga, 1961), *El verdugo* (Luis García Berlanga, 1963), and *El extraño viaje* (Fernando Fernán-Gómez, 1964) are all comedic film narrations that seem to problematize the moment of, and the occasion for, laughter. These are also movies that address—and that in many ways question—the new phase of economic modernization and development that Franco's dictatorial regime entered after two long decades of postwar autarchy. Laughter, dictatorship, developmental capitalism, and cultural identity are, thus, the basic building blocks of this study on Spanish cinema and culture whose critical objective is threefold.

First, I am interested in identifying the conditions of possibility of the *Spanish dark comedy* film genre and, subsequently, in evaluating its place within European cinematic modernity as well as the particular concept of modernity it helped to reframe. What makes all these films *dark* comedies, what makes them *Spanish*, and in what ways they engage with *the modern* are the crucial questions at this stage, questions that inevitably point toward the role played by film genres in the conceptualization of that fraught and contentious entity called "national cinema."

My second objective is to explore the ways in which cinematic texts mediate the socioeconomic context in which they are produced and exhibited. Hence I am interested not only in understanding cinema as cultural praxis but also in examining cinema's relations with the cultural discourses that surround it.

3

Neither reflections nor documents, these Spanish dark narratives are, more exactly, *interventions* in a dictatorship's picture-producing machine bent on projecting images of socioeconomic bliss. A significant reflection on the processes of film spectatorship will therefore be an integral part of what this book does with a series of movies that, first and foremost, do not allow for a moral safe haven from which to watch them.

The third and final objective of my research program is to give an account of the manner in which these film productions contribute to the understanding of a culturally specific identity in the realm of the visual and the province of the comic. In the literature about Spanish cinema, it has become commonplace to invoke the names of the painter Goya and the playwright Valle-Inclán—and their respective aesthetics, *lo goyesco* and *el esperpento*—to elucidate the particularities of the country's film production. The sixteenth-century *picaresca* genre; the work of Cervantes; the eighteenth-century short, comic theatrical pieces with stock social types known as *sainetes*; and even the musical genre *zarzuela* (or Spanish popular operetta) are also liberally used as cultural and aesthetic references in the study of Spanish film. Cultural specificity, indeed, is the name of the game, and the way to play it is to incorporate into one's film criticism not only a distinctively Spanish history (which could include the country's much-discussed belated or "uneven" modernity, its civil war, and the subsequent thirty-six-year-long dictatorship) but also the plastic arts, popular music, and literature. More or less explicitly, *Spanishness* is the frequently invoked term at this juncture, a term whose suspicious essentialism does not spare us from the need to investigate its actual contexts and contours within the country's cultural production. Spanishness is, in fact, the concept that this study will present not so much for consideration but rather as a means for interrogation within the context of cultural and visual studies.

The first chapter of this study will deal with all these questions and establish the theoretical and methodological underpinnings of my research project. Questions of film genre, or "family resemblances," will find a place there, as will disquisitions about imagining rather than imagined communities, the visual expression of nationhood, the modalities of film modernity, and what it means to laugh darkly.

After this introductory section, four chapters—what may be considered the core of this book—focus on four of the movies enumerated above. While *El cochecito* investigates the dawn of a consumerist society that is also the beginning of an uncharted moral order in a brand new world of desires and commodities (chapter 2), *El verdugo* dissects the mechanisms by which an ordinary citizen becomes the accomplice of a totalitarian, oftentimes lethal regime (chapter 3).

While *Viridiana* presents two projects of community regeneration that end in either tragic or ironic degeneration (chapter 4), *El extraño viaje* brings both murder and modernity to the small-village Spain of the early sixties in order to render it deeply sinister and hopelessly naive in equal measure (chapter 5). In what may seem a deliberate simplification at this point, I am ready to say that chapter 2 is essentially about consumerism as well as about the possibility of dissidence under totalitarianism and that chapter 3 presents the prospect that, under those circumstances, daily, widespread connivance with the official languages of propriety and control may be unavoidable. Along the same simplifying lines, I should add that chapter 4 tackles the ethical and visual uses of perversion and that chapter 5 shows how the indigenous and the modern are able to fight and feed each other at the same time. Read in light of one another, these cinematic texts amount to a filmic anatomy of the mechanisms of complicity and the possibilities of innocence within a very specific social and moral order. They also offer a collection of moving images and cinematic figures of lasting influence in the country's cultural imaginary. The last two chapters of the book are dedicated to evaluating the wide-ranging influence of that dark laughter in Spanish film, as well as the new aesthetic and geopolitical uses that young generations of Spanish filmmakers find for it.

In chapter 6 I revisit the first three feature films directed by the most recognizable name in contemporary Spanish cinema: Pedro Almodóvar. Dark humor has a prominent role in both *Pepi, Luci, Bom y otras chicas del montón* (1980) and *Laberinto de pasiones* (1982), his first two productions, the ones he filmed during the years of the so-called *La Movida* and within the time frame of the country's political transition from authoritarianism to democracy. Dark humor is also a prominent factor in how his third film, *Entre tinieblas* (1983), intervenes in the representational practices that both express and respond to newfound national freedoms and anxieties. Almodóvar, then, will be treated here as a dark humorist too, one who adds a particularly disorienting laughter to the transitional years in Spain.

Finally, in chapter 7 I will trace the presence of the Spanish classic dark comedies of the 1960s as they can be found in the new dark comedies of the 1990s. This was the decade in which the country staged its most spectacular and complex display of Europeanness and regionalism: the Universal Exposition in Seville, the Barcelona Olympic Games, Madrid's term as European cultural capital, and the opening of the Guggenheim Museum in Bilbao. *Acción mutante*, directed by Alex de la Iglesia in 1993, as well as Luis Guridi and Santiago Aguilar's *Justino, un asesino de la tercera edad* (1994) will constitute the case studies through which to extrapolate the insights in my first five chapters to a very different moment in Spanish history where, not coincidentally, openness and display (or, indeed, "how to look Spanish") were also the favored terms and issues in the institutional production of national images.

Inspired by Stanley Cavell's *Pursuits of Happiness: The Hollywood Comedy of Remarriage*, this book aspires to be an exercise in thinking *about*, as well as *with* and even *through*, film. The subjects I hope to have thought through by the end of these pages are the epistemic potential of dark humor, the nature of visual modernity, and the workings of cultural specificity.

1

Familiar Questions

I am not writing the history of the genre in question but proposing its logic.

Stanley Cavell, *Pursuits of Happiness*

Some might see it as unworkable to try to cross-fertilize the sweeping and
often outlandishly unrooted claims of comedy theory with an interest in the
historical specifics of cultural representation, but I would insist that each needs
the other if comedy is ever to be fully understood.

Andy Medhurst, *A Popular Joke*

Scholarly discussions of film genre inevitably become discussions of categorization that, in turn, tell us as much about the organization of the critics'
minds as they do about any meaningful connections within any given group of
films. To put it otherwise, a given cognitive model both enables and limits any
exercise in film genre description and formation. Let us consider, for instance,
the following classifications: documentaries, Westerns, road movies, indie films,
melodramas of the unknown woman, cult films, film noirs, short films, action/
adventure movies, chick flicks, prison films, political biopics, the swimming
musicals of Esther Williams, and British war films after the US entrance into
World War II. Such a list of film genres does not seem so far removed from
the famous Borgean animal catalog, which starts with "those that belong to the
emperor," ends with "those that resemble flies from a distance," and takes into
account "those that are included in this classification."[1] The first problem in film
genre studies, then, is one of categorization, which entails having a fairly clear

idea of the kind of conceptual monster a category actually is. Cognitive science tells us that the categories of colors and birds, for instance, not only consist of a different set of members but also constitute, respectively, a class where a member's gradience is the organizing factor and a very different kind of grouping where the chief factor is a prototype-effect structure.[2] Would discussions of film genre benefit more from one or the other? Does it make any critical difference if we identify a prototype from which all the other members of the genre may stem? Does a "gradient approach" make film genre theory a more flexible, decentered undertaking?

To begin one's approach to the methodological problems facing genre studies by quoting Borges and invoking cognitive science is to re-express what a large number of genre theorists have been repeating since at least the 1970s: that genres overlap, that most genres are easier to recognize than to define, and that not even a distinction between genres and subgenres will save us from turning into what Andrew Tudor called "neurotic critics." Once one begins to suffer from such a condition, an anxiety of definitions, a craving for taxonomies, and a nervous policing of borders is soon to follow.[3] Let us, then, specify what cognitive model and which criteria could make it possible to speak of the movies I listed above as a distinctive film genre.

The Spanish cinematographic dark comedy, as a category, is not to be understood simply as a set of films in which all its members share common properties; nor does it need to be seen solely as one in which there is a specific "X factor" that grants membership. Rather, it is all a matter of resemblance — of family resemblances, that is. The term *family resemblances*, as Wittgenstein conceived it in his philosophical remarks on games, does not necessarily entail the existence of common factors among all members of a presupposed category. Family resemblances have more to do with an act of seeing (in the particular way Wittgenstein understands the human capability to do so) that results in the appreciation of "a complicated network of similarities overlapping and criss-crossing: sometimes overall, sometimes in detail."[4] As qualified by Stanley Cavell, this concept acquires more relevance in the study of film genres whose conditions of recognizability depend less on common features among the members of a given category than on each and every member's capability for mutual illumination. Cavell's "comedies of remarriage" constitute a genre "not merely [because] they look like one another or [because] one gets similar impressions from them"; they do so because "they *are what they are* in view of one another."[5]

Even if we have a ready-made category such as the "dark" or, more ambiguously, "black" comedy, the series of movies with which I concern myself henceforth constitute a particular kind of dark comedy when viewed in light of one another. More precisely, they do so when that which is prioritized in their viewing is, so to speak, their grammar. To call them Spanish dark comedies is, of course, to factor considerations of nationality into the discussion of film genre. Yet to determine what makes them Spanish represents a more complex issue than acknowledging their geopolitical coordinates or their production credits. At this stage of the discussion, we are in fact brought to the thorny issue of national specificity with regard to subject matter, filmic narrative form, aesthetics, and, in this case, sense of humor.

I will address all of these issues here, as well as in the film readings that constitute the following chapters. Suffice it to say for now that the notion of family resemblances enables a discussion of this collection of films as a genre for which, as the epigraph that opened this chapter advanced, I will not be writing a history but proposing a logic. I imagine such a task to be germane in some degree to Fredric Jameson's understanding of genre criticism as an undertaking that "does not properly involve classification or typology but rather that very different thing, a reconstruction of the *conditions of possibility* of a given work or a formal practice."[6] By situating my research project in such a way, I seek to avoid a number of genre criticism's pitfalls and inertias, compulsory historicism being the most conspicuous of them. However, in a project that does after all begin by invoking the category of genre criticism, there are a number of concepts, issues, and concerns that, inasmuch as they seem inherent to virtually any discussion of film genre, must at least be touched upon here. Without attempting to rehearse what is already a long, often contentious debate on the critical advantages and shortcomings of genre criticism, I hasten to identify those arguments within that debate that will be of consequence to this study.

The Making of an Imagining Community

Film genre studies, we are told, warrant an approach to movies whereby familiarity is the operative concept and where a dynamics of repetition and variation produces both the satisfaction of recognition and the pleasure of being able to detect differences. As much agreement as this approach would elicit, it seems to bring about some critical qualms as well. If, as Barry Keith Grant notes, genre films "tell familiar stories with familiar characters in familiar situations," we need to ask ourselves at some point where this familiarity comes from and what exactly it entails.[7] Grant links the notion of familiarity to "similar films we have already seen," immediately calling attention to an unspecified first-person plural pronoun, which, as is often the case, could be as much exclusive as it is inclusive.[8] In other words, when it comes to comedy—and especially to dark comedies — who gets the joke and who doesn't is the benchmark for measuring the possible communal and hence exclusionary properties of film genres. As theoretically unsophisticated as it may seem, "getting the joke" is still an apt expression with which to broach subjects such as the workings of cultural *untranslatability* or the possible existence of a "national" sense of humor. Whether the familiarity bred by the movies *we* (i.e., the members of a specific geopolitical cultural community) have already seen either consolidates or unsettles the image *we* have of ourselves, the crucial point is to identify under what conditions the notion of "familiarity" turns film genres, in this case the dark comedy, into a (mainly) visual reflection on cultural specificity.

Film genres, we are also told, are equivalent to social myth. Even if a ritual approach to genre criticism has been both proposed and contested, film genres seem especially conducive to being read in connection with social or national anxieties and hence treated as the expression of a particular Zeitgeist.[9] The escapist value of the Depression-era musical, for instance, has become a critical cliché. Horror and science fiction movies in particular have lent themselves to readings that reveal them as expressions of collective fears or moral concerns. As for comedy in general, its role in the understanding of cultural identity cannot be understated. In James English's words, "comic practice is always on some level or in some measure an assertion of group against group, an effect and an event of struggle, a form of symbolic violence. The inescapable heterogeneity of society, the ceaseless conflict of social life, the multiple and irreconcilable patterns of identification within which relationships of hierarchy and solidarity must be negotiated — these are what our laughter is 'about.'"[10]

Given all this, the methodological problem, of course, is (or continues to be) the relation between text and context. In the particular case of this series of movies, it is my contention that, as a culturally specific film genre, they constitute what I have already called an *intervention* into a certain society under a very concrete set of historical circumstances. To put it in a way that may clarify my verbal choice, whatever these movies are or do, they should not be considered as reductive illustrations of a period, nor should they be seen as texts that merely reflect or document a precise milieu. Within the field of classic genre criticism, Andrew Tudor's take on the matter seems to me to be the closest to my approach. In his opinion, "genre terms seem best employed in the analysis of the relation between groups of films, the cultures in which they are made, and the cultures in which they are exhibited. That is, it is a term that can be usefully employed in relation to a body of knowledge and theory about the social and psychological context of film."[11] More recently, Christine Gledhill has called for an understanding of genre that is capable of "exploring the wider contextual culture in relationship to, rather than as an originating source of, aesthetic mutations and textual complications."[12] Rather than a corpus of movies to be studied, a particular genre can thus be a tool, a means of cultural analysis. A film genre's powers to engage with its sociocultural surroundings could be aptly described as a *contentious entanglement* rather than a *social myth* or a *ritual*. The movies that constitute many a film genre add to that same contemporary world at large that makes them possible: they do not illuminate that world as much as they "burst" into it. Movies, certain movies, usually undo comfortable totalities. Going a step further, they may even be said to constitute and exercise in counter-imagination. This is precisely what I see the particular film genre identified in this study as doing in the Spain of the early 1960s and beyond.

With this selective detour on issues of film genre criticism I have wanted to underline how much the notion of film genre itself overlaps with concepts like "cultural specificity" and "national cinema." We need to remember that genre criticism started as an attempt to identify "national" ways of making movies and that the outcome of many of our most insightful genre studies emphasizes the potential of genres to ultimately *generate* an audience. In a more conventional formulation, we are truly dealing here with the potential of cinema as a social and discursive practice that "constructs national subjects."[13] This would imply that "genre and nation are intrinsically and complexly linked[, since] genre's ability to construct and contain meaning for an audience is very similar to how national discourses interpellate a citizenry."[14] One could even speak of film genre as a set of formal conventions and thematic variations that, first and foremost, enable a viewing or, better, an *imagining* community.

Imagined Communities is, of course, the title of Benedict Anderson's classic study "on the origin and spread of nationalism," as its subtitle reads. It has also become a ubiquitous, somewhat overused critical term, especially popular within literary and cultural studies. A number of film critics and historians have already noticed how suitable the concept is to examine the role national cinemas play in the construction of national identities. And yet, Anderson's groundbreaking book hardly deals with visual images. The first reason why the nation is an imagined political community, for instance, is "because the members of even the smallest nations will never know most of their fellow-members."[15] It has always seemed to me that the use of imagination has little to do with this way of imagining the nation. This is the only occasion in which the imagined condition of the nation as a political community is predicated in general terms. Subsequently, "imagined as" is the expression to introduce the ideas of physical limits, sovereignty, and community itself. This is not to say that the nation is imagined but that some of its attributes are. In Anderson's schema, to imagine is, more often than not, to create mental images mainly out of printed material. The novel and the newspaper are considered the crucial "forms of imagining," or the "technical means for 're-presenting' the kind of imagined community that is the nation."[16] In the second edition of the book, the map and the museum are the "institutions" that add a visual dimension to the imaginings the book analyzes, but only in relation to "late colonial states." In Anderson's book, *to imagine* often means *to assume* rather than to conjure up images of a nation in one's mind. Hence, to determine what is the role of actual visual images in the coming into being of that "cultural artifact" called nationality or "nationness" is how the trail blazed by *Imagined Communities* can be more fruitfully walked. Now, if one is true to the spirit of Anderson's book, to judge the possible role of cinema in the imagining of the nation is to take into consideration the belatedness of film with respect to a community that has been already imagined, for Anderson's book dates the birth of the nation as an imagined community with some precision: the need to imagine the nation (as a mass of fellow members, as a limited space, and as a sovereign, communal entity) begins "towards the end of the eighteenth century."[17] So, rather than collaborating in the creation of an imagined community, film must help in the refashioning (or reimagining) of a community that, historical painting notwithstanding, has been imagining itself with only very limited assistance from the realm of the visual. In other words, cinema supplies the most forceful images, the images that move, in the business of imagining oneself as part of a geopolitical and cultural community.

After the above discussion, it should be clear that in what follows I will concern myself with a genre that engages with the national, or with "nationalness," at several levels and that none of these is more important than the level of image creation. This is a genre, then, that addresses the here and now of a sociopolitical and economic milieu while at the same time engaging with an aesthetic tradition, with a culturally specific representational practice, with what we could call "its visual past."

Film Genre, Culture, and Nation

Determining what makes Spanish films "Spanish" is one of the key interests of this project, as well as a deep-rooted critical and institutional anxiety. I am particularly interested here in a recurrent desire to justify or deny the existence of a national difference (or even recognizability) in film. As previously noted, when one discusses nationality in film beyond certain parameters (e.g., the director's nationality or the production company's "legal" residence), either subject matter or formal/aesthetic tendencies become the critical foci. This certainly makes for a complex hermeneutic undertaking fraught with the perils of cultural nationalism, romantic claims to national exceptionalism, and the overuse of cultural commonplaces. Such pitfalls, in turn, have usually been avoided by taking into consideration our contemporary post- or transnational condition and by gauging the impact of today's global market for cultural products on a stable and even identifiable national culture. On the other hand, intranational differences (usually called "regional" or "peripheral") also factor into what essentially amounts to a healthy challenge to the unexamined links between the nation-state and the cultural production that takes place within its borders. In sum, it is all a question of representativity as much as of representation, one in which geopolitics and culture seem to be in a particular kind of marriage: constantly fighting and making up, always threatening a divorce they both know is not an option.

At different stages of the critical debate outlined above, and with more or less critical care, the term *Spanishness* would make an appearance as the abstraction around which the overall discussion of Spanish cultural specificity revolves.[18] Often, the meaning of such a term seems taken for granted, for it translates as a vague "quality of being Spanish," which, as definitions go, does not help to render the abstraction concrete in any measure. On other occasions, Spanishness, like the notion of national identity itself, gets introduced only to be debunked in the same critical breath. This is the case with a number of texts whose title is or includes the expression "Spanish National Cinema." However questioned, the concept has a market value in criticism as much as the movies themselves do in the economy of festivals and prize-awarding ceremonies. The term *Spanishness*, understood not as the quality of being Spanish but as the quality of being Spanish as it is thought and written about and filmed into existence, is the term I will use hereafter. Spanishness is, then, not a reality but a construct, albeit a construct with very real effects in the thinking as well as in the "making" of a cultural specificity. Hence, rather than being interested in the term's actual existence as a national essence, this study interrogates the array of narratives and images that the term has generated when it is either affirmed or abhorred. As Andy Medhurst does in his remarkable study of popular comedy and Englishness, I enter the debate on Spanishness well aware of the slippery grounds that may lead my critical discourse straight to academic nationalism. Indeed, "when comedy concerns itself, either directly or obliquely, with something as fraught, contested and unstable as questions of 'the nation,'" one needs to be on guard against unacknowledged patriotism (or at least as mindful of it, I may add, just as one must be wary of the temptation to declare the nation extinct).[19]

Paraphrasing Paul Gilroy, I must state the obvious and say that, in the end, "you have to put it [the nation] somewhere."[20] That "somewhere" may very well be an extremely unstable perch that is continuously shaken by multifarious discourses, conflicting symbolic interests, belligerent ideologies, and defiant heterogeneities. Yet there the nation stands, always to be wrestled with and not simply disposed of. My interest in keeping the term *Spanishness* as an operative notion in the analysis of cultural specificity follows from that understanding of a needed "somewhere" to discuss the nation, and to discuss it, in this case, as it has been filmed.

Since virtually the birth of the Spanish film industry, Spanishness has been omnipresent, even an obsession, in describing or in fact prescribing the nature of this particular national cinema. In *Para grandes y chicos: Un cine para los españoles, 1940–1990*, Valeria Camporesi provides us with a useful account of this obsession. Drawing from an ample selection of opinions by filmmakers, film journalists, and politicians, the book documents the ongoing debate regarding the concept of Spanishness (*españolidad*) in film from the 1920s to the early 1970s. The related (and usually pejorative) term *españolada* receives a great deal of attention and is in fact a key term to which I shall return shortly. After her historical survey, Camporesi identifies at least five ways to interpret the concept of Spanishness in Spanish cinema, although here I will take into consideration only the first three.

The first way takes Spanishness in film to be a "synonym of the recuperation and diffusion of the country's intellectual traditions."[21] In this approach to the cultural specificity of the Spanish cinema, the task is to recover "high-culture, precinematographic traditions" for the new medium.[22] A second way to call for Spanishness in Spanish cinema, or to identify it in its productions, is to speak of *costumbrismo*. Understood as the idealized manner in which the everyday is depicted, also thought of as the discourses of the popular or the picturesque that infuse the literary, graphic, and pictorial production of a number of authors during the nineteenth century, *costumbrismo* here refers to a specific film topic such as *bandolerismo* (the bandit movie genre), to subgenres such as the "regional" cinema, and finally to the influence of the *sainete*, a popular theater genre born in the late eighteenth century and still very much in vogue during the 1920s. The third way to understand Spanishness in cinema, according to Camporesi's archival research, is to connect it with the existence of a certain Spanish realism—a realism that, as the more patriotic commentators would have it, stands as "Spain's contribution to the arts."[23]

As previously noted, Camporesi draws from an assortment of views and opinions that may end up having more or less critical weight. In fact, her explicit interest is the remarks that "critics, intellectuals, directors, screenwriters, and movie business professionals in general" make in cinema journals for a "nonspecialized audience."[24] Accordingly, the resulting trio of different yet tangential ideas of Spanishness in film does not lay the foundation for a theory of cinematic Spanishness. Still, these ideas certainly condense a number of instructive conceptions and misconceptions regarding the link between *cinema* and *nation* in Spain. Among the three listed interpretations of Spanishness, two of them (*costumbrismo* and Spanish realism) clearly refer to formal or aesthetic qualities, while the first one (the recuperation of precinematic traditions) could include questions of either style or subject matter. Spanishness, then, has a noncinematic tradition to which it is responding and a culturally specific way of "looking real" or "being popular."

As it relates to the series of movies that constitute my main object of study, their Spanishness has been equated, sometimes in a more overt way than others, to their alleged *costumbrismo*. They have also been associated with the related terms *zarzuela* and, especially, *sainete*. Likewise, most of them have been connected to a somewhat "*esperpentic*" tone, more often than not without any detailing of what such a cinematographic tone would owe to any actual Valle-Inclán play that would warrant such a connection. Both popular reactions and scholarly approaches to movies like *Plácido*, *El verdugo*, *El extraño viaje*, and *Viridiana* rely on identifying national traits because of the characters, the situations, the dialogue, or the representational traditions they invoke.

The notion that something could be easily distinguished as very Spanish (or as very British, for that matter) is the direct outcome of a broad vision of national culture as difference — whose condition of visibility seems to depend on overstatement. What Camporesi's study ultimately makes evident is that Spanishness in film (as a concept, as a topic of serious conversation) cannot be understood without its counterpart, or, better, without its opposite in a dialectic sense: the so-called *españolada*, a term that refers to both bad films and films that offer exaggerated images of an alleged Spanish character. In fact, in film commentary and criticism, Spanishness seems to exist as a term that signals the overacting, the overdramatizing, or the overdoing of national identity as performance. The excessive way to appear Spanish seems to be the precondition to most discussion of the value and meaning of Spanishness, which is to say that the statements on national identity in film have to do with attempts at repressing an excess of representation. If we add to this intricate reflection the fact that, ever since the era of silent movies, the dialectic relation between *la españolada* and Spanishness is inextricably linked to anxieties regarding how to present

the nation to an international audience, then the concepts of display, performance, spectacle, and self-fashioning begin to gain relevance in the discussion
of national identity in Spanish film. Put otherwise, the debate on cultural differentiation in Spanish culture — call it the debate on Spanishness — has revolved
largely around the issue of how to *look* rather than how to *be* Spanish. Ontology
and visuality have been constantly conflated, paving the way to what, for all
intents and purposes, shall be understood as a visual ontology.

I do not wish for this to sound like I am rehearsing, albeit with a different
vocabulary, the classic topos of reality versus appearances. What I would like
to underscore instead is precisely the fracture of this polarity, at least in the
context of Spanish modernity. As Stanley Cavell says of the dichotomy fan-
tasy/reality, "it is a poor idea of fantasy which takes it to be a world apart from
reality, a world clearly showing its unreality. Fantasy is precisely what reality
can be confused with."[25] To some degree, infused by some precise events, appearances are precisely what can be confused with essences, especially because
appearance also means the act of emerging or coming into existence. I am not
ready to say yet that, when it comes to the expression of national identity, appearances are everything, but it stands to reason to infer that they need to be
taken into account as much more than a facade, or a disguise, or a false image
to be redeemed by . . . by what? Reality in this case would be nothing to be seen.

So it is all about how to look Spanish, or, rather, it is about the conditions
of existence of a Spanish look. And it is a Spanish look in both meanings of the
expression: as a particular way to see things (which would of course include
a particular way to laugh at things or find certain things laughable) and as a
specific appearance, as an image presented for others to see. Thus posed, the
question may overlap, yet not exactly coincide, with the question of a national
identity that has yet to be unearthed. Thus posed, the emphasis falls on the
conditions of visibility of a nation whose invisibility within European modernity
has been a national issue to the point of conditioning its difference. As it may
have become evident by now, *modernity* here is a term used in a very expansive
way and always held at the intersection between visuality and cultural difference
in a very specific national context.

Visuality and Spanish Modernity

If we were to write a cultural history of what it has meant to look "Spanish,"
then the opening chapter would be the phenomenon known as *majismo*. In the
context of what has been identified as "eighteenth-century theatricality," that
would be the first moment in which looking Spanish is a question of finding a

place within a modern European context.[26] Associated first with a dress code that contested the French fashion of the new Bourbon dynasty (or, for that matter, the dominance of all things French on the Continent), *majismo* is a defensive way to signal Spanishness that depends on how one looks and behaves in public. The *majo* (or *maja*) was the embodiment of that which was unmistakably national. It fiercely opposed the *petimetres/as*, those who dressed and behaved French.[27] This "battle of the looks" was first a political issue: certain articles of clothing were even banned during the reign of Carlos III, prompting, in turn, a popular revolt. It then found its way into the literature of the period (especially theater) and into eighteenth-century painting (most notably Goya's). The reactive and belligerent nature of the phenomenon, the critical part that exaggeration or excess plays in it, and its synecdochical thrust are the aspects I would like to emphasize in this account of the phenomenon, since they will reverberate throughout future discussions of Spanishness in cinema. In the nineteenth century, French Romanticism, with Mérimée's 1845 novella *Carmen* as the epitome of the European fascination with Spanish otherness, is also complicit in maintaining what Dorothy Noyes terms "a symbolic distance" from the rest of the Continent. In the 1960s "Carmen became the mirror that Franco's government turned back to face its creators in the campaign to promote mass tourism, offering Europeans not an imperfect approximation of their own modernity . . . but rather a holiday filled with difference, as Europe had imagined it." The culmination of this symbolic journey comes two decades later: "What to do about *Carmen* became a key dilemma of Spain in the 1980s as it joined the European Community, a debate dramatized in the 1983 film of Carlos Saura."[28]

This condensed history of Spanish visual and symbolic difference certainly stresses the familiar dialectics of seeing oneself and being seen, the interplay between self-fashioning and spectacle, the crystallizing of national images whose longevity owes to much more than the doggedness of cultural stereotypes, and the obscuring effects of a single, simple image that counterimages of modernity fight against in vain. To collapse all of this into the question of the struggle between the new and the old, between tradition and innovation, would be, in my estimation, too simple. *Modernization* and *modernism* may be terms that lend themselves to a critical equation in which backwardness and even Romanticism are the negative values, but *modernity* is nothing but the name of the equation. In that respect, Spain is, from the very beginning, as *modern* as any other European country. Questions about the tardiness of the country's modernization (understood mainly as its pace of industrialization and the gradual secularization and democratization of its society) are more than reasonable; if anything, they drag modernity's contradictory nature out into the open, so to speak. It is thus a matter of the virulence with which modernity's tensions are evident in this particular country, and not a question of Spain's endemic belatedness.

This is how, drawing on Néstor García Canclini's *Hybrid Cultures*, Helen Graham and Jo Labanyi connect Spain's "belated, uneven development" with the production of a "particularly brilliant artistic, literary and musical avant-garde" that, at the same time, "exacerbated the experience of modernity as contradiction and crisis, rather than in the most advanced capitalist nations where modernity was less problematic."[29] Of course "uneven" can be a very equivocal term, and whether it means rugged or irregular, its theoretical appropriateness should be questioned in this case. "Belated" seems to have a more precise meaning, but it can also elicit some critical questions, since modernity is then just a matter of timing. Modernity is something that arrives late to countries, or something to which countries arrive tardily. I, too, would like to draw on García Canclini's classic, but I emphasize instead what he calls "the multitemporal heterogeneity of each nation" in my approach to whatever it is that European modernity means for Spain.[30] Likewise, I would prefer to speak, as Arjun Appadurai does, of modernity as being "irregularly self-conscious and unevenly *experienced*," rather than to use the adjectives "uneven," "peripheral," and even "alternate" to refer to modernity.[31] In that respect, it would be instructive to take a page from the field of subaltern studies and its challenges to the "uneven development" framework all together. This is, for instance, what Dispesh Chakrabarty does in *Provincializing Europe*, where he writes: "The idea of 'uneven development,' . . . so central to much of Marxist historiography, was treated as a piece of truth, at most an analytical tool, but never as a provisional way of organizing information, or as even something that was originally invented in the workshop of the Scottish Enlightenment."[32]

I am not yet ready to undertake the complicated task of turning Spain into a subaltern country, but my actual analysis of the films in the following chapters will take advantage of the avenues of thought that formulations such as this may open up for a new geopolitics of modernity. Since the emphasis here falls on modernity's conditions of visibility, and since what needs to be stressed is how the complex experiences of modernity are visually expressed and perceived, it is only appropriate to discuss film practices within a broader debate on nation, difference, and visuality. If modernity in Spain looks different from the way canonized centers of European modernity do, this visual difference has to do with a look whereby the modern is seen as friction in a more immediate, apparent manner. But to mention modernity is to open the cage of a multifaceted monster that only adjectives may kill or tame and whose close relationship with different processes of modernization needs to be carefully considered. In this regard, the focus of this book makes me start with that odd pair of adjectives — "happy" and "developmentalist"—in connection with Franco's Spain.

Politically and economically speaking, the early 1960s in Spain represent, among many other things, a selective attempt at modernizing the country by a totalitarian, and in many respects antimodern, regime. The modernizing force that should have propelled the country into a future of prosperity, as it did other European countries, is commodity or late capitalism, which, I would agree, "did not emerge full blown" in the Spain of the 1960s.[33] However, I would contend that it was only in that decade that Spanish culture reached the kind and degree of the type of nation-changing mass consumption and advertising that late capitalism represents. From an economic standpoint, for example, the results of this push toward a new stage of capitalism were remarkable. "In little more than fifteen years," writes Borja de Riquer i Permayer, "Spain went from being a backward agrarian country on the periphery of international capitalism, to one which could be considered fully industrialized, with a strong service sector, fully integrated into the global economic system." As the same author notes, this "made the growth of the Spanish economy incoherent to the point of chaos, prone to sharp imbalances, tensions, and deficits."[34] This, of course, is the economic account of the period, whereas I am interested in a more comprehensive view of what this particular wave of modernization entails, as well as in what it eventually meant for the symbolic life of the country. For that purpose, the concept of modernization should be made more comprehensive too, even at the risk of conflating it with modernity itself. For instance, in Jonathan Crary's formulation, "modernization is a process by which capitalism uproots and makes mobile that which is grounded, clears away or obliterates that which impedes circulation, and makes exchangeable what is singular. This applies as much to bodies, signs, images, languages, kinship relations, religious practices, and nationalities as it does to commodities, wealth, and labor power. Modernization becomes a ceaseless and self-perpetuating creation of new needs, new consumption, and new production."[35] Even though such a view of modernization characterizes a broad period in the history of Western civilization, it constitutes a suggestive frame of reference in the study of the so-called happy 1960s in Spain, since modernization gets "extracted from teleological and primarily economic determinations," and since it "encompasses not only structural changes in political and economic formations, but also immense reorganization of knowledge, languages, network of spaces and communications, and subjectivity itself."[36] If our interest in our investigation is modernization not as the result of the implementation of new economic policy but as a more comprehensive "national experience," then Crary's account lays a good foundation for understanding. New needs, consumption, and production indeed infuse the decade, and the manifold mobility of people, signs, commodities, labor power, and images utterly transforms the country's symbolic landscape together with the country's imaginary. This had not happened before in Spain, at least not at this rate nor with this pervasiveness.

Openness (*apertura*) becomes the overall metaphor, and, along with this openness, the familiar trope of how to be seen by, or how to perform for, a foreign gaze retakes center stage. Markets and frontiers are now supposed to be open in a literal and symbolic way. The latter are open for tourists to enter and for emigrants to leave. Capital and commodities now move with more freedom than the previous two decades have seen combined. In sum, openness and display, spectacle and performance, interior and facade return to the discussion of how to be and look Spanish, and how to do it in a "modern" (i.e., northern European) way. All this takes place while the dictatorship still holds on to its most reactionary founding values and orthodox images, a dictatorship that even showcases its lethal backwardness from time to time, as when it makes use of a capital punishment that utilizes the infamous *garrote vil* to strangle its victims. Film, both as an industry and as a representational practice, could be inscribed in the same process of "spectacular" modernization in which the question, to begin with, is how to be and how to look modern and, more importantly, for whom. The following discussion will set the stage for the critique of visual modernity contained in the subsequent chapters.

A Modern Way to Film Spain

"Please, sir, do you have anything on Bergman or Antonioni?" is the question two youngsters direct to what they assume is a bookseller at a book fair. The person in the booth can hardly understand what he is being asked, let alone recognize the names. "Bergman, Bergman," he replies. "Do you mean the actress?" Ironically enough, he is not a bookseller but a writer and an academician. He will soon write the letter of recommendation that will make it possible for José Luis, the main character of *El verdugo*, to get a job as an executioner for the state. The nominal presence of two of the masters of European modernist cinema in a movie sometimes labeled, more or less contemptuously, as *costumbrista* makes one wonder what this movie is saying about the place it sees itself occupying within the context of modern European cinema. This seemingly trivial dialogue therefore has special significance. It might as well indicate a tacit acknowledgment of difference, an admission of divergence from a film aesthetic found chiefly across the Pyrenees. This realization invites us to address not the place these movies occupy in the country's film history as much as their particular intervention in the decade's debate on how to film Spain in its new sociopolitical realities. The question to ask, then, is what kind of "modern" films were to be made in the face of a national modernization that, as we have already seen, usually deserves the tags "belated" or "uneven," one that comes underwritten by virtually the last dictatorship in western Europe.

In fact, it is my contention that these movies, that this genre, constitute another cinematographic option to respond to, and engage with, the complexities of Spanish late capitalist modernity. In one way or another, they all acknowledge a filmic modernity *out there*, as it were; yet they cannot obviate the precariousness and the tensions involved in the national thrust of modernization occurring around them. As a group, they account for a modernity that is indeed unevenly experienced, and, equally important in my view, they are insistently self-reflexive while they do so. All in all, what I would like to call their several *liminarities* could be the key to appreciating what they collectively bring to a nuanced discussion of cinema and modernity in the Spain of the 1960s.

An approach more committed to doing film history than mine would have these movies striding between the period of autarchy and the phase of "liberal dictatorship" said to have started after 1962.[37] In that year, Manuel Fraga Iribarne, the new *ministro de información y turismo*, reappointed José María García Escudero as *director general de cinematografía*. His return signals the beginning of a timid, mainly propagandistic period of liberalization for Spanish cinema. Young directors and producers were given the mandate to create a quality, festival-worthy cinema to shore up the "new" image that the regime was trying to promote abroad; they were also given new regulations on censorship. The direct result of the new policy was known as the *nuevo cine español* (new Spanish cinema), or NCE, a label that usually designates a generation of directors and technicians formed in the Escuela Oficial de Cine (Official School of Cinema). They embody a diverse praxis, but their films share, if not a common agenda, at least a common foe: commercial, popular cinema.[38]

That hypothetical film history approach would likewise underscore that Buñuel, Ferreri, Berlanga, and Fernán-Gómez belong to the peer group immediately (or distantly, in the case of Buñuel) preceding this "new" cadre of filmmakers. In this view, the truly modern, auteurist way to make films in Spain begins with the NCE productions, and the movies these older directors authored belong, if not to the *viejo cine español* (old Spanish cinema), or VCE, to another type of not-new cinema. I should hasten to emphasize here that this opposition proposes a rigid view of how "modern" films can or must be made in Spain at the time. The most accepted view of what constitutes modern European art cinema would project the idea of a cinematic undertaking that "tells stories about the 'individual' who has lost his or her contact with the surrounding world" and that it does so using certain techniques.[39] In András Bálint Kovács's thorough study of European modern art cinema, the only Spanish movies that qualify as modern are *La caza* (Carlos Saura, 1966), *Nueve cartas a Berta* (Basilio Martín Patino, 1966), *El jardín de las delicias* (Carlos Saura, 1970), *Ana y los lobos* (Carlos Saura, 1973), *El espíritu de la colmena* (Víctor Erice, 1973), and *Cría cuervos* (Carlos Saura, 1976). Judging by this list, Carlos Saura would be the paradigmatic modernist auteur in Spain, with Víctor Erice and Basilio Martín Patino as tokens of a very limited filmic Spanish modernity. It should come as no surprise, then, if I propose a much less strict division between the old and the new in Spanish film.

The cinema that surrounds this series of movies consists of the star-oriented commercial type, with popular singers like Sara Montiel or cute, bankable children like Marisol. There are also producer-led blockbusters, like *La gran familia* (Fernando Palacios, 1962) and *La ciudad no es para mí* (Pedro Lazaga, 1966), that belong to what have been called the *comedia costumbrista del desarrollismo*.[40] Finally, this is also the time for the aforementioned NCE's first productions, the ones that are supposed to compensate for the low quality and the simple popularity of all those commercial films. In a political-economic approach, the movies I group together as dark comedies will also represent an ambiguous place within the decade's production system.

With regard to aesthetics, and assuming for a moment that the battle between realist and aesthete (between Aristarco and Bazin, as Iván Tubau puts it) is as clear-cut as the most accepted descriptions of the cinema landscape of the period would have it, these dark comedies side clearly with a "realist" credo in film practice, or, rather, with one of the realist creeds available at the time.[41] The dichotomy that clarifies the period to the point of simplification is the one that sets the film journal *Film Ideal*, after its Charierist turn, against *Nuestro cine*, or in even simpler terms, the one that pitches *form* against *content*. However, both halves of this too-neat divide seem in need of a nuanced description that would determine, first, in what sense they are mutually exclusive and, second, if they indeed constitute two homogeneous sides of competing aesthetics. For example, as straightforward and conventional as the syntax of the images in the films I study may seem, these films also wrestle with the changing conditions of both the gaze and the spectacle that an orthodox understanding of visual modernity would entail. An extreme, long close-up in *El cochecito*, the famous slow, lengthy crane in *El verdugo*, the disconcerting scene of a character in drag in *El extraño viaje*, the tamed surrealism and the use of parallel montage in *Viridiana*—all these scenes represent momentary flashes of how these films insert themselves into the not so traditional and certainly all too complex visual culture of their times. Before I explore these traits in the subsequent chapters in order to qualify these films' aesthetics, I must note that their realism seems to have been greatly in need of an adjective or a prefix and that the appropriate adjective in this case would tend to emphasize an in-between of sorts once again.

In *Anatomía del realismo* (1965), the prominent playwright Alfonso Sastre already had spoken of "expressionist realism" as a representational option that, rooted in the Baroque writer Francisco de Quevedo and in the Spanish *picaresca*, would fight both naturalist and impressionist practices in theater. Excess and deformation were already key notions in the aesthetic discussion of the 1960s, and they were usually connected with Spanish traditions. Much more recently, in his *Popular Spanish Film under Franco*, Steven Marsh identifies the "constant presence in Spanish cultural production" of what, following Bakhtin, he terms *grotesque realism*. Marsh links this type of realism to Valle-Inclán's *esperpento* yet goes on to describe it as a "twisted subaltern diegesis" that is not particularly Spanish.[42] I would argue instead that only occasionally is the term *grotesque* appropriate or the concept of "deformation" precise enough for describing the aesthetics of the films I have set out to investigate.

A similar feeling of unseemliness surrounds the use of the prefix *neo* either to characterize these films or to qualify their aesthetics. *Neorealism* is indeed a term liberally used in the discussion of cinema under Francoism and refers to the film praxis of postwar Italy. The debate concerning what the Spanish cinema of the 1950s and 1960s owes to that film style, especially after the weeks of Italian cinema that took place in Madrid in 1951 and 1953, has been endless and, in some cases, pointless. Tellingly enough, in any invocation of the Italian model (in and of itself a complex one, too complex in fact to be made into a stable referent), there are qualifications, distinctions, and ways to say "yes, but not quite." Already in 1954 the deposed García Escudero had spoken of a "dark neorealism," which he further subdivided into "somber" and "bitter," and of a neorealism that he qualified as pink (humorous, innocent, and *sainetesco*).[43] This early urge to color the iconic label should serve as a testimony to the limitations of Italian neorealism to measure Spanish cinema's engagement with reality at the time.

The "realism" of the aesthetics of Spanish films in the 1960s often comes qualified not with the terms *excess*, *deformation*, and *neorealism* but with an invocation of the more idealized practice of *costumbrismo*. As we have seen, this is a somewhat pejorative term, and, in fact, it designates a representational practice originally opposed to the achievements of figurative verisimilitude of nineteenth-century realism. Indeed, some critics would align these movies with a Spanish *costumbrista* tradition (*costumbrismo ibérico*) or, in a similar vein, invoke the oft-mentioned *sainete* in their analysis. I will treat in some detail the significance of bringing into play these terms in my discussions of *El cochecito* and *El verdugo* in the next two chapters. In turn, the possible role of a "*sainetesque*" aesthetics will be more fully developed in my reading of *El extraño viaje* in chapter 6. If I mention both *costumbrismo* and *sainete* now as meaningful paradigms of analysis, it is just to recognize the weight they carry to counterbalance the sometimes overwhelming credence given to the aesthetics of expressive deformation in the readings of these films. A case in point would be the compulsion to align these movies with other Spanish aesthetic traditions. In fact, one of the most detailed books on the cinema of the decade sports the chapter subhead *Esperpento y tragedia grotesca.*[44]

The term *esperpento* is particularly ubiquitous and vexing in discussions of Spanish culture in general and Spanish film in particular. To invoke the *esperpento valleinclanesco* is to invoke an aesthetics both theorized and practiced in several written texts, mainly theatrical. In other words, we do not know what an *esperpento* looks like, except in the interpretation of a stage director. More significantly, and as John Lyon shows, "Valle's theoretical statements about the nature of the *esperpento* made after or about 1924, the year *Luces de Bohemia* is published in its definitive version, are not easy to reconcile with the theory as expressed in this first *esperpento.*"[45] Moreover, one could argue convincingly that, even in this unique and paradigmatic *esperpento*, the possibility exists that theory and practice match only in an incomplete or limited way.

The statements in the play that have been taken as the most succinct and forceful definitions of *esperpento* appear in the famous scene 12. They are both uttered by the main character in the play, Max Estrella, who is drunk at that moment. "Tragic heroes reflected in concave mirrors produce *Esperpento*," he says, together with a categorical "Spain is a grotesque deformation of European civilization."[46] Based on these two precise formulations, the theory of *esperpento* that the first *esperpento* advances may be summed up by saying that it is a relational aesthetics wherein the key concept is deformation. The abstraction called "Europe" still dictates what culturally specific representational practices may look like in Spain. As Max elaborates on his theory, the principles of an *esperpento* aesthetics encompass concepts whose degree of tangency or centrality remains to be determined. *Absurd* is the term used most often to describe this work, and, more subtly, the notion of comedy is also applied to it.[47] Max also invokes the name of the painter Goya as the inventor of what he calls *esperpentismo*. One can look at the play in which these seminal statements are made and find all of these guiding notions deployed unevenly and to different effect. One could even find crucial scenes in the play where neither the grotesque nor the absurd nor the comic nor even deformation is a factor of consequence: the scene in which Max says good-bye to a Catalan anarchist worker about to be killed, or the scene that presents the aftermath of a police assault and a mother crying with her dead infant son in her arms.

When extrapolating all this to the film medium and to Spanish film productions, the safer practice is to invoke the tenets of the *esperpento* in its more economical form. This is what John Hopewell does in his pioneering book on Spanish cinema, when, after quoting Max Estrella's maxims, he writes: "*Esperpento* is the grotesque, the ridiculous, the absurd."[48] Leaving aside the fact that one of these terms, the ridiculous, does not belong to Valle-Inclán's discussion, the concatenation of nouns either equates three notions that may not be synonymous after all or defines a hybrid that can be easily invoked whenever the wide range of meanings it connotes are perceived in a Spanish film. This is how Almodóvar's films could be said to revive in the 1980s "an 'absurdist neorealism' based on *esperpento*" and how an Alex de la Iglesia film from 1995 can be called "the best present-day example of *esperpento*."[49]

Helpful or not, clear in its genealogy or still as imprecise as the statements made by a drunk character in a play, the esperpento as a helpful paradigm in film analysis may be first and foremost the symptom for an anxiety. It may reveal, ultimately, an urge to justify the perceived cultural specificity of certain films. Presently, I will satisfy such an urge myself by focusing not on what the *esperpento* is as a representational practice but on the kind of response it represents to the demands of cultural modernity.

Goya, on the other hand, painted (and etched): he indeed worked with a visual medium, and we all seem to have a shared visual reference with which to discuss what the term *goyesco* means. (The different serial etchings and the "black paintings" act as synecdoches for the sign *Goya* itself.) Yet there are few instances of movies, or of scenes in a movie, in which Goya's work is clearly perceived as a direct visual reference, as a translation into the moving image of what he put on the canvas. Something similar can be said regarding the work of El Greco, Velázquez, Ribera, Zurbarán, and Solana, the other painters typically chosen to anchor Spanish film to a national visual tradition.

In hopes that repetition may beget eloquence, I would say once more that the most productive way to create a niche for these movies in the Spanish cultural landscape of the 1960s is to contemplate them as part of a film genre, as movies that ought to be read in the light of one another. All other invocations of the cultural past and of authors and aesthetics from other fields should not be shunned; instead, they must be taken as frames of reference that can mislead as much as they can help elucidate what these films are doing in the medium of the moving image. As part of that cultural past (and a matter of aesthetics as much as of comedy, since it is connected precisely to some of the Spanish traditions and authors just mentioned), dark humor in Spanish film must be approached in a similar way. Dark humor could very well be found more frequently in both the high and the popular culture of a particular geopolitical community (however broadly or narrowly we may wish to define it), and the presence of dark humor could very well be due to historical, anthropological, or sociological factors. However, culturally specific dark humor is just that: cultural. It is also medium sensitive, and if we want to avoid the pitfalls of both generalization and cultural determinism, it is better that we consider it as time sensitive, too. In other words, let us historicize dark humor, and let us relate it to questions of film and modernity.

Laughing Darkly

If we are to believe André Breton's claims, "black humor" (*l'humour noir*) begins with his 1939 anthology, because the concept itself did not exist previously. Furthermore, according to the guru of French surrealism, this particular type of humor is closely related to the experience of modernity. Indeed, Breton speaks of "the specific requirements of modern sensibility" as directly connected to a laughter that either turns dark or finds its sources in darkness.[50] It is not existence in general but modern existence in particular that is the natural habitat of a dark laugher that is either self-protective or belligerent. This alone may be a clarification that can be used to forestall any objection that could refer the question of dark humor back to a tradition of medieval macabre dances, for example.

Simon Critchley makes a claim somewhat similar to Breton's, although he addresses the whole comic field and is bolder in what he intimates about humor and modernity. In his view, "the association of humour with the comic and the jocular is specifically modern, and arises in a period of the rise of the modern nation state, in particular the astonishing rise of Britain as a trading, coloniz-ing and warring nation after the establishment of a constitutional monarchy in the Glorious Revolution of 1688."[51] Critchley here refers to the moment the term *humor* stopped meaning "mental disposition or temperament," but one has the feeling that a somewhat "civilizing" role is at play in this linkage of na-tion, modernity, and laughter. One can also suspect that such a linkage comes saddled with a precise, if unacknowledged, geopolitics. Along those lines, here is Jim Leach reflecting on British humor: "The British not only have a sense of humor but, because they refuse to take themselves seriously, the nation has not succumbed to political excesses, such as fascism."[52] Although Leach is quick to add that such a "national myth" is "open to question," he also claims that it is a myth that "has often worked in favor of the national cinema."[53]

Keeping the role of a national humor open to questioning, modernity, laughter, and the nation may be much differently performed in the case of Spanish dark comedy, and the resulting nexus would be one where the discourse of difference in Spanish culture would remain operative. Once again, I am fully aware of the scholarly uses of nationalism (as I think my engagement with Valle-Inclán's and Goya's aesthetics has demonstrated). And once again, I am equally wary of turning a blind eye to cultural specificity. I believe this predicament is the one Steven Marsh struggles to address in his otherwise brilliant approach to many of the films I study here. He makes a number of important arguments regarding "the popular reinscription of popular tradition" in these films while showing how comedy can become "a source of potential subversion."[54] I shall take up several of his points in my own treatment of the films, although the emphasis of my study will fall less upon carnivalesque subversions than upon the ethical and epistemological effects of dark laughter under a very concrete set of historical and cultural circumstances. In doing so, I especially question the argument that "the operations of clowns exceed temporal and spatial boundaries in all comedy, everywhere, outside of regulated time."[55] And I would preface my dissent on this point with the objection that one could make to any broad ahistorical and universalist statement on comedy, even if it is backed up by Bakhtin's ideas: there may have been clowns and jesters making people laugh about similar subjects or with similar comic tropes across cultures and throughout history, but "comic patterns are still enacted at specific times, in specific places, for specific audiences and to serve specific functions."[56]

Thus nationality and dark humor can be productively conflated in an investigation that would make the latter its main gateway into the specifics of a cultural identity at a time in which how to be and how to look modern (and with what sense of difference) are the key issues. The two more oft-quoted paradigms of Spanish dark humor, already discussed above, are indeed related to the experience of modernity and its discontents. Both Goya and Valle-Inclán translated the perceived backwardness of their country within the context of European modernity into a constellation of images of troubled modernity that became expressions of *modern* representational practices themselves. Rather than taking from the particular aesthetics of both painter and playwright, the movies I analyze here draw upon their way of translating that experience of the modern. Dark humor lies at the center of that translation and is the key factor to take into account in these movies' engagement with both sociopolitical and cinematographic modernity.

As we will see in some detail, dark humor also helps in the process of re-signifying conventional geopolitical aesthetics to make the films a more daring, transgressive means of representing the symbolic life of a nation under very concrete and conflicting circumstances. In the first chapters of this book, these circumstances are the ones that the adjective "happy" poignantly stresses in the expression "the happy sixties," used to refer to this particular period during Franco's dictatorship. The disturbing ripples of this dark laughter would also make apparent the moral dimension of such a comic modality, which is to say, the ethics that are at stake in this process of modernizing authoritarianisms as well as adopting capitalist modernity. This is all done by bringing to the fore-ground the "bitter laugh, the laugh that laughs at that which is not good," or "the ethical laugh," in Samuel Beckett's words.[57] It is via the Irish author that Critchley associates humor with darkness, or, more precisely, with a "black sun" at the center of the comic universe that hinges on the sudden realization that "the object of the laugh is the subject that laughs."[58] So the central question to take into consideration from now on is not what causes laughter but rather what laughter causes in us.

Let me tie the epistemic value of dark humor to the questions of film genre that opened this chapter. Let me go back to and at the same time plunge ahead into "the intersections between given genres and the national."[59] In fact, in the case of the Spanish cinematographic dark comedy, the guiding question should be: "Under what conditions do culturally specific genres arise?"[60] Those conditions, I am afraid, could be traced back to what this admittedly meandering chapter has advanced. They may be traced back to the concept of Spanishness, to the struggles with the idea of modernity as expressed in the realm of the visual, to the discussions of (and the anxieties about) cultural difference, which was poorly understood as lateness or backwardness, and to the reverberation of a dark laughter that is at the same time an intervention in the national milieu and a reworking within the film medium of some of its representational traditions.

In one final attempt at a concluding remark, I would say that with this book I am entering an expression of dark laughter that explores, through the medium of film, questions of national identity and dissidence, the insidious workings of social complicity, the perverse end results of certain regenerational projects, and the interdependence of the indigenous and the foreign in the making of a film modernity that we might as well call *perverse* rather than *uneven*. I will then move to the end of the country's long-lasting dictatorship to see what Almodóvar does with a comedy that essentially questions if it is the right time to laugh yet. Finally, I will proceed to see what dark comedy means within a project of national reconfiguration fixed on looking global rather than Spanish, or on how to still look Spanish in the era of transnationalism. It is indeed time to see how the members of the film genre I call Spanish dark comedy substantiate and clarify what this first chapter has theorized. It is time to read closely without losing sight of the family resemblances that animate the reading.

2

Movement and Paralysis, Dissidence and Identity

Ferreri's El cochecito

El cochecito (*The Little Coach,* 1960) tells the story of an old man's struggle to buy a motorized wheelchair that he may or may not need. Moved by the fact that all his friends have their *cochecito* and undeterred by the reality of his two healthy legs, this senior citizen will strive to convince his family of his dire necessity, proceed to buy the vehicle behind their backs, and ultimately poison them all rather than relinquish his possession. The name of this elderly murderer is Don Anselmo, and, as the story progresses, he may be seen either as a comic puerile *senex* or, more dramatically, as nothing short of an exterminating angel. His vehicle, in turn, may become a mere commodity, or it may represent this man's only chance to gain a semblance of freedom. Whichever way man and object are viewed, the crucial argument here is that they must be contemplated together, that the camera films subject and object, self and thing, as if to twin them.

The first part of this chapter occupies itself with this central insight: Don Anselmo's symbolic ambivalence (as an individual, as a character) can only be truly discerned as *mediated* by the object that turns him into a desiring subject. Taking into consideration that the object in question is also the means to gain membership in an idealized community (that of his handicapped friends), as well as the vehicle that will enable him to take flight from an oppressive one (his family), the character's ambivalent identity inevitably alters how his symbolic dissidence is to be understood. For while the movie has been generally read as a satire directed against Franco's dictatorial regime, a more problematic task is to determine what concrete aspects of postautarchic Francoism the film truly criticizes. Furthermore, the crucial question to ask in this movie seems to be: What is the precise contribution of its ambivalent main character to this film's social and political dissidence? And ambivalent and even multivalent he is, in spite of some notable unambiguous judgments coming from expert viewers. As early as 1962, one can find critical views of the protagonist, like the ones expressed by Santiago San Miguel and Víctor Erice in the journal *Nuestro cine*, where they write: "It is easy to say that man is cruel when we are shown a senile, half-crazed old man as victim."[1] In her influential *Blood Cinema*, Marsha Kinder goes so far as to describe Don Anselmo's crime as an act that ends up costing him "his family, his freedom and his humanity," calling him a "self-centered consumerist killer."[2] Consumerism is, of course, one of the main concepts at which this dark comedy takes aim. However, it would be a mistake to confuse consumerism with consumption in this case, or to assign blame to the individual for the travesties of the system. If consumerism is indeed a target in this movie, it is far from clear if the consumer is to be blamed when the definition of this economic order could be as complex as the following quote suggests: "We may say that 'consumerism' is a type of social arrangement that results from re-cycling mundane, permanent and so to speak 'regime-neutral' human wants, desires and longings into the *principal propelling and operating force* of society, a force that coordinates systemic reproduction, social integration, social stratification and the formation of human individuals, as well as playing a major role in the processes of individual and group identification and in the selection and pursuit of individual life policies."[3] However we want to read Don Anselmo's urge to shop, the implications of his consumerism must be nuanced when what he is actually doing by shopping may range from becoming who he is to acquiring a sense of belonging.

According to the classic work on this subject, Thorstein Veblen's *Theory of the Leisure Class*, it would be just as much of a mistake to decide that all consumption is conspicuous. In fact, one can argue, as I will do here, that consumption can be resignified in such a way that it becomes a strategy of resistance, or, rather, a radical act of nay-saying. I will take on these issues momentarily, since the entire movie—and not only its main character—can be read as a reflection on modern modes of consumption. For now, let us say that I find it useful to enter this film thinking that questions of social and economic order are closely related to the representation of order itself and to the possibility of unsettling it. Matters of economy and matters of comedy are thus fruitfully intertwined if we start contemplating the interplay between order (or structure) and the place of the individual in it.

To that effect, the choice here is to read the film while taking very much into account that it belongs to a comic genre whose definition (and mind how much comedy reminds us of consumerism here) could be, according to Northrop Frye's classic analysis, "the integration of society, which usually takes the form of incorporating a central character into it."[4] More precisely, I will consider *El cochecito* as a member of the "ironic comedy" subcategory, where "a humorous society triumphs or remains undefeated."[5] This kind of ironic comedy renders impracticable the happy ending that in the more common form of classic comedy enables a "kind of moral norm or pragmatically free society."[6] Framing *El cochecito* in such a way (i.e., going back to classic comedy) may occasion some misgivings, but it definitely offers clear advantages. The first one is that comedy is a matter of structure as much as it is a more subjective matter of comic tone. As a corollary, dark humor also has a more significant role in making the film what it is, since, rather than *coloring* the whole story, the occasion for laughter becomes a point of inflexion. Laughter itself and the subject that laughs are indeed the subjects under examination.

This is a constant of the genre that I will broach in different ways and that could be more readily perceived, as we shall see, in Buñuel's perverse modality of dark laughter in *Viridiana*. Likewise, both *El verdugo* and *El extraño viaje*, the films I examine in the next chapters, will make us confront the mechanisms by which laughing stops being just a bodily reaction and becomes nothing less than a modality of knowing and a practice of self-knowledge. But before we get to the darkness and the epistemology of *El cochecito*'s laughter, we must start with the object whose possession could mean so many different things and mean them so differently. We must start with the vehicle whose perception and whose designation seem to change according to the manifold ways it is desired, gazed upon, thought about, and operated.

Object of Perception, Object of Possession

"I am telling you, it's not a motorcycle, it's a handicap car [*coche de cojo*]," cries a nameless youngster in a graveyard. Lucas, Don Anselmo's friend, has ridden his brand-new *cochecito* to the cemetery to visit his late wife's grave. A "motorcycle" is what another youngster has just very enthusiastically called it. Lucas's daughter used the same word several frames before, very apprehensively in her case, since the old man was gleefully speeding away. As much as the latter fears what the former admires in the vehicle, one could safely say that they share the same mythical view of this mobile object. Let us take up the question seriously, then. Let us assume that the confusion the vehicle creates is neither occasional nor reducible to the mistakes in appreciation made by two marginal characters. Let us entertain the idea that, as viewers of this particular object in this particular movie, we can also ask ourselves whether this object is a motorcycle or whether it is a motorized wheelchair. In fact, the correct question in this case would be whether we should even accept a hermeneutic logic that requires choosing one view over the other. A *cochecito* may well offer the same dilemma as the Cervantine *baciyelmo* or cause the same perplexity as Wittgenstein's famous duck-rabbit. With regard to the latter, the fact that one sees it as one thing or the other brings about the realization that seeing an object does not depend solely on the sense of sight. To quote the philosopher himself, "'Seeing as . . .' is not part of perception. And for that reason it is like seeing and again not like."[7]

Throughout the film both Lucas's and Don Anselmo's vehicles are seen as motorcycles because of the rejuvenation they seem to enable in their drivers. Both old men return, however fleetingly, to a stage of juvenile disobedience that mistakes speed for freedom and that couples a mode of private transportation with the dream of an independence that goes beyond the capability to move faster and farther. However, the first opportunity to exercise this independence places these old men in a graveyard, alone and talking about their loneliness. One of them is pushing the other. Later, when the vehicle gets stuck in the mud, they even require the help of a stranger to navigate the necropolis. In this cemetery, Lucas's *cochecito* thus turns back into what it was supposed to replace: a mere wheelchair. Freedom, freedom of movement for now, appears as the first concept subject to filmic investigation. And the first thing to be surmised from such an investigation is that we are definitely dealing with an incomplete, limited freedom: a liberty surrounded by death, to be sure. As seen in the graveyard, the use and the functioning of this first *cochecito* speak, in sum, of an ironic exercise of freedom that foreshadows the ironic way the movie will approach the very possibility of being free. In point of fact, the film will soon invite us to watch the vehicle used as a racing motorcycle. This happens when we witness, fittingly enough, the "primera competición mundial de motos para impedidos" (first handicapped motorcycle world competition). A vehicle for disabled people seems to become the motor vehicle of excitement and rebellion after all, or, at least, it is officially called that.

This is the first instance in the movie of an act of naming that in reality upgrades the object being named. And it takes place, not by chance, in the sequence in which Don Anselmo "encounters" his *cochecito*. It is also the moment in the story when the old man is named as he desires to be named. After a brief, improvised medical exam, Don Anselmo is finally declared a "paralytic." By then, the existential ambivalence of the vehicle has begun to affect the identity of anyone who drives it too. What this vehicle is, what it should be called, and how it should be interpellated are questions already advanced the moment Don Anselmo's daughter-in-law refers to his handicapped friends as *anormales* (abnormal ones), a label that immediately calls attention to the concept of normalcy itself. Ultimately, this film examines the performative value of naming, that is, what naming does to something or to somebody that is not just that: giving a name, christening. In fact, *El cochecito* goes so far as to illustrate the unstable nature of being and naming. In Don Anselmo's case, there is a series of designations that range from *viejo loco* (old fool) to *padre pródigo* (prodigious father). They all contribute to increase the ambivalence that I have considered inherent to the character.

Among these acts of naming, one in particular makes the vehicle instrumental for knowing who the subject that claims to need it wants to be. When Don Anselmo's son asks for the money his father has put down for his purchase, he argues that the buyer is not even a handicapped person. Don Hilario, the owner of the store that sells this kind of equipment, promptly replies: "Paralytic or not, this gentleman here is my client." If the main character's physical condition is the bone of contention that facilitates the articulation of the whole film, and if being called a name or referring to oneself with a very different name is a speech act tantamount to either subjugation or freedom, then to be called "a client" seems to resolve any controversy by suppressing the need to choose. To be a client is, to some extent, to enjoy autonomy. To be a client is to be free, at least in proportion to one's purchasing power. And yet this liberty, taking into account the conditions under which it is gained, remains clearly compromised. In fact, it is a freedom subjected to a brand new set of constraints. Therefore, the question regarding the nature of the vehicle presents us with a third answer to the riddle its mode of existence has become: Is it a motorcycle? Is it a car for disabled people? Or is it, perhaps, a SEAT 600, the first mass-produced automobile for the middle classes in Spain? When Don Anselmo and his family leave the pawn shop where the old man has gotten the money to make the first payment on his *cochecito*, the handicapped vehicle is parked right in front of the family's car, which is that very small automobile made by the government-run SEAT Company and popularly called a *seiscientos*, or a "six hundred" (see fig. 1). That the shot lines up both vehicles in such a way were it not for the fact that they are also compared throughout the film on the basis of the SEAT 600's status as an emblem of Francoist developmentalism.[8]

Figure 1. The *cochecito-seiscientos*

The *seiscientos* is indeed the car that makes popular as well as possible the family weekend outing. In the movie, the family is shown taking off for one of these short trips, more a sign of arrival in the middle class than anything else. Don Anselmo will not join them for reasons that go beyond the ones made evident by the film's plot. He already has his group of friends to picnic with, and we watch him join them too, although still without a *cochecito* of his own. I will nuance my statements soon enough, but I should mention now that it is hard not to notice that, in spite of all the symbolic dissidence Don Anselmo may embody, his *cochecito* could be seen also (or especially) as a *seiscientos*, that is, as the vehicle that implicates him in the economic system that all but guarantees the continuation of the dictatorship. To see the vehicle like this is to understand that this commodity, more than any other, is the one that launches a consumerist period in Spain whose trademark is the purchase in installments.[9] The monthly payments Don Anselmo agrees to, the ones that make him, paralytic or not, a client, turn the vehicle into something less necessary than a handicapped car and something less mythic than a motorcycle. They make the vehicle a commodity and its driver less free. This is the time in the country when prosperity is supposed to diffuse political unrest. These are the years in which the new technocrats announce the sunset of ideologies.[10] However fleetingly, Don Anselmo's dissidence is so closely linked to the spirit of the period's purported "economic miracle" that it may very well make him an accomplice. Don Anselmo is in fact a willing participant in the market economy that is revamping the dictatorship. This "complicity" is the aspect that helps the most in emphasizing the negative reading of *El cochecito*'s main character.

Complicity, and complicity beyond that of a consumerist person, is indeed one of the main concerns of the dark cinematic comedies of the 1960s. *El verdugo*, as we shall see, addresses this concern more deeply and more bluntly. Yet Ferreri's first movie in Spain, *El pisito*, Berlanga's *Plácido*, Fernán-Gómez's *El extraño viaje*, and even Buñuel's *Viridiana* also help in dissecting the vexing and manifold mechanisms of complicity both with a particular political regime and with a socioeconomic order. The so-called economic liberalization, or *apertura*, stirs the country at many levels, one of which is the level of cultural dissent. The critical insight to be pursued here is that cultural dissidence under Francoism truly emerges as such in the early 1960s and that its emergence is already compromised by a self-questioning that results from the blurring of the target for dissent in the new socioeconomic milieu.

These dark cinematographic movies coincide with three significant and interrelated developments in the field of literary production. First, there is the "guilty conscience" of a group of poets who cannot write engaged or social poetry anymore without questioning their social upbringing and, consequently, their privileged position as intellectuals and as citizens. This is the so-called generation of the 1950s, with poets such as Jaime Gil de Biedma, Carlos Barral, José Agustín Goytisolo, and José Ángel Valente. A great deal of their early lyric production could be used as evidence of the intellectual's new conflicted state during the developmentalism stage of the regime. Second, also in the early 1960s, the publication of Martín Santos's *Tiempo de silencio* precipitates the end of the social-realist paradigm and offers another image of a failed intellectual, a doctor who must give up his lofty aspirations in Madrid and seek refuge in a sort of interior exile in the provinces. Finally, the two most prominent playwrights of the time, Alfonso Sastre and Antonio Buero Vallejo, argued, bitterly at times, over what kind of theater was to be written under a politically repressive regime that could easily prevent a play from being staged. That difference of opinion, known as the debate on *posibilismo teatral*, was ultimately an argument about the limitations of representational arts, about the dangers of complicity in artistic restraint, and about the ethics of not taking risks. In all three instances, the cultural elite, and, as a reflection, their protagonists, their poetic personae, and their theatrical heroes, find themselves questioning their origins, their motives, and their credentials. We can safely say that in this new stage of cultural dissidence under Francoism, self-examination appears inescapable, and not even dissent is immediately and unquestionably innocent. In this context, where does *El cochecito* stand as a film that expresses either dissent or connivance? What do the choices of the main character tell us about the chances for fighting back and the inevitability of co-option? Once again, the relation between man and object sheds light onto all these questions.

In order to complicate Don Anselmo's act of consumerism, one only has to compare *El cochecito* to the famous *Ladri di biciclette* (Vittorio De Sica, 1948), a movie in which both the use and the necessity of a vehicle offer hardly any ambivalence. The stolen bicycle is more than a means of transportation: it is, in fact, the only means to make a living, the only hope of survival, really. De Sica's bicycle is, in sum, a vital vehicle, and it bears little apparent resemblance to Don Anselmo's *cochecito*. And yet a healthy, productive provocation would argue that the *cochecito* is as essential to this retiree's well-being as is the bicycle to De Sica's unfortunate worker. The impossibility of seeing the vehicle as nothing more than an old man's whim is the impossibility of overcoming Don Anselmo's family's way of thinking. Likewise, if one only sees in the old man's defiance the embodiment of the incipient consumerist spirit of the times, then one judges the character by principles that, while not being exactly those of his family, surely overlap with them. In the final analysis, the idea that Don Anselmo *does not need* his *cochecito* would prevail if one follows the logic of *seeing as*. So let us not ask ourselves whether he needs this vehicle. Rather, the question at this juncture should be: What concept of necessity gets exposed or is investigated in the film? Better still, the question should be: What idea of necessity, as articulated by the film and its images, goes beyond a dialectics of offer and demand, of need and desire?

Let's go back to the *cochecito*-as-*seiscientos* view. Even if Don Anselmo only uses the vehicle for what amounts to a weekend outing, this does not open any middle-class doors for him. Instead, through the vehicle Don Anselmo gains access to a whole new community in which to feel freer or, at any rate, less lonely. In other words, the paradoxical (or the problematic) aspect in his case is that his use of the *cochecito-seiscientos* redeems the vehicle from its commodity-like condition. Don Anselmo's *cochecito* possesses a use value that does not turn it completely into a *seiscientos*, nor into a motorcycle, nor into a means of transportation for the disabled. This vehicle's usefulness, precisely because it is not the neorealist usefulness of a bicycle, questions the concept of utility itself and, as we shall see at the end, muddles the meaning of the crimes committed to purchase it.

The questions that arise from all this should now be the following: How is this vehicle less a possession and more an object that affirms its owner's identity? Are there images that somehow exonerate the motorized object from being a mere commodity after all? We need to see the vehicle as vehicle, then. More specifically, we need to see it as a filmed vehicle in order to see its driver as more than its owner. A digression is in order, though, to fully appreciate what the genre as a whole says about the meaning of vehicles in these early stages of developmentalism. This is a digression, a detour indeed, that will take us to another illustrious motorized cart in Spanish film.

Of Men and Vehicles

The first images of Luis García Berlanga's 1961 *Plácido* show the title character's vehicle, a *motocarro* (literally, a "motorized cart") with a star mounted on top. This precarious means of transport is otherwise decorated as if all the ornaments could transform the moving object into an abstract entity—into the spirit of Christmas, perhaps, commercialism included. This *motocarro* is, in fact, both a vehicle and a concept, a moving celestial body running down to Earth and preaching compassion and consumption at the same time. The charity campaign to "sit a poor person at your table" that was the inspiration for the script is sponsored by a brand of pots in the film, and a character makes sure to publicize that sponsorship using a loudspeaker that is also mounted on top of this non-horse-drawn carriage. Furthermore, the back of the vehicle is furnished with a table and a pair of chairs soon to be occupied by two persons who play the parts of a rich person and a poor person sharing a meal. The *motocarro*, then, also serves as a shaky float that parades the insincerity and the cynicism of the whole charity campaign.

The name for this vehicle is already an exercise in undefinability, perhaps another specimen showing the logic of the *baciyelmo*, another exercise in *duck-rabbitness*. Its motorcycle soul conjures up the same notions of freedom and urban mobility that the *cochecitos* in *El cochecito* do. The *carro* in it makes it a vehicle that neither announces the advent of modernization nor conveys the thrills of technological progress. This is a means of transport that circulates in the vicinity of the modern. This alone would link this constantly rattling vehicle to the motorized wheelchairs that populate *El cochecito*. A stronger tie—and one surely more pertinent to the focus of this chapter—is provided by the economic mechanisms that facilitate and eventually complicate its ownership.

Right after the first images of the *motocarro*-star are displayed, the film follows the title character underground into the public restroom that his wife runs in order to help bring in some income. In this low, "unclean" environment (where somebody pays for the use of a latrine while Plácido's wife rocks an infant), the first conversation about modern economy takes place. Bank payments are discussed, along with the possibility of the vehicle being impounded. Furthermore, the closing of the restroom door serves as the transition to the following scene, a scene that takes place precisely at a bank, where a door opens to let the director of the bank office go through. In the syntax of the images, one indeed goes from one space to the other as if they were communicable. That one can exit a public restroom and enter a bank office seems like a humorously clear indictment of an economic system that preys on the almost destitute in this case.

Down in the restroom, the talk on economics is symbolically dragged through the mud. Up in the financial institution, Plácido offers to leave a member of his family as a guarantee of payment. All this could be read as an example of "ersatz economy."[11] Yet it is certainly also something else: a particularly graphic description of consumer capitalism deployed on the backs of the have-nots and the indigent. That is, the workings of the new economic dictates are stripped down to their predatory, dehumanizing essence. More than another example of uneven or belated economic development, these scenes could be exposing the ruthlessness of a full-grown system, but in a more crude way. They may be stripping that system down to its very merciless bones rather than representing a yet-to-be-modern stage of consumer capitalism. Be that as it may, the fact is that Berlanga reworks De Sica's bicycle as a vital vehicle not to be lost rather than one to be recovered. Plácido will spend the entire movie trying to make the needed payment so that he does not lose the vehicle that allows him to make a living. And the *motocarro* will make appearances throughout the movie as the precarious vehicle that enables comings and goings, as the commodity that rehearses a chaotic choreography of morals and economics, and, once in a while, as the immobile object that signals the darker realities underlying the collective frenzy.

At last motionless in a film that is all movement, the *motocarro* is but a dark silhouette high and deep in the field of vision as characters fight for a Christmas gift basket in front of it. Seconds later it will figure prominently in the last shot of the movie (see fig. 2). This time the vehicle is filmed from above, looking more broken than stationary. There is an almost spectral aura in the final vision of the vehicle. Its final incarnation is invested with a desolated meaning rooted in nothing but stillness.

Of all the vehicles that populate these dark comedies, Plácido's *motocarro* is the one whose spirit is most closely related to that of Don Anselmo's *cochecito*. The relation seems obvious when economics, deadlines, and payments are discussed, but their moments of motionlessness speak more subtly and deeply about their essence as vehicles and their meaning as things.

In "What Becomes of Things on Films" Stanley Cavell speaks of that moment of "disruption of the matters of course" that inaugurates a mode of sight by which objects are seen in "their conspicuousness, their obtrusiveness, and their obstinacy." One of the best examples of this mode of sight, continues Cavell, is "a tool by its breaking."[12] A motionless vehicle is not by any means a broken tool, yet I would argue that a stationary state makes more visible or more obstinate the essence of this type of object within the universe of things. In fact, the question at this point should be whether these images of still vehicles

Figure 2. The vehicle as stillness and abandonment

reveal, in ways that images of moving ones are not able to, that their essence is movement itself. If this is true, then these objects constitute a forceful trope to think of essences and identities as mobile and unstable, already gone when one tries to pin them down. Gilles Deleuze has a thought-provoking reflection on precisely this meaningful, symbiotic relation between essence and movement in the film medium. "The essence of the cinematographic movement-image," he writes, "lies in extracting from vehicles or moving bodies the movement which is their common substance, or extracting from movements the mobility which is their essence."[13] Within this conceptual framework, it is extremely significant to explore the "essential" value paralysis possesses in *El cochecito*. The task at hand therefore is to elucidate the meaning of those instances in which either bodies or vehicles — ostensibly, obstinately — stand still.

There are at least three shots in which the *cochecito* seems notoriously motionless. These are shots, in fact, that make the vehicle's immobility meaningful. Don Anselmo's handicapped car remains noticeably still, even useless, during what I will call the "reconciliation scene." In the small community of motorized handicapped people to which the old man wants desperately to belong, there is a romantic couple. They have been going through a rough patch by the time Don Anselmo joins the group. In the aforementioned scene, our *senex* forces them to make up. What leads up to the moment in which he stands between the fighting couple is precisely a shot of the old man's still vehicle a few steps away from the group (see fig. 3). The meaning of this stillness (and why it seems to underscore as much uselessness as it does paralysis) partakes of what I will call "Don Anselmo's epiphany," that moment in which he, first, comes to the realization of who he really is and, second, must face what he is unable to become among those who cannot walk. Previously, the *cochecito* has appeared in

Figure 3. The reconciliation scene or the ancillary object

Figure 4. Together indoors: the imprisoned object

the family's apartment, parked in the hall, imprisoned, it would seem, as much as its owner is (see fig. 4).

Confinement is the overwhelming feeling in this shared image of vehicle and man. Here, as much as anywhere else in the film, object and subject become interchangeable: they disclose, as it were, the same captivity. The most comic image of this vehicle's stillness turns the *cochecito* into a cow; better still, it shows the *cochecito* as an object of unstable meaning: a machine or an animal, or both at the same time (see fig. 5). When Don Anselmo brings his brand new *cochecito* to the door of his friend Lucas's business (a dairy farm), one of the employees comes out with what seems like a milking stool tied to his waist. He immediately sits in front of the vehicle and looks at the machine in awe. A curious cow is seen in the background. The dairy farm employee's position and, above all, his nervous inspection of the vehicle seem to underline the puzzlement of a man who does not know how to milk this contraption. This object does not seem to have an immediate use or, say, a natural finality.

If we treat these three moments of stillness as images that underline the symbolic symbiosis between man and machine, the vehicle becomes (1) an ancillary and to some extent inadequate artifact, (2) a mirror image, and (3) an object invested with a puzzling ontological instability. At any rate, in all three shots the

Figure 5. The milking scene: the unnatural object

object is clearly filmed in order to comment on the person who desires it. For Don Anselmo, to desire this object means to confront those representing the dominant social order, which impedes his entry into the community to which he really wants to belong. We are already on the threshold of analyzing *El cochecito* as a dark cinematographic comedy that overlaps with the classic concept of ironic comedy as described by Frye. Let us view the film in this light without forgetting the subject-object considerations advanced so far. Let us also not lose sight of the medium in which this comedic structure is deployed. The importance of the *cochecito* qua filmed object equals that of the main character qua moving body. The relations between subjectivity and movement are paramount in a film where what seems to be at stake in this man's mobility or paralysis is nothing less than his identity and his dissidence.

Ironic Comedy

In *El cochecito* the hero must overcome obstacles to happiness — to the happiness of belonging and the bliss of true communal experience — and these obstacles are set by the social order he wants to leave behind. Since he confronts a family in various ways associated with, and validated by, several overwhelming laws, resistance is futile unless extreme measures are taken. In this case, the main character is the one responsible for what Frye calls the moment of ritual death. "Everyone will have noted in comic actions," he writes, "even in very trivial movies and magazines stories, a point near the end at which the tone suddenly becomes serious, sentimental, or ominous of potential catastrophe."[14] This is a moment that, taking into account the characters and the forces Don Anselmo is battling, can certainly be read as an act of justified rebellion even in its brutality. On the other hand, it is also true that by poisoning the entire family (sweet granddaughter included), Don Anselmo compromises his ethical character. The only way to come to terms with such a disproportionate retaliation is to consider it as the drastic yet necessary answer to a repressive social organism that has gone bad beyond repair. The association of the family with legal, religious, medical, and economic discourses cannot be overlooked, as we shall see. Either explicitly (the son's line of work, his threat to put his father away "con los textos legales en la mano [with the legal texts in hand, that is, following the law]") or in the form of a more tacit visual inscription (the ever-present cross always on his son's desk, later multiplied in the pawn shop), the signs of the family's place among the dominant discourses are well established during the film. Even so, the indiscriminate nature of Don Anselmo's act discredits his good fight, and, more importantly, it does not open the doors to that new society to which he aspires to belong. In that community, our exterminating angel has no place. The vehicle he craves by itself does not grant membership after all. In order to belong, Don Anselmo lacks, of all things, paralysis. Because he can walk, because he can move, he cannot be free. What he can do, what we see him doing seconds after dumping poison in the family stew, is to repair the damage to the social group in which he seeks inclusion by reconciling the estranged couple. Standing on his own two feet, Don Anselmo solves the sentimental problems that threaten the harmony of the handicapped community. Even if Don Anselmo's walking does not seem crucial to this mediating role, the truth is that the *cochecito* is idle by his side, truly ancillary at this point: a marginal object in more senses than one.

I have already noted that the camera films the vehicle as if to underscore its stillness. Moments before this shot, Don Anselmo stood up ceremoniously on his *cochecito* when he finally decided to take charge of the situation and reconcile the lovers. The solemnity of the moment is visually underlined by the shot-countershot syntax and the low angle of the camera. Don Anselmo really stands, if not as a giant, then definitely as a bigger man than the Don Anselmo we have known so far (the timid father in the face of his family's abuse, the old man wandering through the corridors of his own house). Even if the film never questions his walking capability, the effect of this standing up on the same handicapped vehicle he has killed to get becomes, to some extent, a provocation. "¿Está usted impedido?" (Are you disabled?) is the question that precedes this ritual moment of standing on one's two feet. "No, I am not," replies the old man, finally admitting to his true state. Object and subject seem at odds in an all-too-visual way. This is the image that confirms the impossibility of equating the exercise of self-naming with an act of self-liberation. While shuttling back and forth between these two communities, Don Anselmo is at home in neither. In the one he longs to join he can only be a go-between, not a member. So the time comes to stand up and declare his proper nature. Let me underscore once more that it is immediately after Don Anselmo strikes so brutally at the regime that stifles him that he fixes the problems in the community he cannot join. Let me insist that the old man's instrumental role in the couple's reconciliation seems connected with the murderous act that precedes his good deed. The latter action redeems the former. Don Anselmo forces the lovers to make up in a hurry and without explanations. Motives are truly meaningless. The couple's reconciliation is more important for the mediator himself than for the two lovers. Don Anselmo turns into the opposite of what the classic *senex iratus*, the angry old man, used to be: his duties are to facilitate, not to impede.

In a formulation somewhat different from Frye's yet inspired by his work, Cavell points out that classic comedy revolves around the problem of identity, or "what becomes of an individual."[15] In turn, classic comedic resolutions "depend upon the acquisition in time of self-knowledge . . . ; this is a matter of learning who you are."[16] I have identified this moment of self-knowledge in *El cochecito* as the one in which Don Anselmo declares himself to be free of any handicap. It is the same moment in which the camera looks at him from below and in which we know that he is giving up membership in the only community that would offer him both freedom and company. However, this state of newfound exclusion has been foreshadowed by a number of images throughout the film.

Don Anselmo's exclusion is already evident the first time we see him among his handicapped friends. In this image, it becomes particularly noticeable that the old man has worked his way in to occupy the center of the frame. As already mentioned, one of this character's most painful, ironic realities is that he moves by himself, that he can walk. In the first scene with his group of handicapped friends, Don Anselmo advances slowly from a distant background, jumps over the circle of special vehicles that centers the shot, and stands in the middle. He is finally the central human figure in the shot composition, central both in his position and in his difference. Even though Don Anselmo will enjoy a brief moment of happiness thereafter, eating and singing among the small community of handicapped people, the first "shot of loneliness" in the film will take place in the same *locus amoenus*, the same "pleasant place." What I consider a shot of loneliness, by the way, is not a question of numbers or of isolating the human figure but a question of filming abandonment. It is a question of creating images for solitude as a human condition. The most remarkable shot of loneliness in *El cochecito* (the one that forces us to keep watching a human figure) is that extremely slow zoom out of the only *cochecito* that cannot be moved by its rider. As the camera recedes, we see the figure abandoned by his girlfriend, abandoned by the group, and in the process of being abandoned by the camera.

We feel this again in the final shot of Don Anselmo's picnic. After eating, the group leaves without paying any heed to Don Anselmo's pleas to let him come along. The camera stays on him those extra seconds that make the length of time dedicated to human figures in the film feel longer than usual. That extra time of fixation arrests, however fleetingly, the narration as much as it forces the gaze to look deeply into the human figure. Don Anselmo, in the distance, is off center within the frame, and his profile overlaps with the trunk of a tree behind him. He is, in some way, a tree himself, an immobile entity after all. He suffers from the motionlessness of those who can *only* walk in the mechanized world of handicapped speed. In this film, movement is clearly the expression of a mobility that has little to do with the capacity to travel. Movement, in fact, is subdivided into different ways of belonging and exclusion. At home, Don Anselmo continues to translate his movement into forms of in-between existence.

The Proharán household forms a continuum where private space is inconceivable. We know this from the moment we see the old man's room invaded by his French-learning granddaughter. Soon enough, Don Anselmo will guide us through the house's space in the first hand-held camera sequence of the movie. And the first thing to be noticed is how permeable the living quarters are to the multiple noises of the neighborhood; the second thing is the association between the old man and a continuous open and shutting of doors. Without a room of his own, Don Anselmo meanders through the house. His liminal condition and his utter displacement are evident from the very beginning ("Come in, Papá. You sure love to hover in doorways!" complains his granddaughter). Is this condition of being always in between spaces related to the essential ambivalence I recognized in the character? Is it another symbolic clue to the difficulty of naming and judging him? Does this prefigure Don Anselmo's ability to move between communities and not within them? Let us advance for now that his in-betweenness, if not his marginality, coincides with what the movie seems to be saying about identity and dissidence under Franco's totalitarian developmentalism.

Among the few things we know about Don Anselmo's past, nothing is more significant than the fact that he definitely has one, that he is an old man. One of the film's distinctions is the fact that Simone de Beauvoir mentions it in her *La vieillesse* (1970), and another is its frequent comparison with a neorealist classic such as De Sica and Cesare Zavattini's *Umberto D* (1951). As a possible study on old age, the eldest Proharán is not the type of protagonist that has usually embodied the dilemmas of national identity in troubled times. The *nuevo cine español*, most of the midcentury poetry, and a number of the most representative postwar novels will make use of children and youngsters to explore the conditions of Spanishness under such dire historical and political constraints. These characters will discover realities ranging from sex to their country's recent historical traumas in a more or less elliptical way. Theirs will be a future usually represented as uncertain at best. If there is one thing Don Anselmo lacks, in his dissidence as well as in his stage of life, it is a future. His old age is never more evident than in the only close-up in the entire film. It is, to be precise, an extreme close-up of Don Anselmo's face that lasts longer than any of the previous shots. There are indeed a multitude of points one could make about this extraordinary moment, yet I would only underline old age itself, that is, that which underscores the impossibility of a future or of flight. I feel that the images that end the film corroborate this viewpoint. There are images that make visible once more this character's essential ambivalence, especially in his dissidence. There are images that, finally, translate both the possibility of freedom and the limits of transgression into a special kind of movement.

Circularity and Transgression

Along a lonely, gloomy road, Don Anselmo rides his motorized wheelchair toward the camera; he rides past it and speeds away. His *cochecito* is now the getaway vehicle of a crime. In the distance, two *guardias civiles* order him to pull over and turn around. Detainee and guards come back toward the camera on their way back to Madrid. The movie's final images, filmed in a shot sequence, become a 360-degree panorama that emphasizes the impossibility of escape for the protagonist. This camera movement would be tantamount to what in the classic ironic comedy is the hero's return to the fold and the triumph of a "humorous society." The circular itinerary proves the futility of his enterprise. In turn, Don Anselmo's last words in the film ("Will I be allowed to keep the *cochecito* in jail?") seem to make true the claims of those who would consider him a puerile or ridiculous character. Consequently, the disputed motor vehicle cannot live up to being a motorcycle after all, not completely, at least. In the same flawed or failed way, this *cochecito* was also a *seiscientos*, a means of handicapped transportation, and an object that could mean either freedom or belonging. And at this point, it is the ontological undecidability associated with all of this not quite being (or not quite meaning) that needs to be stressed, especially in the evaluation of the supposed final puerilization of Don Anselmo. I insist: what the vehicle says about its owner continues to be a problem. And this is so precisely because of the absurd insistence on keeping the *cochecito* when and where it will mean neither freedom nor belonging. The *cochecito* ends up being some sort of a supplement. In fact, it appears to gain not an economic but an existential surplus value at the end. In the final analysis, the *cochecito* is the absurd yet indispensable foundation for a mode of existence that has been erected against the useful and reasonable discourse that surrounds it. It is dissidence without a clear agenda or a definite goal; it is still saying no in the face of futility.

However, circularity as the metaphor to characterize what this film says about a rebellion that goes nowhere fails to account for Don Anselmo's disproportionate crime. In its cruelty, in its excessiveness, the indiscriminate poisoning of the whole family epitomizes the devastating value that cruelty and excess have within the subgenre of the "integration of a society." Don Anselmo's crime amounts to an act that "does not apply the given ethical standards but redefines them. . . . Once the decision is taken, the very field of choice is transformed."[17] The triumphant "humorous society" does not prevail at any cost after all. Still, the suspicion lingers that, given the conclusion of the film and the fate of its hero, the true transgressive value of his most extreme act could be overstated. The key to it all is, once again, movement. In this case, the key is the circular movement of the camera: a "delinquent" movement in itself.

While it is true that the classic rule of filming that states that the camera cannot pan beyond a 180-degree angle has been broken many times, every transgression of this rule seems to call for especial consideration. A law is a law regardless of how many times it has been broken, so those special violations still signal a moment of transgression that carries a special meaning. In this case, it is worth noting that the 360-degree pan of the camera has a stop and that this stop is occasioned by the two *guardias civiles* who detain Don Anselmo as the shot that follows him reaches its conventional 180-degree limit. It is the representatives of the law, members of one of the police forces more closely associated with repression in Spain, who force the old man to turn around and, in so doing, to break the cinematic rule. Since this is an ending partially imposed by the censor, it is tempting to find in this scene a direct reference to what censorship caused to be broken.[18] However, I prefer instead to point out that this sequence shot represents the cinematic transgression that takes place the moment the one attempted by the main character comes to an end. The transgression hindered by so many obstacles (from Don Anselmo's age to the vehicle's incapacity to represent either belonging or freedom) survives in a technical gesture that disobeys other rules, disarms other automatisms, or contravenes other conventions regarding the way to move a camera or the way to look at something within the film medium. Whether this transgression is merely formal or symbolic, whether it is substantial or sufficient, are surely debatable points. At any rate, it is a point to be connected with the value of transgression, symbolism, and sufficiency that both *El cochecito* and its ambivalent protagonist may represent in the cultural landscape of Spain under Francoist developmentalism. The main character in Berlanga's *El verdugo*, however, seems to be less ambivalent about almost everything he is forced to do to survive under the same political and economic constraints.

3

Complicity Dissected

Berlanga's El verdugo

While *El cochecito* introduces the complex subject of the different modes of complicity with both a political regime and a socioeconomic order, *El verdugo* (*The Executioner*, 1963) represents a cinematographic dissection of widespread connivance with that authoritarian, ultimately lethal socioeconomic regime.[1] The complicity that Berlanga's film dissects is, to be precise, that of the ordinary citizen, that of the "good man," or *hombre de bien*, as he is called in the film itself. In its extreme elaboration on the topic of the everyday citizen's connivance with the forces that keep him down, *El verdugo* goes so far as to question the very possibility of innocence within a certain kind of social order.

In this filmic dissection of complicity, the camera is of course the scalpel, a cinematographic apparatus that does not move as much as it cuts through the characters' motives to examine their degree of involvement with a repressive regime. Correspondingly, space in this movie—filmic, imagined, or iconic—appears as a kind of symbolic limbo in need of an explicit agency on the part of those who occupy it. That would be the way to make space mean something or be meaningful, the way to charge it with ethical demands, in fact. The camera's role (its behavior, if you will) and the various ways spaces signify are then the two guiding aspects in my reading of *El verdugo* as a true anatomy of the conditions of complicity under Francoist developmentalism.

Distances and Heights

José Luis (Nino Manfredi), an employee at a funeral home, meets and eventually marries Carmen (Emma Penella), the daughter of the executioner Amadeo (José Isbert). In order to get the apartment that his brand new father-in-law is entitled to as a government-employed worker, José Luis not only has to wed the executioner's daughter but also must inherit Amadeo's line of work upon the old man's retirement. This is, in any case, the original plan. After a long series of unsuccessful refusals, José Luis agrees to be part of the scheme. Appeased only by the questionable argument that executions are, after all, infrequent, and comforted by the thought that, should the moment to perform his duties come, he could always quit, José Luis starts enjoying his new life as an executioner for the state. He is a closeted slaughterer, as it were, since nothing identifies him as a person who kills on behalf of the state and since his first assignment does not seem to be forthcoming any time soon, if ever. As to be expected, the moment to truly earn his salary finally arrives. Immediate resignation is his first impulse. The "problem" is that the execution is to take place on the very touristy and very appealing island of Palma de Mallorca. Ironically, this first task on the job is also a once-in-a-lifetime opportunity for a really satisfying vacation. The trip will double as the honeymoon the couple never had.

The whole family embarks for the island convinced that the prisoner will ultimately be pardoned. As it happens, he is not. This is the moment of the most famous scene in the movie. It is also the scene from which, according to Berlanga, the whole film springs.[2] It consists of a single shot of the interior yard that joins the jail with the execution chamber (see fig. 6). A very slow crane takes the camera up and away from a rectangular space soon to be known as "the white box," a location in which filming could take place only after the director overcame the producers' resistance.[3] The two groups of people that surround both the condemned man and his executioner walk slowly toward the door that leads to the infamous *garrote vil.* This is an especially gruesome method of execution that was not abolished until 1978 and that basically consists of breaking the neck of its victim. This is the ur-image of the movie, the moment in which José Luis is about to finally do what he is paid to do. The role reversal present in the images is the first thing to notice in this extraordinary sequence shot. The executioner has to be dragged to the execution chamber. A few frames before, he was the one who had showed his family pictures and the one who had asked repeatedly for news of a pardon. Even though they have shown an unmistakable contempt for him and for what he does for a living, the prison guards have had a last drink on his behalf. Now he is the one forcefully pushed toward the *garrote vil* and even the one who faints on his way to it.

Figure 6. Crossing the "white box"

To truly appreciate this seminal scene, it should be underlined that José Luis's struggle on the way to the execution chamber is the last in a long series of rebellious actions throughout the film that proved useless when they were not pathetic. Ever since his coworker Álvarez (Ángel Álvarez) pushed him to go after the old executioner Amadeo in order to give him back the executioner briefcase he left behind, José Luis has been looking for excuses, saying no, backing off, yet always unsuccessfully. Up until now, those failed refusals seemed harmless. When the final struggle reveals that resistance is not an option, the long chain of minor aborted revolts also reveals its true value. The seemingly inconsequential acts of acquiescence, the petty capitulations, are the ones that compromised the fate of this man.

Financial improvement, the right to a decent home, freedom from mean and small-minded family members, sexual desire . . . For José Luis, the motives to act as he does are manifold, and they would seem to touch every single aspect of his life. As was the case in *El cochecito*, in this film the individual is an accomplice of a whole value system as much as of a precise political regime. Berlanga himself describes his movie mainly as a statement against the death penalty but also against "the invisible traps society sets up for us in order to curtail our freedom."[4] A considerable number of pages of criticism on the movie have concerned themselves with the identification of those traps and, especially, with determining who or what sets them up.

For Antonio Gómez Rufo, following the director's lead, the culprit is a very vague and very broad "society."[5] For John Hopewell, what dooms José Luis is a combination of "chance, mishap, chaos and compromise."[6] This reading, of course, puts the blame for José Luis's downfall as much on chance as it does on his incapacity to fight back. Carlos Losilla also focuses on chance when he notes, "It [chance] becomes an unyielding structure that forces the characters as well as the narration to continue on a certain path."[7] Steven Marsh singles out quite specifically what compromises José Luis's innocence when he speaks instead of the "manipulative hand of Isbert/Amadeo."[8] Vicente José Benet makes more concrete the type of society that sets up the traps for our reluctant executioner. For Benet the entrapment comes about because of the "needs and the atmosphere created by developmentalist Francoism."[9] In the same critical vein, Annabel Martín blames the capitulation of our protagonist on "the two totalitarian regimes," the Francoist state and consumerism.[10] As in Don Anselmo's case, the consumerism involved in what the main character does in *El verdugo* would seem in need of careful analysis. The main benefit obtained is, after all, an apartment, a home, hardly a commodity. In any case, this collection of critical opinions illustrates that what is really at stake in the analysis of the film is not only the nature of the satirized entity but also its scope. That which lies within the range of the satire seems to expand or to shrink according to the critic, therefore altering both the depth and the reach of the film as political satire. In fact, a scope or a target either too broad or too ambivalent was the reason to consider the film in its entirety—and not only its main characters—as a cultural product suspect of a twofold connivance: with a consumerist system and, worst, with fascism.

For the Francoist regime (whose spokesman on this issue at the time was Alfredo Sánchez Bella, Spanish ambassador to Rome), *El verdugo* was an anti-patriotic film in which Berlanga showed his true colors as a fellow traveler of the country's enemies.[11] The showing of the film at the Venice film festival took place the same year the regime sent the communist leader Julián Grimau to the firing squad on April 20. Moreover, the premiere was only days apart from the execution by *garrote vil* of two anarchist activists, Francisco Granados Mata and Joaquín Delgado Martínez, on August 17. This, of course, did not contribute to a benign reading of the film by government officials. The dictator himself is said to have called its director "a bad Spaniard." However, in leftist circles, the complicity of the movie was, ironically, with Franco's dictatorial regime. The most extreme accusation came from Robert Benayoun, who, writing in the influential *Positif,* even called the film "fascist," since it portrayed its executioner as a character that inspired mainly sympathy from the audience.[12] There were certainly other opinions, although they were not as virulent in their denunciations, that believed Berlanga's film fell short in its criticism or made its target too vague to be effective. *El verdugo* was indeed a film against the death penalty, but the concrete regime behind all the deaths seemed to be relegated to a too comfortable background. Many of Berlanga's comments on the subject, in fact, helped to depoliticize the movie. Here is one of the most exemplary from this perspective: "I did not make a movie against the death penalty because I was an organized abolitionist or one of those maniacs who organize all sorts of fanatic sects; neither do I belong to any movement against the death penalty. I did

El verdugo because I was terrified of the idea that one day I could go mad and commit a crime for which the punishment is death and that I would be the one condemned. It was a movie against my death penalty. *El verdugo* was born with this purpose."[13] The director was also well aware of the contending thoughts regarding his ideological affinities when, after the premiere of *La vaquilla* in 1985, he declared: "It is the story of my life. For the communists I am a fascist, and for the Right I am an indecent red."[14]

In all the debates on the ideology and the political effectiveness of the film, there was also space for the discussion of aesthetics and difference, as Ángel Quintana's sample of reactions to the movie by the international press shows.[15] Between Jean Louis Comolli's unenthusiastic review in *Cahiers* and the already mentioned contempt from Benayoun, there was the temperate praise by Tom Milne in *Sight and Sound*. For the latter, one of *El verdugo*'s flaws was that some scenes had succumbed to Spanish *costumbrismo*. Quintana's account demonstrates that the European critic still sees this film, and most Spanish cinema of the period, as formally and thematically strange to European cinematographic modernity. And one suspects that those perceived differences, consciously or not, have a role in seeing the movie as ideologically flawed.

At this point it would be worth underlining that the film itself already addresses its ambivalence. In very concrete terms, the film addresses the troubling possibility that sympathy is precisely the feeling an executioner might inspire. *El verdugo* explores, in fact, the morally disruptive effects of certain feelings under given circumstances, in short, the ethics of sympathy.

The first dialogue in the movie that has the figure of a government-paid executioner as its subject focuses not so much on what he is or does as on how he is perceived. As Amadeo leaves the penal complex in which the execution that opens the film takes place, José Luis and Álvarez exchange first impressions about this stout and mild-mannered death dealer. They have not talked to him yet, so they do not have much on which to base their opinions of this seemingly innocuous old man, played by José (Pepe) Isbert, the same actor who played Don Anselmo in *El cochecito*. "The truth is that he seems like a normal person," comments José Luis. "I even like him!" replies his partner. Seconds later, Álvarez speaks of feeling "pity" (*lástima*) for him. Soon enough, Amadeo himself will label as "misunderstood people" all of those who make a living killing in the name of the state. With a flawless logic, he will also bark at José Luis an undisputable truth: "If the penalty exists, somebody must be there to execute it." Before we go any further, it is important to note that in this film, despite the singular noun of its title, there are, in fact, two of these "necessary" public workers. How likable they are or how much compassion they may inspire depends on how they are presented in each case, on their degree of visibility as executioners, and on the different ways they assume the burden of their trade.

The selection of Pepe Isbert to play the old executioner has led critics to speak of an ideologically counterproductive "tenderness" in the character.[16] According to Benet, "it is difficult to distinguish . . . between the character of Amadeo and the body of the actor that plays him. . . . Amadeo is strangely quotidian and lovable; he has the perfect iconography of a tender and kindhearted grandfather who enjoys to the point of ecstasy the prospect of eating seafood or holding on to his funny little ways. However, we know that the narrative has been set up so that everything in him refers to death."[17] Vicente Sánchez-Biosca offers a more forceful opinion: "Between the body of this little man and his terrible job the dark humor of the best Berlanga is born."[18] At any rate, it should be noted that from the very beginning the idea was to depict the executioner in this manner, regardless of the actor who would play the character. In the director's own words, "not only is he a normal person, but from the very first sequence we wanted to portray a likable executioner."[19]

José Luis, on the other hand, has been called a *calzonazos* (henpecked husband).[20] This, of course, identifies the root of the problem as a character flaw rather than a flawed system. There has also been ample discussion about casting issues in his case too. Berlanga complained that Nino Manfredi, an Italian actor, did not look Spanish enough. So we have a very Spanish-looking actor playing the executioner, who approaches his work as the natural thing to do under the circumstances, and a non-Spanish actor being thrown into a situation in which he is called barbaric or uncivilized. Forced by the circumstances of coproduction, casting decisions in *El verdugo* could be read as a matter of ethics and appearances too. In that respect, it must be underlined that what differentiates each executioner from the other is their visibility as the ones who execute the death penalties dictated by the judicial branch of the state. Amadeo is an executioner in plain sight, as it were. He is the one who accepts his trade as a natural consequence of the existence of the law. In contrast, José Luis is never identified as an executioner, not even on his paycheck.

Without the need to pursue anymore all these disquisitions on the executioners' likableness and/or visibility, one can safely advance the conclusion that the films depend on the existence of competing viewpoints and conflicting vantage points (both ideological and moral) to judge the relation of the private individual and the estate. Indeed, *El verdugo* is a filmic text with the capacity to turn affection into proximity and denunciations into detachment. And, as previously stated, the gateway to this ethical spatiality is the use of a camera that constantly underlines immediacy to or remoteness from that which is being filmed. Amidst the hotbed of opinions that, to this day, pull the movie in so many different directions, the guiding question should be: How does Berlanga's camera behave? Such a question is equivalent to asking: How does it display its complicity with or its antagonism toward that which is being filmed? In other words, we have to ask the following questions: What does Berlanga's camera allow us to watch and from where? What subject positions does it force us to inhabit? Are we accomplices with the actions we are seeing? In this series of questions, I want to recognize the influence, at least in spirit, of Godard's (or Luc Moullet's) famous statement: "Tracking shots are a question of morality."[21] In *El verdugo*, not only tracking shots but also cranes, depth of field, the orchestration of sequence shots, and the use of a shot-countershot structure are very much questions of morality. They are all questions of connivance and distance, of emotional attachment or remoteness. They are all about emotions and ethics that get translated into space; they are all about the *spatialization* of a very concrete set of emotions with a moral dimension.

Going back to that foundational white box in the film, what makes that scene really memorable seems to be the noted crane shot that slowly takes the camera up and away from what it films. Among the sound effects, the camera angle, and the shadows projected by the human figures, the movie makes its clearer incursion into what we could call cinematographic expressionism.[22] As a concession to expressionism, the images must be taken first as the projection of a psychological state. However, the slow, upward movement of the camera may be read as a refusal to enter the space for the execution. The distance from which it films is, then, a gesture of detachment. It is, in any case, an explicit act of nonconnivance that should prompt a broader reflection regarding what we are forced to watch in the movie and from which viewpoint.[23] Vicente Benet relates this sequence with a series of instances in the movie in which the shot freezes for a second before the transition to another sequence takes place. These moments of "duration" are the ones that help to change the tone, the ones that force the audience to look differently, more seriously perhaps, in spite of all the comic situations.[24]

Such a sample of quotes from analysis devoted to the same scene should show that this high-angle shot is not only the image from which the entire film may have been born but also the meeting point of all its serious readings. I must rush to add, though, that this shot is neither the first nor the only one of its kind in the film. The first overhead view takes place during José Luis's wedding ceremony, a bird's-eye take with much less commentary. The shot represents the culmination of what has been a long sequence that concludes with an overhead shot of the couple kneeling at the altar. While it is true that this time there is no camera movement, it is also noticeable that the new shooting angle signals a change of tone, just as it does in the white box scene. In fact, this new viewpoint underscores another act of distancing, this time in a sequence unquestionably comical in nature. The wedding ceremony immediately preceding Carmen and José Luis's has been filmed in a way that contrasts strongly with this overhead view of the new couple kneeling. The sequence of shots commences with the lavish church service of that first, unknown couple getting married, but then there is a flurry of activity that aims at stripping the church of all the elements that made it special. The second couple, the undertaker and the executioner's daughter, will have no carpet, no flowers, and no light. The filming of the white box's dead-man-walking scene from a similar angle and from the same height as this second wedding ceremony highlights our conclusion that this wedding ritual feels indeed like a death penalty. This symbolic connection between a wedding and an execution is reinforced by very punctual and poignant touches of dark humor in both the dialogue and the situations. For example, José Luis criticizes his father-in-law for wearing his work attire in the wedding ceremony ("It is my best suit," he replies), and José Luis's professional trip to Mallorca becomes the honeymoon trip that the couple never had.

I should underline at this point that not every overhead or crane shot must mean the same thing in the same way. The heights in this film mean what the whole text makes them mean. The memorable crane shot in *El verdugo* may even gain meaning when read vis-à-vis the other memorable crane shot in Berlanga's filmography and in Spanish cinema: the closing shot of *Plácido*, already mentioned in the previous chapter. In the dissection of forced or feigned charity that *Plácido* is, we see the *motocarro* parked in front of its owner's humble living quarters as a human figure walks away with a prized Christmas gift basket. At this point a camera moves up and away from this reality; the camera seems to comment on this scene with its movement. Here, as in the case of *El verdugo*, we face two overhead views that are clearly not omniscient.

These omniscient views do exist in Berlanga's work, but they serve a completely different purpose. The first scenes of *¡Bienvenido, Mister Marshall!* (Berlanga, 1952) include not only a bird's-eye view but also frozen images from which characters are removed or to which they are returned. A narrator comments in voice-over on what this panoptic gaze simultaneously watches and controls. Neither in *Plácido* nor in *El verdugo* are we invited to look from above in order to satisfy any scopic desire whatsoever. The bird's-eye view in both movies — in rare and therefore meaningful moments — offers an ironic counterpoint that makes evident how dark and how poignant they truly are. Inscribed in a paradigm of closeness and distance that is not only physical but also moral or emotional, these moments exemplify a dynamic present in the profilmic space at ground level as well.

Room to Roam

According to John Hopewell, through depth of field and the use of the sequence shot Berlanga's films underscore how much his characters lack freedom. "The deeper the field," writes Hopewell, "the greater the sense of constriction as whole screen areas are cordoned off by tawdry environment."[25] The location that best exemplifies this claustrophobic use of depth of field in *El verdugo* is the living quarters that José Luis shares with his brother (José Luis López Vázquez) and his sister-in-law (María Luisa Ponte). In this case, distances and heights are again key factors in the analysis of how space is filmed and how it is made meaningful. Likewise, the shot–reverse shot dynamic in key scenes of the movie will be the subject of special attention here, since it is another formal trait that "dialogues" with what depth of field and the long take do or mean in the film.

The apartment in question is really an inhabited basement with virtually no walls and two levels or stages attached by a flight of stairs. The camera alternates its position between these two levels, creating a profilmic space strangely open and claustrophobic at the same time. That this is a space at ground level becomes apparent in a hurry when a street sweeper sprinkles the living quarters as it cleans the street. As the sequence opens, the camera is set up in the first level of the dwelling/basement. Antonio operates a power saw in the foreground, and José Luis enters the frame at the far end of the field of view (see fig. 7). For a moment, José Luis seems to be standing at the farthest limit of the living space. Yet as soon as he moves to his left and disappears behind a steel beam, the camera occupies the position left by the character and shows the space from the reverse angle, with Antonio now positioned in the upper part of the deep frame (see fig. 8). Next to José Luis we can now see one of Antonio's daughters.

José Luis's sister-in-law, with an infant in her arms, will exit the bathroom eventually. The sequence will continue adding characters to the frame, reaching a point in which three levels of depth have been filmed: the two inside the living quarters plus the street when José Luis's friends stop by to pick him up. In Berlanga's hands, depth of field is hence not only a formal recourse that emphasizes the shabby or miserable environment around José Luis but also a means to underline both difficulty of movement and lack of privacy. With each slight reframing, with each brief panning, the filmed space is filled again with people and with things. Berlanga's camera — like Renoir's or Wyler's — is as recognizable as a signature. When it moves it makes what it films more

Figure 7. The dwelling-basement from above

Figure 8. The dwelling-basement from below

meaningful; it even makes movement itself meaningful.[26] Reflecting on Renoir's camera, William Rothman writes that it "is most characteristic when it seems primarily concerned with establishing the contingency of its frame. . . . By this I mean the impression that the world of the film extends beyond the boundaries of the frame, so that any particular placement of the camera is only contingently determined by the world of the film."[27] Beyond the boundaries of Berlanga's frame the world extends itself only to show more obstacles and more dead-end alleys to a character in need of more than a room of his own.

The use of both depth of field and the sequence shot is supposedly related also to freedom, or to a peculiar kind of freedom: the one the audience enjoys as viewers who can pay attention to any of the frames, movements, or characters that at one point or another occupy their field of vision. The classic formulation of this filming philosophy was stated by Wyler: both depth of field and the long take "let the spectator look from one character to the other at his own will, do his own cutting."[28] It is as if the freedom taken away from the character will then be granted to the spectator, a freedom overwhelmed by the fact that, in the case of *El verdugo*, depth of field comes coupled with in-depth staging. In the three planes or three different platforms of the scene I am examining, there are too many things going on at the same time. If we were to take proximity to the camera as the determining factor, we could create a hierarchy of actions; yet the shot–reverse shot structure would continuously undermine any fixed order in this viewed world. In the classic analysis, the systematic use of the shot–reverse shot dynamic in a film reveals a will to show the whole profilmic space. Invoking Bazin, we could speak of a desire for completeness. And the most important aspect of this desire as it is staged in *El verdugo* is that the profilmic space is shown in its entirety only to signal precisely the lack of room and the difficulty of moving within it. The space around the new executioner either is crowded or offers no place to hide. And the latter option must be understood literally. Berlanga's theory on the shot–reverse shot is that it "presents spaces that should never disappear in the story, that it becomes a universe in which the director, like God, must have the characters within reach. Everybody who intervenes in the story and even in the image must be accounted for at all times."[29] In other words, in *El verdugo* José Luis is always well accounted for. And yet, with all his burden of visibility, José Luis's gaze still retains some degree of agency in the articulation of the film.

In one of the first and most detailed analyses of the film's *mise-en-abyme*, Francesc Llinás points out that "within each frame there is almost always either a change in viewpoint or the coexistence of several points of view."[30] Jean-Claude Seguin theorizes this plurality or mobility of points of view when he speaks of a plural shot instead of a sequence shot in *El verdugo*.[31] Acknowledging this plurality of points of view, my reading retains José Luis as the dominant point of view. This allows for a better understanding of the poetics of distance and proximity in place throughout the movie. In *El verdugo*'s choreography of views and visions, there are a number of occasions when the camera either is set up just by José Luis or occupies the position he has just vacated. This is yet another way to stress what the movie has to say about closeness and complicity. Indeed, there are many scenes in which we are forced to look from what used to be the point of view of an executioner in the making. These moments make up a high percentage of subjective or, following Passolini's thoughts on filmic "free indirect style," *semisubjective* shots in the film, shots that translate into the creation of what can be called a *semisubjectivity* in the film.[32] This type of shot recurs during the entire movie, yet its opening scene may very well be the paradigmatic case.

El verdugo opens with the two undertakers entering a prison. They are carrying a coffin on their shoulders, and José Luis's face is not immediately visible. Comic effect notwithstanding, the shot creates a desire to see the only face that cannot be seen, the only one covered, and covered in such a way. This is an exceptional recourse to direct the audience's attention to a face without the need of a close-up. From the very beginning the camera becomes the focal point of that fundamental choreography of getting close and creating a distance that structures the film. The two undertakers will come near the camera and then

Figure 9. Watching from where José
Luis watches

keep their distance in this first sequence shot. Then the camera itself will be set
up next to José Luis after the first cut, as if it were sitting by his side, waiting for
the execution to be over (see fig. 9).

When the prison guard orders the undertakers to come closer, the camera
obeys too. The movement comes to a halt at the door beyond which the execution has just taken place, a stoppage we will notice once more in the film.
Amadeo, the veteran executioner, passes the two waiting characters just as he
passes a camera that has lost all pretense of objectivity. It shares too much of
the characters' (especially José Luis's) point of view. The supposed freedom the
viewer enjoys editing his or her own film is seriously undermined by a camera
movement that creates an emotional attachment with the main character. Nick
Browne called this phenomenon "the spectator-in-the-text."[33] The onlooker is
forced to be everywhere and nowhere at the same time. He or she is compelled
to get into the screen, as it were, and then is immediately invited to leave it. One
is either very close to or very distant from the characters, especially José Luis
in this case. This is, in fact, a truly semisubjective camera not because it stands
in (almost) for the gaze of character but because it becomes almost a subject,
another character who strives to look from where José Luis is looking and then
distances itself from that location, as if movement were used to pass judgment
on what is being filmed.

If camera movement in these profilmic spaces speaks of closeness and distance, of connivance or disgust, the iconic or concrete spaces in the film (the
family apartment, the island of Mallorca, even the whole country of Germany)
turn out to be desired spaces from which to flee to or in which to find shelter.
Put otherwise, in *El verdugo* every idyllic or ideal space can be perceived as such
on account of its moral limbo status. These are spaces where making decisions
is not a question of life or death. And yet it is precisely in one of these spaces of
seemingly suspended agency where our reluctant executioner ends up having
to act.

Filmed Space and Spaces to Be Filmed

Germany in *El verdugo* is frequently mentioned but never seen. One of the most frequent destinations for Spanish emigrants in the 1960s, for José Luis Germany is more a desideratum than a country. In fact, the northern European country is a shelter in which to find refuge and to avoid family responsibilities. The family apartment, the prize to be gained by becoming an executioner, is a space desired in a more concrete way, yet it also becomes another place in which to hide or to delude oneself in the midst of a familiar bliss always threatened by the possibility of a job assignment. Palma de Mallorca, a city immediately associated with tourism, is the last candidate to function as a paradise of inaction. It is even more precarious than the rest, since death in it is nearer. *Et in Mallorca ego* could be the motto here, as if the personification of death itself could stake a claim to this new Arcadia of crowded beaches and north European foreigners. These three desired spaces, all of them with the potential to become idyllic or to be idealized, possess first a contextual value. The Spain of the early 1960s offers a very recognizable background of massive emigration, growing tourism, and a long-lasting housing crisis. However, the film does much more than just deploy these socioeconomic phenomena as background.

The apartment worth killing for becomes the epitome of a desired space whose ideal condition borders unreality. The images that show the apartment for the first time corroborate this unreal rather than ideal status. The apartment is first seen under construction, still a skeleton of a building. The entire family walks around this wall-less space making observations that both attest to its promise and anticipate domestic fulfillment. The kinds of comments the future living quarters prompt are indeed a lesson on distorted vision or, at least, a symptom of how not to measure household happiness. At some point, even the abundance of light in the apartment is praised, although, of course, the apartment could not be otherwise than well lit, since the walls have not been built yet. The unreality of the family home, in fact, echoes the family's unreal expectations of inhabiting such a space, since they have forgotten what had to be done to get it. The fact that the finished apartment bears no resemblance to how the family imagined it during their first visit (it is now essentially claustrophobic and much darker) is but another visual gag that underlines the inevitable ruin of everyone's good intentions. Spaces in this film are not to be walled off from the world of decisions. Spaces of the imagination are needed in order to see if they can serve as a shelter from agency.

For José Luis, Germany functions less as the welfare heaven many Spaniards found it to be in the 1960s than as a way to escape responsibility. During the conversation in which the future executioner contemplates more seriously the possibility of emigrating north, he does not consider the oppressive surroundings he might leave behind but the urgent duty of assuming his role as a father. Carmen, already visibly pregnant, confronts José Luis in his workplace, among funeral vans and wreaths. Both the narrative and the visual imaginary enable us to equate the prospect of leaving mainly with an act of cowardice. Our task now is to decide if this equation can be extrapolated to the meaning of Spanish emigration in the 1960s and, more importantly, if the film is simply saying that leaving the country is definitely not the ethical thing to do under the circumstances.

Emigration was, together with tourism, the most significant factor in the economic prosperity of Francoist developmentalism and, by extension, one of the reasons behind the regime's longevity. Both phenomena alleviated in some degree the disastrous initial consequences of the 1959 Plan de Estabilización. This economic packet of measures was supposed to propel the Spanish economy into Western capitalism, but its most noticeable upshot was a devastating hike in the national unemployment numbers. In the regime's rhetoric, emigration went from bleeding the nation to performing a patriotic duty. In the popular imagination, emigration, especially to northern European countries, became a hybrid of martyrdom and adventure.[34] By creating a series of circumstances that turn José Luis's plans of emigration into an act of cowardice, by making not staying be tantamount to desertion, the film seems to interpret this social phenomenon as another act of connivance with the regime. It is not that we could accuse every emigrant of complicity with the Francoist regime, yet, once again, this film's reflection on the manifold ways to be complicit has room for those who are oblique and even those who are unconscious. Put in a more extreme way, the movie questions the notion that an ethical responsibility could be a well-defined, clear-cut concept.

Tourism also became a social phenomenon of hard-to-delimit ethical dimensions. In fact, tourism even became a chief instrument of the Francoist "mode of governance," as Justin Crumbaugh has extensively shown in a study that draws heavily on 1960s popular comedic films.[35] In the case of this particular movie, to turn the executioner into a tourist at the end of the film is also to make more visible and more dramatic (more dramatically visible) that José Luis has a very superficial grasp of the reality that surrounds him. The tourist who travels to know other places and other people transforms himself here into the one who travels to the very core of what he has become. The classic study that connects tourism and modernity emphasizes the role of leisure in the birth of a certain "touristic consciousness that extends beyond immediate social relationships to the structure and organization of the total society."[36] This kind of consciousness also possesses an ethical and a political dimension. In very broad terms, "the touristic form of moral involvement with diverse public representations of race, poverty, urban structures, social ills, and, of course, the public good, the monuments, is a modern alternative to systems of in-group morality built out of binary oppositions: insider vs. Outsider, us vs. Them."[37] In a totalitarian regime, this us/them divide becomes more pronounced. In the Spain of the 1960s the regime itself acknowledged the propagandistic value of tourism. "I believe that an essential dimension of tourism is the deep awareness that in Spain there are different truths and different forces," declared, somewhat mysteriously, the regime's star minister, Manuel Fraga Iribarne.[38]

In a way very different from what Franco's *ministro de información y turismo* had in mind, *El verdugo*'s ending aims precisely at making these truths and forces painfully visible. The flagrant contradictions that the so-called openness of the regime produces find in this executioner-tourist their most compelling projection. The new phase of modernization in which the country found itself had as precarious an economic infrastructure as it had a bankrupt moral system. I return one last time to the infamous letter penned by Ambassador Sánchez Bella: "What does the old, narrow-minded, traditional Mallorca have to do with the one that today has a thousand hotels and thousands of tourists?"[39] Judging by what we see in *El verdugo*, plenty. It is precisely because Palma de Mallorca can boast thousands of hotels and thousands of tourists that the unreal nature of Francoist *apertura* becomes more evident. It is in precisely this paradise of leisure time where the complicity with the regime must become explicit. And it is here too where we witness that crane that signals the most noticeable instance of a camera distancing itself from what it is filming, a movement and a distancing that we could translate into . . . into what? A moral last stand? Rejection? Disgust? Are we witnessing the end of all the petty complicities into which the spectator has entered? Is the film breaking the spell of an emotional involvement with an executioner who has been primordially filmed as victim? Tracking shots are indeed a question of morality, and so are filming in depth, certain uses of the shot sequence, and the special deployment of crane shots. In this film, they are all formal traits to articulate an investigation of what it means to connive or to condemn. Nearness and distance are here both spatial and moral. Put otherwise, all of these cinematographic practices result in the dissection of a complicity that must be made explicit through agency, where nearness and distance are both spatial and moral terms, and where the filmed spaces and how spaces are filmed are of truly *capital* importance.

Coda: *Costumbrismo* and *Sainete*

After a reading so bent on looking at complex camera movement and a refined use of space in such a supposedly *costumbrista* film, it is only appropriate to rethink the place that *costumbrismo*, together with *sainete*, may have as unmodern paradigms in both *El verdugo* and *El cochecito*. The frequent association with both terms would seem to question to what degree these films are visual expressions of modernity, or how inescapably *indigenous* (and I use the term here fully aware of its charged meaning) they might be after all.

I should start by stressing that the question of filmic *costumbrismo* is a fairly confusing one and that a similar confusion is at play in the frequent invocation of a *sainete* aesthetics or praxis in the film medium. But the lack of clarity is in this case productive, since it points to the ability of some films to expose the geopolitics of cultural categorization. We have seen that *El verdugo* was labeled as *costumbrista* abroad mainly as a way to call it Spanish and hence, tacitly, unmodern. Historically, *costumbrismo* is indeed an aesthetics that idealizes the local and the traditional precisely because the foreign and the modern are felt as threats to a stable sense of national identity. The adjective *costumbrista*, more broadly used to describe a representational practice, assumes other constitutive contrasts: the verbal or visual representation involved is not truly realistic, sophisticated, or complex enough; it is not challenging in its ideological and figurative ambitions. Without space to go into a more detailed discussion of what the term meant in the nineteenth century or into the ways it is used in our everyday appraisals of visual and verbal narratives, I would simply concentrate on the idea that there is no dark humor in *costumbrismo*. Even Mariano José de Larra's humor (one of the less conservative of *costumbrista* writers), acerbic and critical as it may be, keeps the laughing subject at a safe distance from the comic spectacle. Whether *El cochecito* and *El verdugo* can be called *costumbristas*, the demands they make on viewers to self-question the timing and the occasion of their laughter are very different in tone and degree. This is a phenomenon worth noting to qualify the possible *costumbrismo* in these movies, and it is even more deserving of special attention because of the repeated invocations of a *sainete* spirit in them.

We owe to Juan Antonio Ríos Carratalá the most useful discussion of a "*sainetesque*" mode in Spanish cinema.[40] The Spanish critic indeed identifies a number of what he calls "symptoms" that first enable such a discussion. Tellingly enough, the use of the word *symptom* instead of, for instance, *feature* reveals how tentative the extrapolation of the theatrical genre to cinema ultimately is. Ríos Carratalá's list of "symptoms" is long, and it includes a choral structure, the use of stock characters, and the depiction of picturesque or popular scenes.

I could concede that, in some measure, the last two items could be applied to a *"sainetesque"* reading of *El verdugo*. However, since the origins of the genre are theatrically traditional and politically conformist, Berlanga and Ferreri before him (or, as we shall see, Fernán-Gómez) must be using the conventions of the genre in a very subversive way, since these filmmakers continue to be firmly planted in the camp of dissidence during the decade. Fernán-Gómez concedes as much in one of the most eloquent defenses of the theatrical genre in film. According to this actor-director, in the hands of Berlanga, for instance (or in his own hands, I should add), "the genre lost as much in popularity as it gained in sincerity and richness of intentions."[41] In fact, the first meaningful defense of the *sainete* as a viable source of cultural specificity in cinema took place in the mid-1940s. In the film magazine *Primer plano*, the director Edgar Neville published a short essay titled "In Defense of *Sainete*." The most valuable aspect of the piece is that it did not attempt to explain what a *sainete* is or to ascertain what it might add to the film medium. Neville instead stated what the term *sainete* stood against. In the 1940s the *sainete* opposed the historical superproductions that used to re-create both the recent past, such as *Raza* (José Luis Sáez de Heredia, 1942) and *Los últimos de Filipinas* (Antonio Román, 1945), or the distant, mythical one, like *Alba de América* (Juan de Orduña, 1951). As a cultural practice, it also stood in opposition to the universal or, at least, the exportable. To make filmic *sainetes* was to thrive on the local and hence to embrace the condition of being too exclusive, too vernacular, or too untranslatable. We could equally say that, in the 1960s, to take from the *sainete* tradition meant to undermine the attempts at the creation of a national cinema that could be easily read by others. The crucial point in this view is that this mechanism of untranslatability was less an expression of nationalistic pride than an act of resistance in the face of the compulsory mandate of making Spanish reality more palatable to foreign tastes (the implicit command to NCE directors, for instance). Once again, the type of humor the movies used or deployed was the key factor to overcome the conformist tenor of the *sainete* genre. As much as all the formal traits I have laid bare in *El verdugo*, dark humor itself undoes what some of these movies have of a *comedia de costumbres* or of a cinematic *sainete*. With Buñuel about to enter the scene, and hence with the possibility that an auteur discourse can sweep away these generic considerations, it is vital to emphasize that modernity in these films is a question of both aesthetics and laughter.

4

Don Jaime's Laughter

Humor and Perversion in Viridiana

> In reality, *Viridiana* is a picture of black humor.
>
> Luis Buñuel

Just as he is about to write his last words before committing suicide, Don Jaime (Fernando Rey), Viridiana's scheming uncle, pauses for a moment to stroke his beard and reflect on what he is about to do (see fig. 10). He seems to be contemplating what his decision, whatever it is, will bring about. And he chuckles. The future that his words on a white piece of paper will help materialize seems to amuse this man. His most recent past, what has just happened, is nothing but deadly serious. He has asked his niece, a novice nun, to dress in his late wife's wedding gown. He has proposed to her, and, with the help of his servant, he has drugged her, kissed her in her sleep, and made her believe that she is not a virgin anymore. Viridiana (Silvia Pinal) leaves in spite of the many lies and truths Don Jaime produces in a desperate attempt to make her stay. Now the old man can only look out from his office window as the carriage that takes her back to the convent drives away. When he turns away from that window, on his way to his writing desk, he is already smiling. We will be able to conclude later that what Don Jaime is about to write is his last will and testament. His estate is to be shared between Viridiana and his long-estranged natural son, Jorge (Fernando Rabal). It would be hard to argue that, in writing this will,

Figure 10. Don Jaime, or the "pervert" screenwriter

Don Jaime can anticipate all that will befall innocent Viridiana. She will share her uncle's mansion with a womanizing cousin who wants to modernize their property, while her plan is to turn the estate into a homeless shelter. She will be sexually attacked by one of the beggars she has helped. Finally, she will end up falling into Jorge's clutches in a famous final scene where an ironic ménage à trois with Jorge and the servant Ramona (Margarita Lozano) is implied.

This chain of events may not be what Don Jaime foresees as he chuckles, yet he is certainly envisioning a situation in which two individuals who signify two opposite views of life and who hold conflicting moral codes will have to live together. This is, incidentally, one of the original ideas Buñuel and Julio Alejandro used to write the screenplay.[1] Hence one could say that Don Jaime is not so much writing his last will as he is authoring a script or, at least, coming up with a scenario. According to Tom Conley, in Don Jaime's "scene of writing . . . he is seeing, hearing, and soon writing as might a director staging the very sequence as it might appear in the film."[2]

As a stand-in for the screenwriter or the filmmaker, Don Jaime seems to be as perverse a character as any character could be in the first part of the story. He is also as perverse as many spectators have imagined the man behind the camera to be, a notion that never ceased to perplex Buñuel. Since Freud, of course, perversion has always been measured against the standard notion of normalcy.[3] Since Lacan, Kant cannot be understood without Sade. Even though the Spanish director recognized his debt to the latter, Buñuel's "perversion" as a filmmaker can be related simply to the way he makes us derive pleasure from the moving image, a way that challenges the pleasure conventional filmic narratives are supposed to provide. This is in essence the thesis of Paul Sandro's *Diversions of Pleasure*.[4] In contrast, it is more complicated to gauge the transgressive pleasures involved in Don Jaime's perversion as a fetishistic, necrophilic *metteur en scène* because of his manipulation of Viridiana and Jorge.

If perversion is indeed "a specific mode of desiring and making sense of the world," if it is most of all a practice that exposes "the fantasy of the other and the various social lies that such fantasy necessarily enforces," then the question regarding perversion in *Viridiana* (1961) becomes: From what moral order do the various perversions in the film get their meaning?[5] Or, to put it in a more extreme way, the question in this case would be: What kind of desiring and thinking represents those two perverts, Don Jaime and Buñuel? The perversions of both filmmaker and character do entail ways of looking and making others behave. They both indeed direct Viridiana. They make her do things, act, and dress in a certain way. And the subsequent questions to be posed to both Don Jaime and Buñuel are: Why treat sweet Viridiana this way? What has she done to deserve this? The character played by Fernando Rey and his creator may come up with two different sets of answers to these questions. To the suggestion that the movie's main object of criticism is Christian charity, Buñuel responded that it is rather about its counterproductive nature, only to disavow the idea that Viridiana is an anticharity film in the same sentence.[6] In fact, the film, according to its author, is not "anti-" anything, another curious, disconcerting authorial statement.

Now, even if we take the title character to be the embodiment of Christian charity, this cannot play a role in Don Jaime's plans for his niece. For Don Jaime, Viridiana has mainly meant innocence, sexual attraction, and rejection. So more questions beg to be answered: Is revenge the motivation for his scheme? Is Viridiana's fate arranged or envisioned out of spite? Or is her fate an act of, once more, perversion? Judging by the laughter Viridiana's envisioned fate draws from the "pervert" screenwriter, perhaps it is appropriate to consider Don Jaime's plot the natural outcome of nothing but a very particular sense of humor, precisely the type we have in mind when we speak of a perverse one.[7] The laughter that makes the one who laughs uncomfortable is indeed a staple of Buñuel's filmmaking. The connection between perversion and laughter is, hence, at the center of my approach to *Viridiana*, as it is the double lineage of what Dominique Russell has called Buñuel's "style gags."[8] For if it can be argued that the remnants of surrealist jesting are still operational in Buñuel's nonsurrealist movies, then the case for the Spanishness of the director's humor has equal weight in considering either what he laughs at in his movies or what he makes his audience laugh about in them. Repositioned as a member of the cinematic genre this book examines, *Viridiana* represents another intervention, another explosion of dark mirth in the rocky course of Francoist developmentalism. The concept the movie puts forward as a detonator is, in many senses, close to the notion of perversion, namely, degeneration. Perversion and degeneration then lead the way into the black comedy that *Viridiana* is in reality.

"De-Buñuelizing" *Viridiana*

A "comedy of transgressive desires," *Viridiana* is routinely recognized as one of the most idiosyncratic works authored by its creator.[9] This is a film, if not *the* film, in which Buñuel's recurrent themes and obsessions are as evidently personal as his sense of humor. In this the critics follow the lead of the director himself, who has said as much in interviews. For me, *Viridiana* is also—in fact mainly—a dark cinematographic comedy of Francoist developmentalism. Its dark, perverse humor is Buñuel's; but, then again, it is not only his. In fact, the most interesting critical discussions of Buñuel's humor seem to me to be those that revolve around questions of nationality and universality, of author and tradition, or, ultimately, of the local and the global. With this director in general, and with this film in particular, humor appears to be first and foremost a question of location.

Famously, Buñuel stated that even though *Viridiana* was not a surrealist film, its meaning and its humor certainly were surrealist. So it is the epochal dark laughter of the avant-gardes that this film conjured up first, the same laughter André Breton thought so close to a modern mode of existence. In a short piece written in 1929 to introduce a series of silent comedy shorts, Buñuel asserted that the equivalent of surrealism in cinema could only be found in the films that were about to be screened, films that featured classic silent comedians such as Harry Langdon or Ben Turpin.[10] Man Ray's films, the Spaniard continued, have nothing on, say, Buster Keaton's buffooneries or, rather, on "his poetry." Provocative as these remarks were intended to be, they clearly identify the spirit of surrealism in the medium of the moving image in productions that had almost no plot, were not European, and did not look up to the novel or try to resemble the theater. The break from the past is also a dislocation in space and an affirmation of newness tantamount to the rejection of tradition.

Speaking precisely of Buñuel's early surrealist films, Jean Cocteau asserted that Buñuel had invented what he labeled the "tragic gag." For Dominique Russell, the gag in general has a central place in the director's filmography, yet it is also "inflected with Spanish black humour."[11] In this view, the comic in Buñuel seems to mix the cosmopolitanism of the historical avant-garde with indigenous stock. Robert Stam even locates in time that second ingredient in the mixture when he writes that Buñuel "forges a direct link between the formal and thematic transgressions of the avant-garde and the medieval heritage of carnivalesque irreverence."[12] At first, these two practices of comic subversion are described as simply "European," as in "a proud European countertradition of comic desacralization."[13] However, in the same discussion, and in connection with the famous last supper scene in *Viridiana*, Buñuel is also quoted invoking the "Spanish tradition of blasphemy." A national strand is always brought into the discussions of Buñuel's humor. And this is not always prompted by any nationalist agenda. The location of humor is an exercise of locating aesthetic practices too, a question of discerning a filiation.

In a pioneer 1951 text on *Los olvidados* (1950), for instance, André Bazin claimed that "Buñuel's surrealism is combined with a whole Spanish tradition," a tradition Bazin summarized as follows: "The taste for the horrible, the sense of cruelty, the seeking out of the extreme aspects of life, these are also the heritage of Goya, Zurbarán, and Ribera, of a whole tragic sense of humanity which these painters have displayed precisely in expressing the most extreme human degradation — that of war, sickness, poverty, and its rotten accessories."[14]

Even though there is no mention of humor here, many of the elements recognized in this "whole Spanish tradition" overlap with the ones deployed in many a discussion of that "tragic," macabre, cruel, or black nature of Buñuel's comedic ways. The invocation of Goya, in fact, would suffice in this case. If one remembers that another of the well-known quotes on Viridiana by its author is that "it is not a fantasy, it is another instance of that famous Spanish realism," then questions of laughter, aesthetics, and nation are finally meshed together to form a construct in need of close analysis. I hope to address this need with a close reading of some of *Viridiana*'s key scenes, those in which the confluence of comedy, mode of representation, and cultural specificity is more intriguingly actualized.

The Unmotivated Spillage, Comedy below the Waist, and Voyeurism

Very early in *Viridiana*, while the title character is having an improvised lesson on how to milk a cow, Ramona's young daughter, Rita (Teresa Rabal), turns to the animal and, for no apparent reason, dumps a mug of milk on its head. I would call this seemingly gratuitous act the first gag of the film, arguably the first moment to pinpoint as "comic." For that reason, it also represents the first occasion to interrogate what comedy truly means in this context and how easy a concept it is to isolate. The young girl's action can be called comical not because of what it may mean but because of its relation to meaning. In other words, neither meaningful nor meaningless, such an unmotivated spillage refers back to the connections between laughter and logic. This is obviously the connection that surrealist humor feasted upon. In taxonomies of comedy, it is also a recurrent theme tied to the so-called incongruity theory. In order to make this moment in the film dovetail with what seems to be a guiding concept in the analysis of Buñuel's filmmaking, one can also consider it, as I will here, as an instant of disruption.

Motives to behave in certain ways have been very reasonable up until this point in *Viridiana*. The first scenes, for instance, took pains to set up the encounter between Viridiana and her uncle as a logical consequence of the novice being so close to taking her vows and the fact that Don Jaime has been her lifelong benefactor. The mother superior is the voice of reason in this case. Rita's action, in turn, is the first moment of gratuitous action, even if it comes from a child, even if it looks just like mischievous behavior. I would argue that this moment is funny because it is odd, because it disrupts the logic of what we are seeing, because it does not serve any narrative purpose. In fact, this is precisely what the cinematographic gag does in and to the fabric of the film narrative. That is to say, "the cinematic gag can be defined as a striking and disjunctive 'effect' that suspends the temporal orientation of the narrative by turning our attention back to an unexpected cause in the consciousness of the character who performed the effect."[15] Or, as Dominique Russell puts it, a gag in film is "a momentary interruption of the viewer's immersion in the story world and an awareness of the hand behind the screen."[16] Does what I have called the "unmotivated spillage" represent all of these?

As I advance this reading, I can hear the objections of all psychoanalytically inclined readers of this movie pointing out that the spillage may not be disrupting but downright culminating a phallic, crude joke. After all, Viridiana is timidly holding the teat of the cow as if it were the penis she would not know how to handle. Rita adds to the obscene undertones of the scene by saying, "Don Jaime knows how to do it very well." This, by the way, does not look or sound like the stuff sophisticated Freudian jokes are made of. All the readings that stress what is intimated here of Viridiana's sexual repression notwithstanding, the scene instead looks and sounds like the brand of humor below the waist, the one we describe as popular or crass. So which is it? Is Rita's spillage a disruption equal in nature to the pie-in-the-face quality of the early cinema film gag? Or is it an integral part of a sexually charged joke that in turn is capable of eliciting either psychoanalytical appreciation or plain old lewd laughter? Of course, I set up this either-or dilemma to immediately forsake it. I also want to set the stage for an analysis of what humor brings to this film narrative as a structural device. After all, "to disrupt" also means "to throw into disorder," and Rita's spillage may represent just that: "disorderly" conduct insofar as it affects the flow of the narrative, the course of visual and logical concatenations, and the linkage of humors, so to speak. While to laugh at the penis joke is to laugh because one recognizes, knows, or gets it (either sophisticatedly or crudely), the laughing that the unmotivated spillage produces does hinge on not understanding. Laughing, then, is also a matter of knowledge, and, in the case of dark laughter, it is also a matter of perversion, as in addressing the question of what is normally and abnormally comic. Minor animal cruelty, for instance, as is the case here, clearly hints at much more disturbing acts of comic cruelty toward animals yet to come in the film — and yet to figure prominently in my analysis.

Even if film gags can be described as "the potholes, detours, and flat tires of narrative," in contemplating their place in the fabric of the film, it is equally vital to consider that the interrelation of "nonnarrative and narrative features is quite complex, precisely because narrative acts as a system of regulation which ultimately absorbs nonnarrative elements into its pendulum sways."[17] Likewise, as much as the unmotivated spillage can be read as a moment of disruption, it can also be placed in a lineage. It can obtain its meaning from other scenes and images in the movie not exactly in the vicinity of the milking scene. Rita's action, after all, is also the first moment in the film of ultimately pointless actions involving animals. Famously, a bee, a dog, and a dove are "saved" in *Viridiana*. All of these rescues are invested with a very noticeable irony that, as usual, tilts toward the darker side of whatever laughter they can inspire. Don Jaime saves a bee from drowning in the midst of a conversation on how he neglected his illegitimate son and just minutes away from entrapping his innocent niece. We witness Don Jorge saving a dog from inhuman treatment only to see another dog pass by in the exact same situation. The lovingly protected dove is to be killed at the end, her feathers thrown into the air during the beggars' orgy. Acts of kindness to animals are inevitably undermined by a cruelty that may prompt a smile, enable an ironic insight, or make one laugh at what is but grim and heartless. So the unmotivated spillage is also part of a series of visual gags that place the question of ethics and laughter at the core of the black comedy that *Viridiana* is. Perverse humor becomes, once again, a matter of laughing against the grain, so to speak; it is about decentering the proper object of laughter. In *Viridiana* that decentering starts with a variously disruptive gag, with an actualized moment of comedy in the narrative that can be first tied to a theory of humor as disruption and then examined alongside the scenes that develop the themes of humor and perversion. A very different matter is how this first part of the movie is deemed as comic in its entirety. In this, as in many other insights in this chapter, I take Dominique Russell's cue. "Don Jaime's necrophiliac obsession with his niece," she writes, "is played for dark laughs."[18] The question this statement raises is: What accounts for the pervasiveness and the perverseness of dark humor in this first section of the film? Or, put differently,

Figure 11. The voyeur-fetishist scene

how exactly are Don Jaime's perversions funny? How can perversion itself be something to laugh about? The image of an old man trying on woman's clothes is a suitable place to start looking for an answer to these questions (see fig. 11). The camera pans right, leaving the lighted chimney it was framing to show a clock that tells us that it is already two in the morning. It quickly resumes its movement, tracking this time for a while until it stops in front of Don Jaime's room. The door is wide open. Inside, we see Don Jaime trying on a woman's shoe too small for his foot.

If sometimes voyeurism is a term too readily brought into play to describe the experience of film watching, this time the scene itself fully justifies its use.[19] The time of night, the open door visible in the frame, the subsequent alarm in Don Jaime's face when he hears a noise and rushes to hide his dead wife's wedding garments—the filmic potential for turning spectators into voyeurs is clearly realized. We are definitely watching intimate behavior not meant to be witnessed. This private behavior, in turn, involves both fetishism and cross-dressing. If we favored the Lacanian approach to perversions in which they have to do more with "structures" than with behaviors, in this case we need to recognize that two perversions inform one pole of the structure of another (voyeurism). To understand the variety of perversions at play in the scene is crucial if one is interested in teasing out the conceivable pleasures and the possible laughter at stake here. Or, to repeat the question posed before but in plainer terms: How is this funny?

The immediate answer would invoke again the idea of oddity or of momentary incongruity: it is the spirit of the gag once more, this time mixed with the humor that the sight of somebody dressing in the other gender's clothes can occasion. The comedy in this sudden spectacle of aristocratic, manly, old Don Jaime may stem indeed from the discrepancy between appearance and behavior. The solemn classical music heard throughout the scene helps to emphasize this feeling of general incongruity. This would certainly be a way to explain why such a scene could inspire laughter, yet it does not address what is comic in the sight of perversion. For that we need an answer that reflects on the structure of voyeurism, one that, as a matter of fact, will also reframe the comic meaning of Don Jaime's perversions.

First, let us remember that the voyeuristic pleasure most readily associated with film spectatorship has presupposed a male, heterosexual gaze and the image of women in different degrees of nakedness. Laura Mulvey's famous 1975 article started the discussion on the subject, and since then it has been refined by Mulvey herself, among others.[20] It has also been expanded to include other possible viewing positions and a broader sense of visual pleasure. Yet the female body being looked at and desired from a vantage point of invisibility is still the paradigmatic filmic moment of voyeurism. In fact, Buñuel has offered us one of those model instances just a few scenes before we are surprised/amused by the sight of Don Jaime admiring his half-bare leg with a half-fitting woman's shoe on his foot. During her first night as her uncle's guest, alone in her room, Viridiana stands in front of a mirror and sets her hair free from the constraints of both habit and headgear. She then sits down on the bed and proceeds to undress. The camera tilts down to show her baring her legs. No subjective shot anchors this erotically charged view. It is we, the spectators, who are surreptitiously watching a woman undressing. A straight cut will take us to the figure of Ramona outside the novice's room. She will kneel down to look through the keyhole, but we will not be granted access to what Don Jaime's servant sees. Even though this act of looking has been repeatedly called voyeuristic, there is no sexual content in Ramona's action, nor is she enjoying watching without being seen. She just reports back to Don Jaime her interpretation of what she has witnessed.

If sometimes a cigar is just a cigar, sometimes spying is just spying. So the vision of Viridiana's bare legs is there just for us to see. It is a spectacle to entice us, but it does not prepare us for the view of Don Jaime's leg. The joke is then on us, gentle viewers, comfortable in the conventions that have regulated (and produced) male heterosexual desire in the film medium. Buñuel's perverse humor comes this time in the form of a question: Did you equally enjoy those two bare legs? Did you obtain the same pleasure from both of those scenes? And here is where we should be pushing a Lacanian rather than a Freudian take on voyeurism. Not two but three gazes are at play in Lacan's structure of voyeurism. According to Slavoj Žižek, "it is never just me and the object I am spying on, a third gaze is always already there: the gaze which sees me seeing the object."[21] Then could our laughter at Don Jaime's perversions owe its existence to our nervous awareness of an observer who knows he is being seen as he sees something he is not supposed to see? The spectacle that signals a more troubling type of voyeurism in the film medium does so because it imposes on us the knowledge that our watching is there to be seen by the big Other. This is indeed not the laugh that betrays an idea of superiority toward its object or the laugh triggered by the encounter of incongruity or absurdity in the world. It is not the laughter that means relief either. This is the laughter that interrogates, the laughter that even interpolates the one who laughs. Seizing the image of Don Jaime in his fetishist moment against his will in fact leads to the possession of a troubling knowledge that has more to do with us than with him. The perverse laughter sends us back to the notions of self-knowledge and the ethical order. Is the other notable instance of ostensible spectator's voyeurism in the film doing the same? As we shall see, it is a moment that once more involves a complex structure of scopophilia where a pair of perversions (necrophilia and incest this time) comprises one pole of the voyeuristic experience. If, as quoted before, we can agree with Russell in principle that "Don Jaime's necrophiliac obsession with his niece is played for dark laughs," then does that laughter depend on a perversion that we discover in ourselves through the gaze of the big Other?

Don Jaime has finally resorted to drugging Viridiana in order to possess her. To do so is to possess his late wife also: the wife whom Viridiana resembles so much, the wife who died during the wedding night. With the help of Ramona, he has taken his unconscious niece to the bedroom and now asks to be left alone. With the camera filming from an objective point of view, the old man literally unveils the young woman dressed in his deceased wife's wedding gown. He fixes her crown of flowers. He positions her left arm so that her hands are crossed over her chest. He finally arranges the pleats of the gown to provide the perfect image of a dead body in the conventional final resting position. All this mortician activity ends with a close-up of Don Jaime looking at the resting body, excited with anticipation. It is at this moment that the camera setup changes to a view from behind Don Jaime's left shoulder and then zooms over him to give us a semisubjective shot of Viridiana as a radiant white and blonde corpse. The degree of identification we can measure in this camera work depends, as always, on what kind of viewer we are able to posit in front of the image. We are changed from momentary necrophiliacs to subjects incapable of moving, while the scene mobilizes all the pleasures and anxieties the depiction of sexual gratification with an unresisting and unrejecting partner can create.

Our passage from voyeurs to participants is, however, a key factor to bear in mind in the libidinal economy of the sequence. Things get complicated the moment Viridiana and Don Jaime are watched by somebody else. The final close-up of Viridiana's face as seen by the spectator/Don Jaime is followed by a close-up of young Rita looking up at the window of the room in which this incestuous and necrophilic scene is taking place. The two faces of innocence about to be ruined follow one another as if to equate them visually one last time. Rita climbs a tree to peer through the window. Up in the room, we, the audience, are still the ones witnessing this behavior. The camera is set up this time at the other side of the bed, where Viridiana lies at the mercy of her uncle. Don Jaime is noticeably struggling with the idea of what he is about to do. He walks away for a second, unable, it seems, to bring himself to carry on. But he ultimately goes back to the bed, lifts his niece's body, and kisses her passionately, only to fall back either in despair or with remorse after his transgression. It is only then that Buñuel cuts to Rita approaching the window and looking inside. When he cuts back to the couple Rita is watching, the point of view of the scene has changed (see fig. 12).

The camera is now at the bed's headboard, and Don Jaime and his victim are shown from a high-view angle. There is no window at the head of the bed, yet the impression, however short-lived, is that this is Rita's point of view. The new angle is in fact the vantage point from which to share Don Jaime's view, the only one that enables such a clear view of Viridiana's semibare breast as he unbuttons her gown. Rita, like her mother, has repeatedly been read in this scene as a stand-in for the spectator/voyeur. Yet the truth remains that nothing in her gaze aligns her with the voyeuristic structure. Even the most revealing viewing position is not hers. She has stumbled into a scene she most likely does not understand and from which she can obtain no pleasure. Rita represents virtually the opposite of what the viewing position from the bed's headboard might embody. Hers is an innocent gaze that enters the voyeurism of film spectatorship as an interruption, as a pure gaze of innocence that literally comes from nowhere. Indeed, a review of the different shots of the bedroom in which the scene is taking place shows that the only window in it is situated at the other side of the bed's headboard, relatively distant from where the camera is placed to film the partial undressing of Viridiana. Not only is there no direct line of sight for Rita to watch Don Jaime kissing his niece, but when Don Jaime suddenly stops and stands up, that lone window is directly behind him, and Rita is nowhere to be seen. However, the subsequent shot is a cut to Rita stepping back from a window, a window that has to be the one in which we did not see her in the previous shot. There is no possible viewing position for a gaze that, however, helps in articulating (or disrupting) the grammar of these images and this scopic field. Now, in this detailed analysis of the structure of perversion that organizes the sequence, questions must be posed again: How is this funny? Where is the comedy? And where is the potential for dark laughter in it?

Figure 12. A vantage point of view to
Don Jaime's perversions

As is the case with the scene of voyeurism, fetishism, and cross-dressing I addressed earlier, a solemn, religious music also scores this succession of images where voyeurism, necrophilia, and incest find a meeting point. The discrepancy between image and sound adds more than just somber irony. Of course, the natural reading here is that of a blasphemous juxtaposition of perverse deeds and religious spirituality. Yet it is also reasonable to find as much overlap as contrast in this coexistence of music and images. Being true to one's desires is musically transformed into a sublime experience; one's urges can have the sound track of Communion. Aware of the gap, or caught in the overlap, the audience as listeners — as much as seers — have no "outside" to the spectacle from which to laugh comfortably.

Indeed, there seems to be no safe, detached position for the one who laughs in the workings of perverse laughter. Laughing is but the main way to participate in or to enter into the structure of the perversion. There is definitely no Hobbesian sudden glory to be felt here, since there is no superiority to be recognized. Is this also the case in the second part of the movie? Is there an innocent viewing position from which to laugh at what happens in the other movie *Viridiana* becomes as soon as the pervert, Don Jaime, removes himself from the film?

Laughing at (and Not with) Others

After her uncle's death, Viridiana decides not to return to the convent. Instead, she embarks on a project of private and, one would say, indiscriminate charity. To that effect, she rounds up as many beggars as she can in the village and offers them shelter at her estate. At the beginning of their first meal together under Viridiana's protection, every one of her saved souls states the skills he or she brings to this newly formed community. The ex-novice has announced to the beggars that from that point on everybody will need to work, an announcement that prompts a comic reaction shot of a startled tramp. His name is Manuel, and he is the same character who very soon will share with the group what he can bring to the community. "What I am good at," he says, "is to make people laugh." Viridiana's answer could not sound more like a cliché: "Then we will all laugh with you here; but I will not allow anybody to laugh at you." What Viridiana does not want anybody to do is obviously what we do not stop doing during the entire movie. This is particularly the case the moment the assemblage of beggars makes an appearance. Laughing at each other is of course what the beggars themselves do time and again.

The coming together of cruelty and humor raises more questions regarding where the laughing subject stands vis-à-vis the object of laughter. It also invokes cultural traditions that may be at once popular and highbrow. For many critics, when *Viridiana* enters its second part it also enters into a clearly demarcated aesthetic tradition. Francisco Aranda, for instance, considers *Viridiana* as the equivalent in film of Quevedo's classic Golden Age narratives *El buscón* and *Los sueños*, to the *picaresca* genre in general, and to nineteenth-century Galdós's prose (although there is no mention of titles in this invocation of the Spanish Realist novelist par excellence).[22] Víctor Fuentes sees Goya-inspired *disparates* (follies) and *pinturas negras* (black paintings) all through this second half of the film, while Vicente Sánchez-Biosca identifies the film's "roots" in "Spanish autochthonous traditions such as the picaresque genre and the *esperpento*."[23] Of all these allusions, the *picaresca*, Goya, and the *esperpento* function as a holy trilogy of references, as outlined in the first chapter of this book. Interestingly enough, they all draw heavily from a dark and cruel conception of laughter. Broad claims of resemblance and/or influence animate most of the invocations of the sixteenth-century narrative genre, the eighteenth-century painter, and the twentieth-century playwright in the critical reading of Buñuel's movie. I refer to the introduction of this book for my take on what these shortcuts for cultural specificity may entail on the whole. In the case of *Viridiana*, it is important to note what these references mean as efforts to find an ancestry for the movie's humorous cruelty. The scene in which they all coalesce is the famous beggars' bacchanal: the climax of a mode of the comic that incorporates cruelty.

When every figure of authority must leave the estate for a night, the group of recently homeless persons takes possession of Viridiana and Don Jorge's mansion. It all starts as an urge to snoop around; it ends with a luxurious dinner at the master's table that collapses into pandemonium. There is excessive drinking, fighting, infant neglect, sexual aggression, and the wanton smashing of fancy tableware. The crown, veil, and corset Don Jaime had Viridiana wear as part of his wedding night re-creation are now paraded by the character all the other beggars have shunned for allegedly having leprosy. As he dances in such attire, he tosses in the air the feathers of the dove he had saved earlier. Leonardo da Vinci's rendition of the Last Supper is famously re-created so that one of the women can pretend to "take a picture" by lifting her skirt. Most of this happens to the tune of the "Hallelujah" chorus of Handel's *Messiah.*

That the entire sequence has a carnivalesque tenor to it seems fairly obvious. What this carnivalesque atmosphere may mean is a different matter. As a way to address this issue, I return to Robert Stam and quote in its entirety what I only partially quoted before:

> The "Last Supper" sequence of *Viridiana,* meanwhile, melds an iconoclastic assault on high art—Handel's *Messiah,* the da Vinci painting—with orgiastic sacrilege in the tradition of the medieval "Coena Cypriani," which like this sequence also parodied the Last Supper. . . . Such sacrileges, in Buñuel, constitute a prolongation through film of what Buñuel in his autobiography calls the proud Spanish tradition of blasphemy, in which "extraordinary vulgarities— referring chiefly to the Virgin Mary, the Apostles, God, Christ and the Holy Spirit, not to mention the Pope—are strung end to end in a series of impressive scatological exclamations." Buñuel's attacks on the church, in sum, derive less from "surrealist provocations" than from a proud European countertradition of comic desacralization.[24]

As suggestive as any association between the Bakhtinian carnival and Buñuel's films is, there is also something missing in a reading that uses only the lenses of the carnivalesque to measure the transgressive nature of this humorous sequence.[25] The key factor here is the place laughter has as a concept within a Bakhtinian theory of carnival. Many other concepts that spring from this theory can indeed be related to the beggars' orgy as filmed by Buñuel. Drawing from Stam's list alone, we could distinguish the "concatenation of life and death, Eros and Thanatos as crystallized by orgiastic sacrifice," the "corporeal semiotic celebrating the grotesque, excessive body," or the "rejection of social decorum entailing a release from oppressive etiquette, politeness, and good manners."[26] Yet, in the final analysis, Bakhtin's reflections on the complex essence of carnival laughter do not help us in thinking through the workings of Buñuel's perverse laughter in this momentous succession of images. This is the most pertinent passage from *Rabelais and His World* on the subject: "[Carnival laughter] is, first of all, a festive laughter. Therefore it is not an individual reaction to some isolated 'comic' event. Carnival laughter is the laughter of all the people. Second, it is universal in scope; it is directed at all and everyone, including the carnival's participants. The entire world is seen in its droll aspect, in its gray relativity. Third, this laughter is ambivalent: it is gay, triumphant, and at the same time mocking, deriding. It asserts and denies, it buries and revives."[27]

Expanding on his second point, Bakhtin distinguishes the "festive people's laughter" from the "satirist whose laughter is negative because he places himself above the object of his mockery." Finally, the Russian critic ends up stressing "the special philosophical and utopian character of festive laughter and its orientation toward the highest spheres."[28] It would be hard to recognize people's festive laughter in the laughter associated with the beggars' sequence. Bakhtin's notion of a laughter directed at each other, and the ambivalence he distinguishes in carnival laughter, may at first sight seem to capture the essence of this explosion of comic enjoyment. Yet the communal, utopian nature intrinsic to what Bakhtin sees in carnival laughter does not match the cruelty, the violence, or the scorn the beggars direct at each other. It does not fit either the possible split the act of laughing itself creates between spectators and performers. Deep down, the carnival laughter, in spite of everything, could still be closer to Viridiana's naive "laughing with you" approach than to a true laughing at others that results, perversely, in laughing at ourselves—laughing at ourselves, mind you, without any cathartic, communal, or utopian component. The crucial moment in the sequence to take into account here is the one in which the alleged leper re-enters the dining room.

As already noted, this previously ostracized beggar is wearing the wedding garments we saw first in Don Jaime's possession and then adorning his niece's body. Whether the beggar is degrading Viridiana's pureness or ridiculing Don Jaime's perversion, this problematic transvestism is not calling into question the social construction of gender roles à la Bakhtin. There is something crueler in the performance, something harder to laugh at—something that hardens laughter, perhaps—since it includes the feathers of the saved-to-be-sacrificed dove falling to the ground around all the dancers' feet. I would argue that this sudden instance of what Raymond Durgnat calls "harsh, belligerent laughter that comes from secretly gritted teeth" precludes the possibility of any utopian modality of people's laughter.[29] It is not that we assume the position of laughing spectators as morally superior beings; it is not that there is a release of accumulated tension or energy either in the laughter occasioned by these images; nor is it an occurrence of comic incongruity beyond the one signaled by the disconnect between music and actions. The key factor at stake here is that laughing is not innocent, it does not make us feel better or superior; instead, we become the object of a troubled, perverse laughter ourselves. When Lola Gaos raises her skirt and takes her famous picture with her genitals (or "the camera her parents gave her"), she is, after all, taking a picture of us, mocking us too. Buñuel has cut to a frontal shot of the woman. We suddenly stand as the centered viewer, as the object of the joke and the exhibitionism. To be accurate, we actually share the point of view of the blind beggar at the center of the table: he is the only one incapable of seeing what is going on, the only one not getting the joke.

This is the perverse laughter that the dark comedy *Viridiana* really brings to the table. Customarily, it has been thought as a sort of explosion in the face of Francoist developmentalism. It may be seen also as a spectacle that goes off in the face of the spectator. We have been previously drawn into the structure of perversions and are now enmeshed in the visually and morally chaotic beggars' bacchanal. So the last question I will use as the link from one section of this chapter to another is: How is this laughter related to the one we have seen so far in *El cochecito* and *El verdugo*? In other words, what adds to the reading of *Viridiana*'s dark laughter the fact that it belongs to a series of dark comedies in the Spain of the early sixties?

Developmentalism and Degeneration

Virtually every piece of writing on *Viridiana* mentions the fact that it represented a public relations move that backfired on the regime. Buñuel was allowed to film in Spain again so that the officially trumpeted liberalization of the Franco regime could be more readily accepted. His movie was then chosen to represent the country in the Cannes festival so that the alleged openness of the regime could have a wider resonance. A comic strip by the cartoonist Alberto Isaac is often mentioned as a sort of visual synopsis of what the movie did as a poisoned gift. Buñuel himself makes reference to the three-panel cartoon in his memoirs.

In the first panel of the comic strip, the dictator is shown welcoming the exiled director while a figure in the background yells, "Prevaricator!" This angry protester is supposed to represent Spanish exiles and their reaction upon learning of Buñuel's Spanish project. In the second panel, the director is shown abandoning the frame and leaving behind a smiling Franco. The dictator holds a wrapped gift with the name "Viridiana" written across it. The character in the background now shouts "Death to Buñuel!" In the final panel, the gift has exploded in the dictator's face: both he and the figure in the background look stunned. What the movie did to the regime, how it embarrassed it, how explosive a product it was seem to be clear.[30] How the film itself (in its narrative, in the grammar of its images) accomplished this is something not as easy to recognize. The anti-Catholic thrust of the film usually becomes the main argument in the diegetic analysis of *Viridiana*'s anti-Francoism. Yet Don Jaime's estate — subsequently Jorge and Viridiana's — is such a cloistered, disconnected space that it is hard to distinguish the Spain of the early 1960s in the narrative.

In spite of the ahistorical feeling of the setting and the story, one can argue for the existence of a connection with the contemporary world at large. Dominique Russell puts it best: "Buñuel anchors the story in the particularities of the Spain of the late fifties and early sixties, as it was emerging from ultraconservative autarky into consumerist culture. Both the conservative tenets of Catholicism and the modernizing 'American know-how' of the Opus Dei technocrats, who wielded power in Franco's cabinet at the time, are skewered. Buñuel clearly understood that faith in God and washing machines worked in tandem during the Franco years."[31] In this reading, Jorge, the modernizer, would represent the new technocratic impulse that swept the Franco administration at that time. Yet the movie does not present us with clear images of the consumerist culture the country is entering. Less anchored in the socioeconomic specifics of its time than the other movies of the genre examined so far, *Viridiana* clearly presents religion and modernization as two competing discourses. That the tenets of that modernizing project do not plainly point toward a late capitalist society is something to ponder upon, though. Put otherwise, there are no washing machines clearly visible in Don Jaime's property, even after his more modern natural son takes over. By the end of the movie, we discover Jorge still giving instructions to get the house ready for the arrival of electricity. Furthermore, his previous modernizing endeavors were no more than a very modest and very anachronistic land reform. Even the modern music in the final scene hardly functions as an index of the times in which the movie was produced. The rockabilly song "Shake Your Cares Away" no doubt represents the opposite of what the music by Mozart, Beethoven, or Handel might bring to the film, but it is after all rockabilly, a style of rock-and-roll music already fading by the beginning of the 1960s. Only the presence of Pepsi-Cola and Coca-Cola signs in the crucial scene that divides both halves of the film seems to "indicate that we are at a moment where the commodification of Europe is taking place."[32]

Viridiana is about to get on the bus that would take her back to the convent when a representative of the local civil authority and two rural policemen, or *guardias civiles*, arrive to prevent her from doing so. This simple premise is visually articulated in a fairly complex sequence-shot structure. The villagers, dogs, carriages, and time-worn columns of the square we see offer the image of a provincial, impoverished background to a still-distressed Viridiana. In his detailed analysis of the sequence, Tom Conley concludes that we are witnessing a "highly cinematic world in which the people are caught in the frame of or *cadre* of a milieu set in strong contrast to the 'originary' site of Don Jaime's farm."[33] In this world, "the Coca-Cola signs refer to what seems to be a world *off*, that of Spain of 1961, that is nonetheless held within the originary frame."[34] Conley is of course drawing heavily on Deleuze's "originary worlds" concept as it is developed in *Cinema 1* in connection with "naturalism in cinema." This is a mode of filming whose great masters, according to Deleuze, are Erich von Stroheim and (who else?) Buñuel. In Deleuze's elaborated paradigm, "the originary world only exists and operates in the depths of a real milieu, and is only valid through its immanence in this milieu, whose violence and cruelty it reveals."[35] The originary world is also the world of the impulse, and the impulse is first described and then connected to the concept of perversion in the following manner: "The impulse is an act which tears away, ruptures, dislocates. Perversion is therefore not its deviation, but its derivation, that is, its normal expression in the derived milieu."[36] In other words, there is no need for washing machines in *Viridiana* after all: the Francoist developmentalist milieu is distilled, as it were, in a collection of impulses springing from within, derived from it. Or, rather, the Spain of the early 1960s is "diagnosed" as a state of widespread and utter degeneration, the ultimate outcome of all emancipatory discourses in the film. Whether they speak the language of spirituality or the vernacular of instrumental rationality, these emancipatory promises result in collapse. They may even collapse into one another. "Beast of prey or parasite—everybody is both simultaneously," says Deleuze in reference to Buñuel's originary worlds just lines before mentioning *Viridiana* in his reflections.[37] Some pages before, he has written that "the male and female lover, the holy man himself are—according to Buñuel—no less harmful than the pervert and the degenerate."[38] Deleuze refers here to Buñuel's *Nazarín* (1959), but it would not be difficult to substitute holy man for holy woman to make the dialectic between holiness and perversion remain in place in *Viridiana*. Now listen to Adorno speaking of the concept of enlightenment: "Promiscuity and asceticism, excess and hunger, are directly identical, despite the antagonism, as powers of disintegration."[39] Degeneration, degradation, disintegration, perversion, even entropy reveal themselves as the true obverse of the modernizing enterprise. And in this film—or in this film genre, for that matter—such an epiphany comes along with the dark laughter that laughs at that which is not good, the selfsame dark laughter that does not spare the one who laughs. Cut to the final shot of *Viridiana*.

After her ordeal, after what Jorge, referring to her cousin's sexual aggression, calls the "scare," Viridiana sets her hair free for good, looks at herself in the mirror, and heads for Jorge's bedroom. Ramona is already inside. After the two women exchange some uncomfortable looks, Jorge insists that the three of

Figure 13. Intimations of a ménage
à trois

them should play cards together. As they all sit down to do so, Jorge is the only one speaking. His final utterances are steeped in double entendre. He always knew his cousin would "end up playing cards" (*jugar al tute*) with him. "All cats are gray at night," he tells both women. The pure, innocent ex-novice abandons her chastity to enter a ménage à trois, a fate that has been repeatedly offered as the ultimate evidence of Buñuel's dark and perverse sense of humor in this film. The final image of *Viridiana* frames the three characters sitting at a table inside Jorge's bedroom (see fig. 13).

The camera will soon initiate a receding traveling, as if it were backing away from such a tableau. At this point, it is crucial to realize that, before that camera movement takes place, the initial setup of the apparatus is almost identical to another key setup already discussed here. From that setup we saw Don Jaime trying on his late wife's nuptial finery. From almost the same spot we watched the spectacle of Don Jaime's fetishistic necrophilia, and, in so doing, we effectively entered a complex structure of perversion scored by Handel. We back away now to the sound of a rockabilly song that tells us to shake our cares away. This time the spectacle is very different in nature, and the voyeuristic overtones are not there. They would be, but only if we stayed. There is nothing more to be seen, and the camera makes us abandon the scene; it makes us retreat, fully aware of the bitter irony plainly visible in this final state of affairs.

What are we walking away with here? Whatever we have learned, whatever wisdom we have gained about desire, perversion, degeneration, or innocence, comes by way of the "ethical laughter." Knowledge and dark laughter are clearly interconnected in the final analysis. This is how Paul Sandro puts it: "Often enough in Buñuel's films laughter has a hollow ring to it. There is only a partial or momentary discharge of tension in this kind of laughter, only a partial distancing, followed by a moment of residual identification in which the viewer is contaminated by the aggressivity of his or her own laughter. This black or perverse humor turns the spectator's attention inwards again upon the act of viewing and telling itself."[40] This process, with the appropriate nuances, applies to the different analysis of laughter and spectatorship undertaken in this chapter. It resonates in the humorous incongruity of the unmotivated spillage. It is a clear factor in the comic articulation of visual perversions. It is definitely inherent in the cruelty of laughing at others and not with others, improper object of laughter and all. And then there is the question of how all this is socially and historically pertinent.

Francoist developmentalism, the real milieu in whose depths *Viridiana*'s originary world can exist and operate, appears crisscrossed by a laughter that becomes the impulse that "tears away," "ruptures," and "dislocates." In this regard, Buñuel's movie is a member of the genre that subjects historical and geographical specifics to a more thorough process of sublimation. It is not about Franco himself; it is not about an isolated source of discernible evil. It never is with these dark cinematographic comedies. It is about something bigger and broader. It is about perversion and innocence this time. Most remarkably, it is about the impossibility of innocence, an impossibility tantamount to certain hopelessness in the existence of an innocent viewer and a harmless laughter. If perversion, as noted earlier, rather than a behavior, is a structure, then the possibility exists to participate in it without being oneself a pervert. Is this not what spectatorship means in all the key moments of *Viridiana* in which laughter turns into something closer to a dreadful knowledge about oneself? And is it not a perverse humor that questions what there is to laugh at that does not compromise our desire? In a time when, and under a regime where, commercial film comedy was beginning to be the genre to laugh innocently or to laugh in connivance, the perversion and the darkness of Buñuel's *Viridiana* undo the innocence of comedy as much as *El cochecito* debunked the myth of harmless consumerism or *El verdugo* disavowed the existence of nirvanas of nonagency. The stage is set for another black comedy to take some of the preoccupations of the genre a step farther. This strange voyage will take us, in fact, farther into the province to find more Coca-Cola billboards and also to meet with Alfred Hitchcock in a village not very far away from Madrid.

5

Modernizing Desire

Fernán-Gómez's El extraño viaje

C onsumerism, dissidence, and complicity; vehicles that mean more than
movement; decisions that transfigure the very field of choice; spaces that
cannot hide or shelter from ethical demands; the perverse realization that innocence can be as harmful as connivance . . . To the series of questions covered
so far, we now need to add a reflection on the place desire occupies within modernity. Desire certainly played a major role in all the purchasing, killing, and
compromising done by ostracized old men, secluded fetishist, ironic modern-
izers, and reluctant executioners. However, the production and reproduction
of desire within a certain modernizing project need to be placed center stage at
this point in this research project with the analysis of the movie that more clearly
put them on-screen. Enter Fernando Fernán-Gómez and his strange voyage.

In a small village near Madrid, Fernando (Carlos Larrañaga), a musician
from the capital, starts a romantic relationship with the very chaste and very
cursi (corny) Beatriz (Lina Canalejas) while he meets in secret with Ignacia (Tota
Alba), the eldest (and harshest) of the three rich orphans who comprise the Vidal
family. The grim interior of the Vidals' mansion, together with the village's
"social club," unpaved streets, and humble squares, provide the main settings
in which this story unfolds, a story that includes episodes of voyeurism, a disconcerting occurrence of cross-dressing, three murders, and the theft of a corset.
One of the bodies ends up dumped into a large wine vat (the local custom is to
submerge cured hams in this vat so that the wine tastes better). Eventually, the

86

murderers will be murdered, and this second crime, the police will learn, has been committed so that the criminal can get married and fulfill his dream to start a zarzuela, or comic operetta, company.

Even in a plot summary as brief as this one, it becomes apparent that the quality of the film narrative oscillates between the *costumbrismo* of a small-town movie and a darker, even grotesque, whodunit. Another way to underline the film's hybridity would be to describe *El extraño viaje* (*The Strange Voyage*, 1964) as a film in which the *sainete* and the psychological thriller combine forces in order to put at center stage the workings of a variety of desires within a provincial space. This is a space where gossip and murder coexist, where rock-and-roll and zarzuela intermingle, and where Arniches, the paradigmatic *sainete* author in the twentieth century, meets Alfred Hitchcock.

Starting with the silent classic *La aldea maldita* (*The Cursed Village*) (Florián Rey, 1930), Spanish cinema has created a series of canonical films in which the small town is both background and microcosmos. Analyzing precisely Fernán-Gómez's movie, Steven Marsh writes that "the Spanish pueblo is the unpredictable 'home' at the centre of the nation's Arcadian imagination."[1] At the beginning of the 1970s this narrative began to reach a broader audience. The future prime minister of Spain Adolfo Suárez, by then director of TVE, brought the nostalgia of the small-town space directly into Spanish homes when he promoted the creation of the TV series *Crónicas de un pueblo*.[2] The small town, the village, and even the province were definitely hijacked by the regime and repackaged as spaces untouched by modernity. Throughout this stage of Francoism, the regime indeed seems to have been pushing for socioeconomic modernization while dreaming of a premodern reality that amounted to, say, an autarchy of the soul. Almost a decade before *Crónicas* popularized this fantasy of idealized public and private spheres beyond the reach of the modern, *El extraño viaje* offered images of a rural community suffused with the stuff capitalist modernization is made of, including images, as noted earlier, of desire, images of a new set of cravings seen everywhere, even in the spaces the regime imagined as pristine.

So let us start at the beginning. Let us start with the first sequences of the film in order to read them symptomatically. After all, they become a succession of images that reveal, among other realities, how new desires are connected to new ways of looking and, no doubt, of filming. For cinematographic modernity is also a question of desire, the desire to look different. In a movie that seems to flaunt its *costumbrismo* and to acknowledge its bonds with the *sainete* tradition, filmic modernity is (and I must repeat the point that the book has argued on every available occasion) a question of interrogating the very idea of what the modern may be (or look like) within the medium of the moving image and under a very particular set of geopolitical and historical circumstances. Accordingly, we can say that *El extraño viaje* accounts for a reorganization of the interplay between gaze and desire that shakes up the entire scopic regime. With both desiring and observing subjects equally disturbed or transformed, Fernán-Gómez's film shows that in developmentalist Spain the institutional desire for modernization cannot be separated from the urge to modernize desire. This is precisely the question he takes to the paradigmatic unmodern spaces of the small town and the province. And it all begins with the things one can see attached to, or projected against, walls: those blank spaces for display and enclosure.

The Writing on the Wall: Desire Bound and Unbound

El extraño viaje opens with images of printed matter. As the opening credits roll, the camera slowly films the front page of different newspapers as well as the covers of a miscellaneous collection of journals and glossy magazines. They all hang from ropes with clothespins to form a makeshift press kiosk display. *El caso*, the periodical that has epitomized sensationalist crime reporting since the early 1950s in Spain, dangles next to an issue of the gossipy magazine *Hola* and is one publication removed from the Spanish edition of *Life*. The right-wing daily *El Alcázar* is displayed in proximity to the "syndicalist" *El pueblo* and not far away from the very conservative *ABC*. The famous comic book *La codorniz* is seen twice, and so is the popular film magazine *Cine en 7 días*. Besides providing both a context and some forebodings, this mishmash of words and images attests to the tumultuous coexistence of a variety of social, political, and cultural discourses at the time. Sophia Loren (and her cleavage), Jordan's Prince Hussein (during an official visit to Spain), the future queen of Spain (on her wedding day), and a number of female actresses and bikini-wearing models hang out together; that is, their pictures on magazine covers do. In fact, the feminine figure becomes one of the first foci in this opening, paving the way for the prominence of women on display or as commodities in the film. Even the first prop is an object, a piece of clothing really, that is closely associated with both restraining and exhibiting the female figure.

As the camera finishes its slow panning over printed words and captured images, it stops at the white wall behind this rudimentary press display. Soon enough a hand enters frame right brandishing an undergarment, a corset, to be precise. "It was just like this one," cries the person we will later know as the always-angry haberdasher (María Luisa Ponte). "They stole from me one just like this one." So a corset is the first truly cinematographic object in this film: an object of desire, an object on which every gaze converges and whose where-abouts will be of some consequence in the plot.

The corset is, as Valerie Steele puts it, "probably the most controversial garment in the entire history of fashion" and, I would add, arguably one of the most cinematic.[3] Closely associated with the mechanism to control and to objectify the female body, the corset can also mean, and I follow Steele again here, "social status, self-discipline, artistry, respectability, beauty, youth, and erotic allure."[4] From an instrument of quotidian, self-inflicted Victorian torture to the iconic attire of the dominatrix, this piece of clothing seems to constrain as much as to empower. Moreover, as Alberto Mira Nouselles reminds us, at the time *El extraño viaje* was filmed, the corset belonged to a category of cloth-ing items that could not be shown on-screen, not even by itself, away from the human figure.[5] In the actual way it is shown and talked about in this movie, the corset means different things to different people. In fact, its meaning in each instance depends on competing readings of the object. In other words, because the corset means immorality for the choir of old women in the town, it can mean modernity and transgression for the characters who want to steal it and wear it. I would advance now the argument that this *contentious production of meaning*, already discussed in regard to precarious moving vehicles in chapter 2, is key to the understanding of cultural modernity and paramount in analyzing the place desire occupies in it.

After the irate merchant denounces the theft, one of the old women mutters to the other: "It serves her right, since she brought those filthy things [*porquerías*] into town." The stolen corset will reappear later on in a scene on which I will comment extensively. Still, I cannot pass up the opportunity to point out now how the first images of the movie frame against the same white wall bikinis and corsets, bits of garments that exhibit the body they at once cover and constrain. In fact, I should underline as well that walls form one of the privileged spaces of meaning in *El extraño viaje*: they seem to offer an ironic counterpoint, a biting commentary to what the characters who move or stand in front of them are and do. Gaze and desire are mobilized once again in a way that stresses that to be wanted is to be looked at or to be on display. The rest of the opening credits sequence confirms this intuition.

As more words appear and disappear on the screen, the haberdasher crosses the town square, followed by her small choir of old women, to confront Bea-triz, her employee. At the entrance of the social club (called El progreso with the same irony that the ladies' shop is called La Parisienne), they have a brief argument before Beatriz goes back into the building. The movie cuts then to the interior as Fernando's girlfriend enters through a curtain, leading the camera through a space where the walls are covered with posters that invite us to drink Coca-Cola, enjoy a certain brand of liquor, and take a summer vacation in a popular tourist destination. It is commonly held that commodity capitalism intends to create desires instead of just products, and this is exactly what this second part of the opening credits sequence makes evident in Fernán-Gómez's movie. The production of desire is the process filmed. First and foremost, it is the production of sexual desire, as we shall soon see, but also the more restrained longing of the village's *cursi* for the out-of-towner she hopes to marry. Let us concern ourselves with the latter first, which means, by the way, that we must invoke the discourse of *cursilería*, a concept that could be translated as "cheesiness" or "tackiness" for now.

In Beatriz's case, desire comes with no need for a close-up. The desiring subject and the object of her desire do not have the clear visual structure in which a usually male and usually heterosexual desire is filmed. Beatriz's desire appears as an undifferentiated, hard-to-distinguish look across a crowded room. Before the scopic field is reorganized around the spectacle of Angelines (Sara Lezana), the young, sexy female dancer, the camera films a woman desiring a man as something that happens across a room, as something that has to be recognized in a crowd. Let us say that this modality of desire drowns all the other ways in which much modern desire fills the screen. As it slowly pans from right to left, the camera also shows the posters from afar that invite us to consume through sexual innuendo. In such an environment, they look like exotic inscriptions on the wall. The chaste and restrained desire of Beatriz is literally bracketed by these invitations to consume, by these first clear instances of what Wolfgang Fritz Haug called "commodity aesthetics." As such, they partake of "a beauty developed in the service of the realization of exchange value, whereby commodities are designed to stimulate in the onlooker the desire to possess and the impulse to buy."[6]

I will go back to these images and to the possible critique of advertisement inscribed in the film later in this chapter. For now, I want to linger on the fact that it is against such indexes of consumerist capitalism that the town's *cursi* sits, with her disempowered desiring looks, being the object of nobody's gaze, subjected, instead, to the desire of being gained or possessed through marriage. *Cursi* is the name she is called several times during the film, and, judging by some of the overly sentimental dialogues she has with Fernando, she appears guilty as charged. Now, as Noël Valis's classic on the subject has shown, the discourse of *cursilería* is about much more than exaggerated or outmoded sentimentality. In one of her more succinct formulations (which I partially quoted when I commented on Beatriz's position in the first sequences of the film), "lo cursi is really a form of disempowered desire."[7] Equally interesting for this particular reading of Beatriz is the fact that Valis also speaks of *cursilería* as "cultural inadequacy" and that she tracks its historical basis to "the shift from a traditional to a more modern society, moving toward increasing industrialization and consumerism."[8] Valis also suggests that *lo cursi* persists "partly because it is a recurring (and unstable) historical sign of the uneven processes of modernity that have characterized nineteenth- and twentieth-century Spain."[9] As for the presence of *lo cursi* during the Franco regime, it persisted "in part because post–civil war economic hardships and material shortages brought out more sharply the gap between appearances and reality, in part because the ideology of Francoism demanded it, in the sense that the regime's values were self-consciously modeled on an obsolescent code of behavior and beliefs."[10]

All this, of course, resonates deeply with what *lo cursi* means or does in *El extraño viaje*. Beatriz is surrounded by the markers of that supposedly new society moving toward new ways of consumption, while her moral code and her behavior are, at best, conservative and, at worst, complicit with the regime's mantra on woman's chastity. She refuses to be kissed before marriage or to hold hands in the presence of others. Her codes, one supposes, are also informed by romantic or melodramatic sources, since she will allow her boyfriend to kiss her as soon as she learns of the made-up tragic story about Fernando's nonexistent, very sick brother. Either way, Beatriz's codes and morals are still those of a woman who is *cursi* because she is not modern, or, put slightly differently, because she feels the anxieties of the modern. Following Valis's groundbreaking research, I posit that *lo cursi* not only has to be thought about in the context of modernity but also has to be placed within the realities (and the pressures) of modernization.

In a very poignant exchange between Angelines and the always-angry shop owner, this critical bond becomes hilariously evident. When the former wants to buy a bathing suit similar to the ones worn by magazine models, the latter resents the suggestion that her business would be thought to carry "such things" (*esas cosas*). "What a *cursi* town!" replies Angelines. "We are not as modern as you are, thank God" is the shop owner's comeback. The dialectics between *cursilería* and modernity are stated as if one were the opposite and yet the requirement of the other. The very comic moment points toward a very serious distinction in the understanding and the imagining of what can be called modern in developmentalist Francoism. Angelines shows the shop owner a cover ripped from a magazine similar to the ones we have seen in the opening credits sequence. For her, *cursi* reeks of something that is backward looking, reactionary, prudish.

Modern, for the shop owner, means daring, sexual, indecent. Whatever break or interruption the modern means for this village (or for this country) is here stripped down to questions of images of women and sexuality. *Lo cursi* is definitively about much more than outmoded displays of sentimentality. It is surely about provincialism and most likely about repression. Hence Beatriz is to be contemplated not only against a background of seminaked models but also in conjunction with her counterimage: Angelines. *La cursi* and *la moderna*: they are paired up from the very beginning, and they are kept as each other's contrasting image all through a film that shows them crossing paths, standing side by side, and finally bonding in their desire for an elsewhere. Before the moving images of this film spell out this dynamic of similitude and difference, I need to go back to their first visual juxtaposition. That is, I need to go back to the social club where Angelines disrupts the initial combination of *cursilería* and consumerism that opens the film.

An attractive woman performing for an audience has become a commonplace of classic cinema. That performance takes the form of either a song or a dance that interrupts the flow of the action and forces all gazes to converge on a female figure. The degree to which the camera sexualizes her of course changes from film to film, as do the demands of identification made on the audience. The spectator is usually shown both the performer and the built-in audience watching her. They are mostly male and customarily lustful. In Angelines's case, her dance has been read as a "barefoot imitation of [Silvana] Mangano."[11] The reference here is to the famous dance performed by the Italian actress in *Riso Amaro (Bitter Rice)* (Giuseppe De Santis, 1949). While this is indeed a young, sensual woman dancing without her shoes to a piece of modern music, her suggestive movements and the way they are filmed or watched may also invoke other precedents. In fact, I would like to propose another visual reference: John Houston's *The Asphalt Jungle* (1950) and the famous scene of the jukebox dance. This is certainly a less automatic visual quotation, yet, I would argue, it is a much more revealing one, since the process of identification it sets in motion is much more disturbing, for Silvana Mangano is watched and desired by the audience almost exclusively through the gaze of Vittorio Gassman, a character with whom the typical male audience member would have no problem identifying. However, Houston's character's look of desire for a much younger girl means a much more unsettling process of making the gaze of the audience and the gaze of a character converge.

Virtually every commentator on the sequence has noted that the spectacle of sensual Angelines is filtered through a multiplicity of viewing subjects. Hers is a dance that choreographs motions and emotions, pulsions and mores. As

Figure 14. Angelines's dance

Figure 15. The nonreaction shot

the camera oscillates between filming her dance and the subjects looking at her, Angelines's contortions cause excitement as much as reprobation. Old men look at her from behind a very symbolic barred door, while old women, sitting closer to her, shake their heads in disapproval. She will dance by herself, in front of young villagers who obviously lust for her, and also to and with the camera. Yet one gaze — one face, one reaction shot — interrupts this feast of invested looking. The reaction shot to one of the most provocative views of Angelines (twisting her body down and offering a generous cleavage to a downward-filming camera, shown in fig. 14) consists of the image of a very serious villager backed by the ever-present poster that invites us to drink a particular brand of alcoholic beverage (see fig. 15).

This particular frame, the one with the expressionless peasant, evidences both the proximity and the distance between the human face and the inviting world of "sensualized" commodity displayed behind him. Unmoved by either the music or the movement, this countenance also points to the distance between the onlooker and the suggestive spectacle right in front of him in a reaction shot that could more aptly be called a shot of nonreaction.

To judge the meaning of this expressionless countenance I would like to go back for a moment to a classic in film experiments. When in the 1910s and

1920s Lev Kuleshov intercut a freeze frame of an actor with shots of diverse spectacles (a plate of soup, a dead child, an attractive girl), the audience reportedly saw different reactions in what was just an expressionless face. Designed to champion montage as the essence of the cinematographic art, the results were taken by André Bazin to prove precisely the opposite: what makes possible the Kuleshov effect is precisely the human face in all its expressiveness—in all its raw potential to convey meaning. And yet it seems as if this particular face during this particular scene in *El extraño viaje* displays utter inexpressiveness. There is a profound disconnection between shot and countershot, between countenance and spectacle at this point. Among the lusty looks of the villagers literally behind bars and the looks of reprobation by the village's women, there is this short-lived gaze of an unmoved peasant. It is a third modality of looking that does not seem to respond to the brand new world of sights and commodities to be watched and desired. The world of desire the movie puts on display has then, so to speak, a built-in visual disclaimer. If we take into account that the face clearly belongs to one of the nonprofessional actors in the film (truly a stand-in for the face of the pueblo), then this countenance may also bring a certain "reality effect" to the film. Both the performance (the film) and the performance within the performance (the dance) are briefly yet abruptly halted: this might as well be a nonactor nonacting. Nonactors have meant different things in different moments in film history, yet the concepts of rawness, sincerity, and authenticity seem to recur in the discussion of their occurrences. When Flaherty, Pabst, Eisenstein, and De Sica employed nonactors, they were countering comparable foes in the medium of film.[12] Either redeeming cinema from its ideological sins or saving it from its commercial, overprofessionalized ways, nonactors represented a dosage of reality. This is what this face means here too: the reality of a look and a gaze that short-circuit the entire scopic field and compromise the free circulation of desire. Although when it comes to analyzing the gaze and desire, or desire filmed in a disconcerting way in this film, there is one sequence that must be discussed at all costs: the sequence of Fernando's cross-dressing (see fig. 16).

This is the most famous scene of the film, the one with the most potential for scandal in 1964, and the one most likely to cause puzzlement still today. Even sophisticated film critics have called this scene simply "the weirdest in Spanish cinema of the time."[13] To be fair, the scene *is* strange; that is, the images of Carlos Larrañaga parading around in women's outfits amount to a radical change in the way that looking, appearing before others, and desiring have been handled throughout the film. The scene could also be called perverse, if by perversion we understand, once again, a deviation from what is orthodox that

Figure 16. Fernando's fashion show

in turn calls attention to a stable concept of normalcy. Nothing before in the movie prepares the audience for this sudden apparition of cross-dressing in such a cinematic blend between thriller and *sainete*. More important, women have not been looking at men like Ignacia looks at Fernando in drag. Fernando's deposition to the judge is what triggers these images, and, as part of a flashback, they actually feel more like a dream than like something that did happen. Hitchcock is very much present in them, since it is hard not to see in Ignacia's dress and in her figure a reference to Norman Bates in his killing uniform — the original act of lethal cross-dressing, if you will. The fact that she is sitting in a rocking chair underlines the reference.

The visual gag and the comic feeling of the images (a feeling reinforced by the soundtrack) are now a much more sophisticated affair than all those jokes that had lusty old villagers in them. The scene with such characters peeping through windows to see Angelines in a makeshift swimsuit seems indeed distant, as if it belonged to a different movie. Thinking back to all those bikini-clad models selling drinks or destinations in the opening sequences, we could say that we have been taken from the realm of commodity fetishism to the sphere of sexual fetishism, or from Marx to Freud, in a voyage strange indeed because of its sudden transitions this time. We have borne witness to the more normalized varieties of desire only to be shown those mediated by objects, by articles of clothing, in this case. These expressions of sexuality were called sexual deviations at some point, and, if we take deviation to mean an act of defiance, this is very much true of these images and this gaze. As such, Ignacia is the desiring subject, the one in control. Ignacia is the subject who choreographs a screen desire that has been both hidden and repressed. Yet this surprising new space for a feminine, sexual gaze is indeed tumultuous and unstable. Female desire does result in disorientation.

The sequence ends with Fernando walking toward the camera in his most

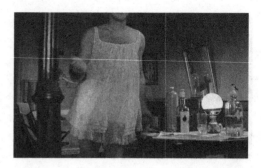

Figure 17. The final garment and the
empty rocking chair

revealing garment yet (see fig. 17). With this movement, the character essentially
disrupts the shot-countershot structure that articulates the entire sequence. The
spectator was indeed a witness of this private fashion. We were looking now at
the model, now at the observer in the scene. As this sudden cut to Fernando's
body coming toward the camera takes place, it becomes evident that the apparatus does not stand for Ignacia's gaze anymore, since she is clearly sitting at the
other side of the room. Or she was, because her rocking chair can be seen empty
now. Ignacia has disappeared from the space of desire she helped to articulate.
It was her desiring gaze that, for all intents and purposes, had reorganized
the space of sexual desire in this movie. To the disempowered, passive look
of Beatriz, we have to oppose this Norman Bates type of Ignacia and her very
empowering manner of looking and desiring. And to calibrate how desire (and
its displacements) is filmed here, we need only pay attention once more to the
walls enclosing the action and what appears on them. As Fernando does his
modeling, a mirror on the wall behind him reflects the image of a still-made
bed. Now, the compositional and symbolic role of mirrors in visual modernity
is yet to be written. Beyond what has been already said about Velázquez's most
famous looking glass in *Las meninas* or about those deforming mirrors in *Luces
de Bohemia*'s Callejón del Gato, there is something to be said about mirrors that
return the images of desire, even if they do so in such an elliptical way. There
was one of these revealing mirrors already in *Viridiana* (see fig. 18), this time
perhaps foreshadowing the fate of the ex-novice.

At the same time more humble and subtler, the existence and the role of
Fernán-Gómez's mirror in *El extraño viaje* speak of a triangulation of desire that
has no need of beds and, ultimately, of the mechanisms by which desire itself
is reorganized, disturbed, or redefined. The latter, I argued at the beginning,
pertains both to the act of looking and to the art of filming. A modern way of
doing both is at stake in this film, a modern way that turns to Hitchcock for
something more than custom design and the visual echoes of a rocking chair.

Figure 18. The reflected bed in *Viridi-ana*

What Is Hitchcock Doing in a Film like This?

The subtle presence of the master of suspense in the cross-dressing scene is but the culmination of a Hitchcockian strain in *El extraño viaje* that can be felt very early in the movie, as early as when the action moves from the "happening" social club to the unnerving space of the Vidals' mansion. Coincidentally, in this new profilmic space the walls are also inscribed with messages that make reference to a libidinal economy. A prominent handmade sign seen on several occasions very tellingly reads: "Abandon lust for a month and it will abandon you for three." In this new setting, *costumbrismo* and *sainete* make way for that first Hitchcockian mode of the film. Not only does the camera film this new space as the view of an unidentified character slowly and apprehensively walking along a dark corridor, but, soon enough, a stuffed seagull on the wall will invoke more specific works by the English director. The question then presents itself in unequivocal terms. What is Hitchcock's "murderous gaze" (William Rothman) doing in a small, provincial Spanish village ruled by a dictatorial regime and besieged by commodity capitalism? This is, of course, to ask once more about modernity and film and to factor in, in addition, the notions of the foreign and the autochthonous. It is also, as we shall soon see, to ask about the meaning of crime and transgression within a specific type of filming and in a very particular milieu.

So far, the answer to the Hitchcockian question in *El extraño viaje* has pointed in two different directions. For Santos Zunzunegui, Hitchcock is in this film mainly "a stylistic reference."[14] *Rebecca* (1940) provides inspiration for the characterization of Ignacia, and several motifs and camera movements refer to *Psycho* (1960). For Steven Marsh, the "Hitchcock" in Fernán-Gómez's movie "is very much a comic rendition of the original . . . a hammed up, spoofed version of [it]."[15] With different degrees of explicitness, both critics acknowledge that the Hitchcockian overtones cannot be read in isolation from the more clearly "native" elements of the film. The master of suspense's presence is to be noticed, yet (one cannot help but conclude from Marsh's and Zunzunegui's readings) it is noticed as something that is, in some degree, ancillary. Zunzunegui, for instance, brings up the inevitable *esperpento* reference and adds the zarzuela genre as subtext. Marsh uses the word "cannibalization" to describe what such a Spanish film does with Hitchcock. I would argue that intertextuality and parody are two terms that do not take far enough what the presence of the English director means in and to this film.

First of all, to invoke Hitchcock is to conflate the categories of auteur and genre as well as those of entertainer and artist. Truffaut was, if not the first, surely the most adamant advocate of a Hitchcock auteur. Furthermore, for the French director the latter was a filmmaker "at once commercial and experimental."[16] Truffaut thus reserved for Hitchcock the role of both forerunner and first practitioner of a modernist thrust in the medium of the moving image. Gilles Deleuze would claim as much some years later, when he situated the master of suspense at the juncture between what he terms classical and modern cinema, or, using his words again, at the intersection between the movement-image and the time-image.[17] Most recently, John Orr, after giving an account of the master's interest in the high modernist productions by an Antonioni or a Bergman, argues that "with *Vertigo*, *Psycho*, and the *Birds*, Hitchcock had already proved his modernist credentials without fully realizing it."[18]

I want to make mine the line of thought that would require full awareness of all these disquisitions regarding the master of suspense when looking for his footprints in *El extraño viaje*. Put otherwise, it is not simply about quoting from the master of suspense, nor is it about aping his style. It is, instead, about a very concrete choice to engage with the modern through film. It is, in fact, about a certain degree of self-consciousness regarding the place this movie occupies between the elsewhere of a cinematic modernity and the here and now of very local, seemingly unmodern representational practices. If Hitchcock style is, more than style, a creation of mental images that pushes "classical cinema" to its limit, his presence in the Spanish movie must have an effect in it that goes beyond the acts of quoting and lampooning. In fact, I would argue here that the presence of Hitchcock in *El extraño viaje* has to be taken seriously. By this I mean that it must be read as substantial to how this film builds a complex logic of imagery as opposed to a mere hybridity of crass localism and fancier visual quotes. The comic effect—call it the ironic relocalization of a Hitchcockian gaze—is also a matter of serious regard. Actually, by asking about the seriousness of Hitchcock in Fernán-Gómez's film, I am imitating Robin Wood's gesture regarding Hitchcock himself in his pioneering 1965 study. "Why should we take Hitchcock seriously?" was Wood's question. The answer came, of course, in the form of a serious study of both formal and thematic aspects in the English filmmaker's oeuvre by Wood himself and then followed by many others. I find no better way to undertake this serious reading of the Hitchcockian in *El extraño viaje* than to follow suit and embark on a close reading of key scenes in the movie so as to "put into words the thinking inscribed in [its] successions of frames."[19] For that purpose, I need to rewind once more and go to the first scene in which the mood of the suspense-horror film is clearly perceived.

  I have said that the camera moves slowly and apprehensively along a dark corridor. The previous establishing shot showed the whole mansion from the village square, briefly illuminated by lightning. The switch in tone possesses an unmistakably generic mark, a convention that prepares how the interior is to be felt and read. Immediately afterward, the camera starts the slow traveling shot already mentioned. It first approaches a partially open door that creaks as it allows the apparatus through. It is as if the camera were pushing the door open. Only much later will we discover (actually, we will need to assume) that the camera stands for the gaze of the character (Fernando) who enters the mansion. Initially, the scene develops without a reverse shot of that moving being, so our first encounter with these images presents us with a cinematic apparatus that has a life of its own. There is no sound of footsteps, no shot of feet, back, or shadow, none of the auditory or visual clues that would intimate that an actual person organizes all this walking and all this looking. Interestingly enough, the fact that we are not clearly shown that there is a person behind this point of view is an ignorance of consequences for what the movie does with a genre it has so topically entered.

  First of all, these subjective views without the anchor of a known or seen person — these subjective shots without a subject — do not allow for a clear reading of this moving gaze, whether it signals menace or whether it itself is a sign of danger. Either assassin or victim, the recording apparatus moves, and all we can do is look and walk with it along this dark corridor. As it does so, the camera slightly pans left to allow a glimpse of a closed door with a wall telephone to its left. The camera then pans back to the right as if fixated with another door at the end of the corridor, presumably its final destination. To the left of it, the shadow of a bird seems to mark this second door as the ominous one. The camera dollies forward as the interior of the mansion is fleetingly illuminated by another stroke of lightning. A second later, there is a rattling noise followed by a straight cut to a door moving. It looks as if somebody is trying to open it from the inside. This sudden cut is the cause of some meaningful disorientation. At first, it seems natural that the close-up of the rattling door would be the door that the camera was approaching, since it was the door last seen. However, it is the door just beyond the one we are seeing, which entails a forty-five-degree turn in the point of view.

Right up until this moment, the camera has followed the convention of behaving like a head, of rehearsing a well-known anthropomorphic point of view. It will resume this behavior shortly, panning right as the rattling subsides and bringing us back to the view of the door at the end of the corridor, this time with the stuffed seagull and not its shadow in full view. The traveling resumes, and the camera eventually reaches its goal, opening and passing through this gloomy yet silent door. The spatial disorientation created both by camera movement and by the syntax of the shots represents the first moment of tension between the generic marks that frame the scene and its actualization. In horror and suspense films, these ambiguous gazes are at some point cleared of their double meaning. The objective shot becomes the shot of, say, a killer. Here, the mysterious, deeply equivocal way the camera moves and makes us look is maintained all the way through. What is more, one can even read the scene retroactively and relate its meaning to the ambiguous criminality of each of the four characters in that mansion. How much of a criminal is Fernando really? What are the nature and the reach of Ignacia's evil? In what sense and to what extent are the younger Vidal siblings, Paquita (Rafaela Aparicio) and Venancio (Jess Franco), victims or villains? Certainly, this is a set of questions foreshadowed by the camera movement that opens *El extraño viaje*'s Hitchcockian mood.

Soon enough, the first human figure in the sequence, Paquita, will emerge from the rattling door left behind. She is no Hitchcockian heroine, to be sure. The master did prefer them blonde, after all, blonde and sophisticated. Rafaela Aparicio was primarily a well-known comic actress, and her dumpy, familiar figure on the screen is certainly a clear signal of comedy. She will proceed to enter her brother's room, bump into a piece of furniture, and fall clumsily, certifying with slapstick that this suspense movie within a movie is also to be read in conjunction with other genres and other moods. However, this does not invalidate the, say, seriousness of the first part of the sequence, nor does it turn the Hitchcockian presence into parody. In *Shadow of a Doubt* (1943), for instance, the deadly seriousness with which Uncle Charlie's murderous inclinations are filmed shares the screen with a small-town America of odd and mostly lovable characters. In fact, this movie could be a productive point of reference in the reading of *El extraño viaje* as an invocation of a Hitchcock universe not because the American movie's plot or characters are anywhere noticeable in the Spanish film but because of all Hitchcock movies it is the one that most clearly works with a small-town setting disturbed by an outside murderous presence. And this is an aspect in the movie that has to do with moods or tones as much as it has to do with the avatars of the plot. In Rothman's words, "Part of *Shadow of a Doubt*'s originality resides in its deliberate juxtaposition of the dark world of film noir and the cheery world of sentimental Americana."[20] The juxtaposition in Fernán-Gómez's film is of course of a different sign, undoubtedly more extreme: the dark world of the suspense-horror film and the comic—at times grotesque, at times ridiculous—world of provincial, developmentalist Spain.

Yet let me reiterate how seriously the film takes its entrance into what I have called a Hitchcockian strain or mood. The ambiguous meaning of that camera movement and the disorientations it causes are not erased by the irruption of these two characters, overacting included. Fernán-Gómez is in fact working with genre conventions that thrill and scare us as much as the master did. Early on in Hitchcockian criticism, it was argued that suspense in Hitchcock is the main tool to delve into questions of a moral order (sharing the fate of the characters, fearing for them, dreading yet hoping that we will see another murder, etc.). Hitchcock's "moral ambiguity," writes Tom Gunning, is "based in ambiguous identifications."[21] The Spanish director is equally serious in pursuing this marriage of suspense and ethical investments in the process of spectator identification.

To illustrate this point we can take a look at another extraordinary moment in the film in which camera movement forces us to address questions of spectatorship. It is another Hitchcockian moment par excellence, since it involves opening a door and venturing into a room where neither the characters nor we know what to expect. Of course, this is a paradigmatic moment of suspense and horror films, yet what Hitchcock did with such a stock moment is a different matter. The exemplary Hitchcockian moment in this respect can be found in *Psycho* when Lila, Marion's sister, is searching Bates's house. In Rothman's very suggestive analysis, when a camera setup that represented Lila's point of view is reprised with the character in it (her back to the camera), the suggestion is that "Lila has crossed a barrier, as if she has stepped into her own dream."[22] Now let us take a look at the scene in *El extraño viaje* in which a similar passage may be taking place.

Intrigued by some noises, Paquita and Venancio enter Ignacia's room in the middle of the night. They are initially filmed from above, a ceiling lamp somewhat obstructing their figures. A crane movement brings the camera down below eye level to show the two characters holding hands and looking in amazement at the spectacle of what seems like the remnants of a private party. At first, they are shown from a distance in a shot that holds both of them in the background while the first source of their astonishment is in the foreground. Then the camera tracks forward to get closer to the couple's faces and immediately pans left. When the camera starts surveying the room from left to right, it seems logical to assume that camera and characters share the same point of view. They do seem to be looking at the often-seen handmade sign on the wall that urges us to abandon lust and then, in succession, at a potted plant, a shelf under the sign, the frame of a picture, a nightstand, the bed with a portable radio resting on it, and finally a mirror by the side of the door through which they have just entered the room. But as the circle is complete (suddenly, strangely), the two characters enter the frame: they are still standing where they originally were, trembling and looking straight past the camera as if they had never looked around, as if the camera alone was doing all the looking. This second moment of notorious spatial disorientation in the film may be said to create the illusion of characters who look at themselves looking. These individuals have entered their own field of vision, and they wait, literally scared stiff, for something terrifying to happen. At that precise moment, Ignacia opens the door behind them, and we are provided with the promised scare the characters themselves seemed to be expecting. It is as if the characters know the type of movie they are in. It is as if the audience was made aware that this film is simultaneously playing with a genre and rehearsing what an auteur did with that genre. This film, to be sure, is going for the thrill (and for the laugh), but I will go so far as to say that it also extracts from the gaze a particular modality of spectatorship in which images cause both uncertainty and self-consciousness. In sum, this remarkable sequence shot in *El extraño viaje* speaks of Hitchcock as much as the very notorious stuffed seagull does, a bird whose presence I also consider as much more than a funny prop or a humorous quote from *Psycho*. As D. A. Miller says of a particular Hitchcockian moment in a Claude Chabrol movie, "If everyone recognizes the extended *Psycho* moment, will anyone easily be able to state the point of it here?"[23] In this case, rather than an "extended moment," we contemplate a particular object that invokes what in *Psycho* amounts to an extended motif. Let's go back, yet again, to the first sequences in the Vidals' mansion to revisit the apparition of this very conspicuous seagull.

After Paquita wakes up Venancio and tells him that she has heard somebody enter the house, they work up the courage to knock on Ignacia's door. There is another subjective shot of the ominous door guarded by the stuffed seagull as the two characters move closer to it. The gaze that belonged to no known subject seconds ago is now a dual gaze, one that could belong to either of the brothers or to both of them. Then the camera tilts down to reveal light inside the room. There is a cut back to the two brothers, who are now filmed in profile from a low angle. "Look, there is light," says the sister. "Thank God she

Figure 19. The ominous stuffed seagull

Figure 20. The stuffed seagull and the mean sister

is awake," replies Venancio. He then approaches the door, and the camera, in a different setup, pans slightly right, revealing the stuffed seagull with its beak literally hovering over the human figure (see fig. 19).

Ignacia opens the door, and we see her from a low angle between her two brothers: she is dressed in black and is thin, tall, mean looking. As if to underline the physical and symbolic separation between these siblings, there is a cut to a two shot of Venancio and Paquita as they get closer together, seeking each other's protection. Finally, a frame very similar to the one that had the stuffed seagull facing them presents the bird now by their older sister's shoulder, as if perched on her (see fig. 20).

More than anything else in the film, this stuffed bird and its placement in the shots seems to scream Hitchcock at us. Of course, the motif of the stuffed bird in *Psycho*, as it is presented in the famous motel's parlor scene, seems like a much more complex presence than this lone seagull in *El extraño viaje*. *Psycho*'s stuffed birds are looked at by the characters, talked about, compared with other characters (most significantly with Norman's mother), and associated with other actions in the film (the notorious Norman's observation "You eat like a bird" directed at Marion, whose last name is, of course, Crane). However, the "bird motif" is there mainly, if not solely, to indicate that Norman Bates is a predator.

Fernán-Gómez's seagull, on the other hand, is just that: a seagull. In other words, it is not an owl or a hawk. It is not even a raven or a crow. If the natural reading of the bird's presence is that it represents an extension of Ignacia's figure in the frame, either anticipated or visible, the natural inference could be that this is a much less menacing figure than it seems. We may even take it to signify that the whole film is a lesser Hitchcock, that the movie itself acknowledges what it has done with a filmic constellation so at odds with this particular setting and this particular set of characters. Yet a "Hitchcock" it is, deadly serious in its technical choices and definitely bent on making these choices clash with the nature of spaces and figures as un-Hitchcockian as the ones provided by this small Spanish village, where cured hams make wine tastier. This is a town whose lack of sophistication has a role in this reframing of Hitchcock that ultimately points to ways of filming, ways of looking, and criminal ways. For the other major aspect to address in what I have called "taking Hitchcock's presence in *El extraño viaje* seriously" is to try and elucidate what the Spanish movie says about crime and evil or about transgression and punishment.

Since the very first attempts at identifying a serious "Hitch," made by Eric Rhomer and Claude Chabrol in 1954, the aforementioned concepts have been deployed in many a discussion regarding the director's commentary on the nature of modern existence.[24] Criminal acts and criminals in particular are usually seen as possessing a double ambivalence. First, one can say that, in regard to Hitchcock's most notable criminals, one can scrape the surface of a villain and find a victim. On the other hand, crimes in Hitchcock can be either the outcome of a sick mind or the expression of a social malaise. In a more general formulation, Robin Wood saw Hitchcock's films as belonging not only to the author but also "to the culture, its institutions, its values, its ideology, its internal conflicts and struggles."[25] If Hitchcock's presence is as ostensible in *El extraño viaje* as I have made it out to be, one should wonder about the import of these matters in the Spanish film too. Criminal acts and the individuals who commit them are, hence, the first components of the narrative in which to anchor discussions of order and transgression in Fernando Fernán-Gomez's movie.

The first villain, the first murderer to be examined, is the outsider, Fernando. From the very beginning his moral fiber is very much in question, as he lies to Beatriz about having a sick brother and then proceeds to "kill" him to hide the lie. Later on, he also helps the Vidals hide their crime, only to murder them on a beach at the end. The ulterior motives for this gradual escalation of criminality are worth examining. In his confession to the judge, Fernando tries to justify all his misdeeds by saying that they gave him the opportunity to marry Beatriz and to finance his own zarzuela company. The zarzuela is a very traditional, very Spanish genre: a type of musical theater that does not reach the lofty heights of opera. So the crime cannot have a more conformist, traditional, bourgeois motive. If it is true, as John Orr claims, that in Hitchcock's American phase "his narratives rotate around a recurring theme — the internal violation of bourgeois order," then Fernán-Gómez's movie turns that theme on its head.[26] These are crimes committed to establish such an order and to paint it Spanish, as it were. In Fernando's case, one scratches a villain and finds a traditionalist and, to some extent, a *cursi* too. A harder question to answer is: What would one find after scratching Ignacia?

From the very beginning of the most sinister part of the narrative, everything points toward the elder Vidal sister as the villain in this film. Her actions are secretive and despotic, her words are harsh, her attitude is menacing, and the visual clues on and around her figure are disturbing. Of course, she ends up being the first victim in this story, a fact that may even force us to reread that stuffed seagull as a disclaimer. Ignacia's evil, after all, boils down to a plan to leave town with the family's money, ditch her siblings, and run away with Fernando. Additionally, she has other mean plans that result in what cannot be truly qualified as the deeds of a criminal. She has kept hidden, we will soon learn, Paquita's and Venancio's childhood toys in the same closet in which she stashes her liquor and her stolen sexy lingerie. This meanness, however, feels like a very serious crime in the way the narrative unfolds. It also seems to be somehow connected with Ignacia's death. That deliberate act of cruelty, that apparently harmless hiding of toys, seems to be the key evil deed among all these other clumsy, supposedly involuntary homicides. And I call it "key" because of its meaning or, better, because of the modality of its significance. To make this claim meaningful, I need to revisit the night of the murder.

Venancio maintains that he killed Ignacia in order to defend Paquita. "She was going to kill you," he contends. He also claims that there was no "ill intention" (*mala intención*) in his action. These two characters are indeed simpletons, and nothing in the narrative prepares the audience for the eventuality of such a murder. The way the crime is filmed, however, seems to disavow Venancio's self-justification. In a struggle that commences as a clumsy chase between such caricature-like characters and that is counterpointed by the traditional *pasodoble* played by the band outside, Venancio's outburst of rage seems as unexpected as Fernando's drag scene did. He whacks his older sister's head up to six times with a bottle, the last two blows when she is lying on the floor. One is tempted to think that the only reason the beating stops is because the murder weapon breaks. Ignacia's murder is indeed filmed as if to conflate the two main strains of the film (the comedic and the *sainetesque*) with the Hitchcockian element. First, from the time Paquita and Venancio enter Ignacia's room until the time those six fatal blows are delivered, the sequence showing the murder is intercut with the events taking place in the village's central square. The musicians have been in a traffic accident, and the villagers seem to be on the verge of turning into a mob for two reasons: because the band is late, and because it may not play after all. The film reaches one of its *sainetesque* nadirs when the mayor himself exclaims, "What a vulgar [*ordinario*] town!" in front of his unruly constituency. Once the mystery of Ignacia's killing is solved at the end, it becomes evident that the parallel montage serves the purpose of accounting for the whereabouts of all the main players on the night of the murder. Yet, taking into account that the weekly dance has already been established as a sublimation of sexual desire, the rage of this crowd, which is ready to act violently if its collective desires are not satisfied, seems to be somewhat connected to Venancio's sudden brutality. At the very least, both bouts of violence feed symbolically from each other. Indeed, the realization that a disturbing, vicious core lies hidden under the likable appearance of these ordinary small-town folk makes its way through the film, as does the capacity for viciousness in an otherwise cowed and puerile Venancio.

Second, the brutality of Venancio's killing appears as a violent, belated retaliation after a life spent under the tyranny of Ignacia. Simultaneously robbed of a happy childhood and kept in a perpetual state of infancy, Venancio is indeed exploding rather than just defending. Tempting as it is to see Franco's dictatorship allegorized in this visual meditation on violence and repression, I would not want to make the film simpler with my reading. So let us conclude that the surplus of viciousness in Ignacia's murder and the suspected rage lurking under the surface of the affable townsmen are symptoms of a disturbing undercurrent running under the good-humored, *sainetesque* texture of this strange journey. As in the case of *El cochecito*, *El verdugo*, and *Viridiana*, the latent violence under the regime's jovial new ways is what gives pause to all our smiling and laughing. It bears repeating that this dark laughter is not the liberating, utopian comic discharge commonly thought of as an alternative or indeed an antidote for despair. This is no "entropic humor," as Patrick O'Neill would describe it, for instance.[27] Instead, this is the more disquieting laughter that forces one to confront all that is wrong with both laughing and the object of laughter.

As for Ignacia and her gratuitous, mean way of keeping toys from her siblings . . . well, it is back to the seagull. Is it not the seagull that preys on small fish? Or, better still, is it not the bird that either scavenges opportunistically or steals from both humans and other animals? And, in spite of what I said before, is it not the seagull that is the first dangerous bird in Hitchcock's *The Birds*? Is this too much symbolism? Is this too much reading into a prop that others may rightfully take as just a fun reference? And, then again, is this not also the Hitch-cockian "density" of meaning, especially with objects, that so many critics have gone to great lengths to prove? The master of suspense is also the master of sur-plus meaning. He is the king of maddening invitations to overread, the virtuoso of the *sinthome* (understood as a network of significations) rather than the very punctual meaning production of the *symptom*, in Žižek's Lacanian parlance.[28] Surrounded by the unrefined, the indigenous, and the tacky, encroached upon by the traits of either the *sainete* or the zarzuela, and, in theory, weighed down by the overacting typical in both, this movie is still a "Hitchcock": it is a filmic exploration of what the look has to do with moral choices and ethical conduct. Now, taking into account that the movie is virtually contemporary with *Nueve cartas a Berta* (*Nine Letters to Berta*) (Basilio Martín Patino, 1966), the most cel-ebrated production of the already mentioned new Spanish cinema, it seems worth our while to see both films not as an old and a new way of doing film in Spain but as two opportunities to engage with the modern given such cultural and geopolitical circumstances. In another attempt at a winning formulation of my critical obsession, let us say that, should we accept this movie as a modern one, however heterodox in its visual modernity, then the concept of modernity in film itself has to be thought differently.

Last Stop, Voyage Over

Basilio Martín Patino's *Nueve cartas a Berta* has been described as "a manifesto and a compendium of sorts that shows the film movement's virtues as well as its weaknesses."[29] This "movement" is certainly polemic, as it befits a series of films promoted by the regime, made with international festivals in mind, and being mostly "social cinema," which was successful as such only in small intellectual circles. As government-sponsored productions, NCE films have been deemed complicit with the Franco regime and its public relations campaign of the 1960s. There would be much to discuss in how *Nueve cartas a Berta* actually engages with the dialectic of the old and the new underpinning the cultural production of the times. Simply put, the old in this film is the location itself. The old is the stagnant provincial city of Salamanca and the traditional views that thwart any real men-tal and moral progress in the country. The new in the film is the way this reality is put into images (freeze-frames, 360-degree shots, a camera that dollies past its subjects, etc.) and the main character-narrator in the film, a young university student who has been abroad and is now imbued with European (i.e., foreign) ideas. Do these points allow us to pitch this kind of film production against the supposedly old way of making Spanish film, the way with which *El extraño viaje* flirts? In the following I answer this question by condensing many of the other questions on the meaning of "Spanish" filmic modernity that I have anchored to a movie in this and the previous three chapters.

"The modern Spanish cinema begins with the modernization of Spain," states John Hopewell.[30] Agreed; but the process of modernization is complex and crisscrossed by internal conflicts, one of which is precisely the place the old occupies in the workings and the imagining of the new. What is extremely interesting in this case is that Hopewell goes on to see modernization as a process of differentiation, not of homogenization. In other words, while modernization has been seen as a process that essentially would make Spain more like the more modernized nations of the Continent, Hopewell goes against the grain in tying modernization to difference. Just after linking modern cinema with the country's process of modernization, he continues: "Most Spanish films are not immediately universal. But it is just this 'otherness' that gives them a vital authenticity, and an ability to snap the spectator out of his usual way of looking at things."[31] Now, let us reflect upon what this statement presupposes regarding the interplay among modernization, universality, otherness, authenticity, and spectatorship, for all these seem to be the concepts puzzlingly and suggestively at play here.

First, in Hopewell's view, otherness is predicated on a concept of spectatorship in which cultural background or even cultural competence is a factor that can be used to understand the unusual quality of the spectacle in front of an audience. Here modernity in film seems to imply a movement away from universality; otherness, in turn, is a guarantee of newness in how films are watched. In other words, the quintessential gesture of modernist cinema (waking up the spectator from his or her visual slumber, or, in more technical terms, challenging the institutional mode of representation) rests precisely on the existence of the local/authentic/other as a disturbance of sorts, as a jolt to the spectator's visual expectations.

Now, if the explicit agenda of the NCE, as advanced by García Escudero, was to modernize Spanish cinema, and if that meant basically to Europeanize it, is it not the perceived local component of the film that would truly add the measure of strangeness that would snap the audience out of its comfortable viewing practices? The relation between the local and the modern certainly works paradoxically here, as does the relation between an audience-that-is-supposed-to-know and the kind of spectacle of desire that is there to be dislocated or reorganized. The modern Spanish cinema of the 1960s is the cinema that questions modernity itself as a linear progress or as a train to catch. It is a cinema where the local is not something to be merely overcome nor where the foreign is an attainable model of both visualizing and looking. Modernity in film and in Spain is a strange voyage indeed, one in which films like *El cochecito*, *El verdugo*, *Viridiana*, and *El extraño viaje* have pride of place, so much so that they constitute the foundations of a film genre in which dark humor creates an imagining community whose ethical laughter "dis-locates" as much as it returns us to a very specific locale.

The last ten years of the dictatorship will see other instances of cinemato-graphic dark humor, most notably, Carlos Saura's 1970 *El jardín de las delicias* (*The Garden of Delights*). But we will have to wait until the early years of a still tender democratic state to find a dark laughter as geopolitically and aesthetically relevant as it was in the years of developmentalism and dictatorship. We will have to wait until the arrival of that dark humorist called Pedro Almodóvar.

6

Almodóvar Interlude

Transitional Laughter

When in November 1975, after thirty-six years in power, the dictator Francisco Franco died of natural causes, we did not contemplate, not even symbolically, the death of the nation's father. In Spain that death, and the political transition it set in motion, may have been the cause of mourning for some and of trauma for others, but it was also the occasion for much celebration and certainly a reason for laughter. The meaningful (and manifold) confluence of death and comedy has been a constant in this book. At this juncture, then, it is only reasonable to ask whether there is a relevant role for dark humor within the analysis of the sociopolitical process that took the country from dictatorship into democracy. In other words, does the laugh that laughs at—or in the aftermath of—such a momentous death provide some insights of consequence regarding the nature of the Spanish transition? The question could be posed in simpler terms: Is the transition from dictatorship to democracy in the Spain of the midseventies serious business or a joke? To put it so crudely is of course to be asking for trouble. On the other hand, the crudeness of the question underlines what this chapter aims to point out: how, in the analysis of the transition, the success/failure or celebratory/damning paradigms are equally unsatisfactory in their ultimate either/or simplicity. The chapter also aspires, albeit more tacitly, to move beyond the "analytic imperialism of the Oedipus complex" that has dominated the critical discourse on Spanish cultural production during and after Francoism.[1] For Oedipus can only be of so much use. The desire to kill one's father still keeps the father-son relation as the overarching structure in the imagining and the understanding of a national milieu. Even if that father figure is the object of repressed hatred and imaginary violence, it remains a father; that is, the figurative role the dictator reserved for himself is kept in place. There are, there must be, other symbolic ways to deal with dictators. Both the people who have been repressed and the critics who assess the culture of dissidence under and after a dictatorship need different ways to imagine those dictators.

In this chapter, the films of Pedro Almodóvar offer the darkness and the laughter I need to reconsider the hegemonic discourses on the Spanish transition or at least to make room for competing ways of understanding it. Along the way, I also expect to revisit Almodóvar's role within that moment of artistic and youth-culture exuberance after the dictator's death known as *La Movida* and to rethink the director's place within the transition itself. If a presumed "post-Francoist" moment, "typically discussed in the context of the *Movida*," can be "characterized by a fairly widespread desire to be done once and for all with the dictator, to forget and ignore him," and if Almodóvar's early productions can be seen as enacting, among many others, that particular desire, then there is much to be said for the possibility of finding an anti-Oedipus Almodóvar.[2] In consonance with the arguments of Deleuze and Guattari, this would imply the existence of a schizophrenic Almodóvar, an Almodóvar turned into a nonneurotic producer of desire. At the same time, the alleged apolitical essence of *La Movida*—for which the director's first films are sometimes seen as exemplary—may compromise the filmmaker's place in a transitional period whose lack of engagement with the country's legacies of authoritarianism has been progressively deemed as a political and ethical flaw. Can both the Franco/father metaphor and the Oedipal narrative be disavowed only at the price of being complicit with a culture of political naïveté and historical amnesia? This seems to be the critical corner I have painted myself into after combining the first films of Pedro Almodóvar with an anti-Oedipal thrust in them and the possible role of *La Movida* within the socio-ethical shortcomings of the Spanish transition. However, I do not mind walking all over the fresh paint in order to find in dark laughter the key to a cultural analysis that may go beyond the either/or approach in trying to understand the interrelations between film, culture, and politics in such a foundational moment in present-day Spain.

In what follows I will concentrate on Almodóvar's first three feature films, the ones he authored in the early 1980s, *Pepi, Luci, Bom y otras chicas del montón* (*Pepi, Luci, Bom, and Other Girls on the Heap*, 1980), *Laberinto de pasiones* (*Labyrinth of Passions*, 1982), and *Entre tinieblas* (1983), or *Dark Habits*, as it was retitled in English. The first two films comprise the *Movida* diptych in Almodóvar's early career as a filmmaker. They are the most underground, punk, pop, or campy in the Almodovarian corpus, and they can be alternatively thought of as just the outcome of the wild times in which they were produced or as frenzied texts in which to find the themes and the obsessions of the future craftsman. How the comedic in them is evaluated seems to have determined these two approaches.[3] Ultimately, how seriously to take them is, in my estimation, the main challenge they both offer. I am afraid my analysis of them will be piecemeal and that I will favor *Pepi* at the expense of *Laberinto*, but I still want to treat them as a diptych and call them Almodóvar's *Movida* movies for reasons that will soon become apparent.

His third feature (let us call it the first post-1982 Almodóvar film) is still within the time frame of *La Movida* but in its later stages, after democracy in the country appeared to be on solid ground and a new socialist government had entered the cultural scene. Even though *Dark Habits* cannot be neatly isolated from the subsequent productions of the director's filmography, this film signals a new turn in the director's career, and it represents a new way to engage with the transitional times it still manages to chronicle. This comic melodrama of drugs and lesbian love extrapolates the dark humor of the incongruous, first found in madcap comedy, to the secluded space of a nunnery. The darkness of this film seems to be inversely proportional to the brightening of a political process finally moving beyond the last gasps of hard-core Francoism, yet it remains attuned to a bleakness in values and circumstances, keeping its distance from any sense of sociopolitical optimism.

There are several questions one could ask regarding the role of comedy in this trio of films, yet the most pressing for the purposes of this book is this: Where is the laughter of these movies situated vis-à-vis the serious business of making a political transition? As I said of the dark cinematographic comedies studied in the previous chapters, these Almodóvar productions *intervene* in their social milieu (in the transitional years this time) as much as they are enabled by it. In the analysis of the three films mentioned, I hope to clarify the particularities of that intervention. Yet before I get to the films (in fact, in order to be able to get to them), I feel I have to cross through critical zones where, in spite of their names, movement is only slow and difficult: the transition itself and *La Movida*.

What Does a Transition Feel Like?

In 1978, with the dictator already dead for three years, Spaniards approved a brand new constitution for the country through a popular referendum. Since a number of politicians born and bred within the Francoist apparatus still ruled the country via the right-center party Unión de Centro Democrático (UCD), the ties to the previous regime felt, if not strong, at least still holding. The year 1982 saw the electoral victory of the Partido Socialista Obrero Español (PSOE), which meant the arrival of the Left to power and a de facto break with political Francoism. In February of that year, the still young Spanish democracy passed its most perilous test when it survived a coup attempt masterminded by the military and executed by members of the police force known as the Guardia Civil. In 1986 Spain was finally accepted as a member of the European Community. "We are already Europeans!" is the ironic exclamation, pronounced with a marked regional accent.

This neat string of momentous mileposts tells a story of accelerated democratization and foreseeable integration, of normalization and Europeanness. Like any success story, it also silences the false starts, the compromises, the dead ends, and, most importantly, the realities left unsaid or untouched. These eleven years may paint a picture of unstoppable progress and historical inevitability, yet the process, hailed as the model of an unwavering and effective race from totalitarianism to parliamentary representation, has been replayed again and again in a search for cheating shortcuts. The result of this search is a counter-narrative that speaks of incompleteness, traumas, wounds, specters, simulacra, silences, oblivions, and even "*intransiciones*" (nontransitions). Either exemplary or deeply flawed, the transition delivered the promised land of political representation, but it accomplished that feat at a price.[4] It either healed through compromise or created traumas.[5] It inflicted wounds that are still open, set loose ghosts, and even created a sort of abstinence syndrome.[6]

Initially viewed as a political process orchestrated by politicians and embraced by the citizenry, the transition has been reevaluated and resignified by historians, political scientists, and journalists. In turn, the cultural critics have revised the transition done by artists, writers, and youth subcultures and have discerned in it the several symptoms of the nation's current maladies, the absence of closure, truth, or reparation being the most troubling. In all this, it becomes apparent that the more we discuss the transition, the less feasible it is to make an aseptic distinction between politics and culture, between the business of building the democratic city and the task of providing it with narratives, with its images, and, ultimately, with a poetics. As Germán Labrador Méndez puts it, the transition at some point ceases to mean a process that generates political and institutional structures and alludes instead to "the group of practices, modes, languages, and values that are transformed at that moment."[7] Along the same lines, one cannot but underline that this particular moment in the history of Spain has been approached more affectively than cognitively. In other words, the transition seems to have been easily and frequently translated into feelings, affects, moods, or emotions. The eleven years one might describe as the transitional ones are indeed crisscrossed by collective feelings of hope, fear, anxiety, elation, uncertainty, disappointment, perplexity, mourning, and sheer joy. Yet when the emotional dust settles, one feeling appears to enjoy some sort of structuring dominance: *el desencanto*, or "disenchantment."

How an entire nation can be disenchanted is a sociological phenomenon that needs to be abundantly nuanced. I have argued elsewhere that the all-explaining powers of such a mood need to be reexamined in great detail.[8] Even *El desencanto*, Jaime Chávarri's 1976 documentary film, the one that may have most helped to make that feeling hegemonic in the analysis of the transitional years, is a filmic text in which anger, irony, and confrontation have major roles. I would add here that the emblematic movie of all things disenchanted also displays telling moments of humor — of dark humor, that is — and that those moments have the effect of liberating the film from being constantly reabsorbed by ominous, mournful appraisals.

Covering almost exactly the years of the transition, *La Movida* offered the possibility of adding joy and celebration to the spectrum of moods and feelings predicated on the nation as a body. It also presented the challenge of articulating its place and its value vis-à-vis the overall gloomy tenor of the hegemonic approach to the transitional years. First, as Jorge Marí points out, some of the "positions, interests, desires, and anxieties" besieging the critical discourse on *La Movida* "are also very much present, in practically the same terms, in a great number of approaches to the transition."[9] Among these I would single out the fact that both the political process and the cultural moment share the same celebratory/damning paradigm in which the ethics of reading what happened responds to very concrete ideas on where the country stands as a modern European democratic state. *La Movida* has been equated with an uncompromising outburst of freedom, especially sexual in nature.[10] It has also been made part of a broader "process of remarking a democratic Spain and democratic Spaniards in the wake of the dictatorship."[11] At the same time, as Rosi Song and William Nichols point out, it has been "used as evidence [of] the country's incapacity to purge its authoritarian past."[12] *La Movida* has also earned the scorn of those who see the movement as either brightly burning or co-opted by party politics and market forces in equal measure; yet it has also deserved a nostalgic treatment when contemplated as that exciting time of almost teenage democracy not yet fully conscious of the seriousness that life has in store. Furthermore, in spite of all the definitions that make use of the terms "liberation," "energy," "creativeness," and "exuberance," *La Movida* has also been soaked in disenchantment and melancholia.[13] Finally, to speak of *La Movida*'s "dark side" has become a subgenre within the studies dedicated to the phenomenon. Drug abuse and the breakout of the AIDS epidemic in the early 1980s have made for a somber, self-destructive end to the movement, an end that, in turn, facilitates the extraction of moral lessons.

At the risk of repeating myself, I would like to state once more that it is within this charged realm of feelings, affects, and even visceral reactions connected to the transitional years through *La Movida* that I would like to search for laughter and, more specifically, for the kind of dark laughter I have studied within the context of Francoist developmentalism. The searching grounds are, as noted, the Spain of the early 1980s and the first films of Pedro Almodóvar. A filmmaker internationally celebrated for his alleged postmodern, eccentric ways, Almodóvar will be contemplated here as a very local dark humorist filming during the transitional years or, in effect, darkly filming a transition while posing the question of how seriously we must take it.[14]

Seriously Funny

The scene takes place in the outrageous, low-budget, and technically flawed first Almodóvar feature film, the already mentioned *Pepi, Luci, Bom y otras chicas del montón*, the one I have called *Pepi* for short. Dressed in the typical *castizo* garb — the costume diehard *madrileños* would wear to show off their traditional roots — and obviously lip-synching one of the most recognizable songs of the popular zarzuela genre, a group of young people beat up what they believe is a fascist policeman in the street. The assaulted man is actually the policeman's innocent twin brother, and it was the policeman's rape victim, Pepi (Carmen Maura), who commissioned a beating she paid for with some marijuana plants. She is even watching the assault from a street corner, visibly excited by the spectacle. The perpetrators, the ones dressed as *chulapos* and *manolas* (Madrid men and woman of the people), are in fact the members of a punk-rock band both in the fiction of the film and in the reality of Madrid's nightclubs at the time.

To find this act of violence funny is to recognize, first, its incongruity but also its excess and, more importantly, its cultural distinctiveness. A policeman is being beaten in a country where police brutality is still part of the country's everyday reality, while the punks who punish him disguise themselves with the clothes of the unmodern. Ultimately, the comedy here is rooted in a context-specific, hard-to-translate knowledge. Arguably the most international of Spanish directors, Almodóvar has displayed the local as something humorous (as well as disturbing) from the earliest stages of his career. One could even say that in Almodóvar the local, the traditional, or the autochthonous is something to make fun of or have fun with. If we take into account that this comic treatment of the local quite frequently comes paired with a topic that questions the limits of laughter (street violence and revenge in this case, and murder, rape, or drug overdose in future films), a very vigorous strand of Almodóvar's humor appears to be exploring the unpleasant truths of who we are, which may include the troubling likelihood that we are sexist and homophobic. In Simon Critchley's words, humor "puts us back in place, whether the latter is our neighbourhood, region or nation."[15] Turning himself into a case study, he continues: "As an eager cosmopolitan, I would rather not be reminded of national differences and national styles, yet our sense of humor can often unconsciously pull us up short in front of ourselves, showing how prejudices that one would rather not hold can continue to have a grip on one's sense of who one is. . . . If humour returns us to our locale, then my point is that it can do this in an extremely uncomfortable way, precisely as thrown into something I did not and would not choose."[16] Laughing at others (because they are foreigners, because they are different) may indeed forge or reinforce a sense of community. Finding ourselves ridiculous — and uncomfortably so — might be equally foundational and self-defining.

One of the most recognizable of Almodóvar's auteur credentials, the ludic (and lurid) use of the local — of conventional signs of Spanishness, really — will recur with more or less aesthetic and narrative weight throughout Almodóvar's films. *Matador* (1986), the tragicomic tale of serial killing and bullfighting, represents the director's clearest incursion into putative marks of national specificity. Yet at this initial stage in his film production, Almodóvar's dark, homegrown humor still ought to be linked to that irreverent moment of youth subculture that his first two movies are said to record.

Indeed, and following the director's cue, it is not uncommon to treat Almodóvar's first two feature films as documentary in essence. In a very loose sense of the term, they are said to document precisely the initial phase of *La Movida*, its most raw, un-co-opted early years. The authentic locations and the cameos by the director's friends, some of them key participants in the "scene" of the early 1980s, support these films' claims to documentary quality. In a still looser sense of the term, one could say that the movies also document the type of humor that pervaded many of the cultural manifestations associated with *La Movida*: the underground comics of a magazine like *El víbora*; the graphic art of Ceesepe, Nazario, or El Hortelano; the paintings by the pair of painters known as Las Costus; the lyrics of some of the early songs by bands like Orquesta Mondragón and Siniestro Total; or a number of the colorful photographs by Ouka Lele, to name, as the cliché goes, only a few.[17] The hedonistic, outlandish, pop- and punk-inspired climate of the 1980s youth subculture in Spain's capital displayed a sense of humor where excess, provocation, scatology, sexual humor, screwball, and the bizarre made for a unique mix. The common perception would have Almodóvar outgrowing this type of humor at the same pace that the country itself is thought to have grown up and left behind the early stages of immature, carefree cultural manifestations. Reality set in, and the director became a more somber, controlled jester at the same time that *La Movida* started dying of overdoses, AIDS, and success. Or so the story goes. For this common view, of course, circumvents the fact that death and violence were all around the transition and *La Movida*. It does not pay heed to how Almodóvar himself may have dealt with that violent, uncertain national milieu in his early works. The years 1978–80, for instance, were especially deadly in Spain, with more than three hundred mortal victims of political violence caused mainly by the Basque separatist group ETA (Euskadi Ta Askatasuna) and the Maoist GRAPO (Grupos de Resistencia Antifascista Primero de Octubre) as well as by neofascist groups and police repression. *La Movida* may very well have been an interregnum of long-overdue, happy-go-lucky partying where cultural production was not patently political, but it had to contend, in a more or less tacit manner, with the very real violence and the very concrete anxieties of its times.

"El horno no está para bollos" (an idiomatic expression that could be translated as "the situation is very hot"), Pepi tells her marijuana-paid thugs after reminding them that she does not want the policeman dead, just beaten. In fact, the terrorist groups ETA and GRAPO make a cameo in Almodóvar's first movie. The former appears on the front page of a newspaper one of the characters is reading. The latter finds a rhyme in the lyrics of "Murciana," the punk song Pepi dedicates to her masochistic housewife lover, Luci (Eva Siva). Luci's husband, the fascist policeman (Felix Rotaeta), voices the right-wing sentiments that could have fueled the assassination of five people associated with the Spanish Communist Party and trade union in Madrid just one year before the first scenes of the film were shot. When this caricature of a sexist, ultra-right-wing cop expresses his doubts regarding "where all this democracy is taking the country" and adds that "these communists need to be taught a lesson [*darle un escarmiento*]," it is hard not to find this parody of the lingering hard-line Francoist outlook chilling. Yet it is equally hard not to find it frivolous, since it comes embedded in a film practice where the bizarre and the caricaturesque have such prominence.

What to do with all these contextual references, however anecdotic they may seem, in precisely this type of movie is of course the problem. Deadly serious statements in the mouth of a caricature are not automatically ridiculed.

The world out there does not become inconsequential just because it is recontextualized in such a madcap, comic narrative. As Paul Julian Smith very aptly puts it, Almodóvar showed, as early as 1975, a "love of comic confrontation . . . inseparable from serious concerns."[18] The vital question would be to assess what that inseparability means at a historical juncture with so many national concerns and the potential for so much confrontation. My provisional answer to this question is that, above all, the comic in this director's films confronts the audience with the task of laughing *with no orientation*. I then speak of comic disorientation in Almodóvar's films, a disorientation I imagine to be but a variation on the comic principle of incongruity.[19] Moreover, beyond what the classic formulation of that theory has to offer, I would like to advance a theory of the comic incongruous where *that which is not consistent within itself* and *that which is lacking in propriety* are the meanings to be emphasized. The disorientation I have in mind, then, may be caused by the implausibility of the situations in already convoluted plots. This explains the proliferation of the adjectives "bizarre," "eccentric," "estranged," and, more simply and commonly, "weird" in Almodóvar commentary. More prominently, however, the disconcerting effects of his humor are due to the ideological quicksand zone on which one is forced to stand while witnessing the comic spectacle. In other words, it is the demands of seriousness that the topic or the moment make on a nevertheless laughing audience that makes his comedy disorienting, hence my stressing of a potential lack of propriety in the meaning of the adjective "incongruous." I will give the grounds for this claim presently, but the essential point here is that these sources of comic "disorientation" point to how laughing during the transition was equally an uncertain business. One could laugh at the mores and traditions of the old regime, and this is immediately apparent when Almodóvar targets family, gender roles, and religion. Yet the newfound liberties are also the object of an ironic treatment that can even be confused with derision in his films. Feminism and new gender roles in general, sexual identities, sexuality itself—they all figure prominently in films whose liberatory ethos makes use of double-edged provocations. These provocations ultimately test the limits of what can be said and done in the country, including the ones that demarcate what is an appropriate object of satire. *Pepi*, for instance, combines the discourse of pornography with images of female solidarity and an ambiguous message on lesbianism and sadomasochistic practices. It also constitutes an exercise in queer celebration not entirely devoid of disconcerting aspects.

Pornography, to begin with, or the "new wave of eroticism sweeping the country," as Luci puts it, is in fact a key component of the comedic in *Pepi*. Its opening scene might be called porno without nudity. In such a genre, it would seem that all possible humor, however questionable, might come only from improbably blunt and forced dialogue, bad acting, and naughty puns. The movie seems to make use of all three sources. Famously, right after the first general election in forty years took place, in his first feature Almodóvar stages a penis size contest called "General Erections" that ends with oral sex for the winner. In the opening scene, Carmen Maura, virtually the only professional actress in the film, objected to the line that could roughly translate as "And speaking of sucking: What do you think about this juicy little pussy," a line she nevertheless delivers with the characteristic overacting of the genre the film is quoting.[20] Before legendary Hollywood divas like Bette Davis and Joan Crawford would provide inspiration to the Spanish director, he mentions the likes of Bárbara Rey, María José Cantudo, and Agata Lys, sex symbols of the so-called *destape* (undressing) during the transitional years and stars of movies where plots were just an excuse to show female nudity. *Pepi* absorbs these low forms of popular entertainment and pleasures and proceeds to lump them together with the said protofeminist stance or with an all too evident queer joie de vivre.

If, as we saw, the comic recontextualization of political violence finds a small but potentially disruptive place in *Pepi*, then sexual relations and sexuality are the major battlegrounds to test how disorienting the laughter generated by Almodóvar's movies might get. His "battle of the sexes" films are, rather, sexual battles where the pain is not always only emotional, nor is it always unwelcome. In *Pepi* that battle pitches husband against wife, masochistic housewife against lesbian punk singer, and rapist against his victim. And at the end, it is hard to reconcile the resolution of Luci's story line (the masochist housewife, married to a fascist cop, who eventually finds happiness with him as she lies severely injured in a hospital bed) with any progressive, instructive message. The same could be said of the treatment of pornography within a liberal, or *progre* (progressive), discourse. While the seemingly ubiquitous policeman is shown directing lewd looks at a porn magazine, and hence lustful machismo seems very obviously reviled, a number of key scenes in *Pepi* are too central to the fun the film is having with pornography to find in them an indictment of the genre. The ironic use of pornography to advance a politics of freedom (of expression, of representation) is of particular consequence to the effects and the value of arguably the most scandalous scene in the movie. Right after Luci meets Bom (Olvido Gara, a.k.a. Alaska) in Pepi's apartment, the punk teenager urinates on the forty-something masochist housewife. The moment in the movie that most forcibly signals the arrival of an unrestrained freedom of expression and representation, the scene that most cheerily revels in nonnormative sexual acts, happens to owe its existence to porn, since in no other genre is a golden shower scene likely. Low, "disreputable" freedoms are linked to loftier ones to the point of inextricability. Taking into account that one of them (say, the freedom to film sexual acts and show them to an adult audience) can infringe upon other liberatory discourses (the classic feminist contention with pornography and its sexist representational politics), the pornographic intertext in *Pepi* could be even more bewildering. Of course, Almodóvar does not film a porn scene when he films one character peeing on another. The parodic traits are important to note (the music, Bom's melodramatic diva entrance, and Luci's love-at-first-sight stare), and so is the matter-of-factness with which the characters live the unusual, the out-of-the-ordinary, and their perceived weirdness. A pious reading of this trait would hold these moments as representative of a "what is weird to you is normal for others" kind of message. I would contend that the line between normality and weirdness is never stable or irreversible in Almodóvar and that the seriousness of his humor in the face of difference (sexual or otherwise) resides in the realization that the weird (or the queer, for that matter) is something you hardly laugh away. This brings me to a related set of problems regarding the seriousness of Almodóvar's first comedies, or how seriously they may or ought to be viewed. It is in fact a series of issues that have to do with the representation of homosexuality and, more precisely, of "queenery" in this first Almodóvar.

Held up as the artist who did the most to make the queer visible in the post-Franco years, Almodóvar in these first films also showcases a more problematic image of the gay as court jester. In particular, the effeminate queen is the character who displays all her ideological ambivalence as source and object of comedy. Of course, it would be preposterous to detect the slightest hint of homophobia in Pedro Almodóvar's films. Yet some of his queer characters in these first two movies have the potential to become a comic stereotype, one that is being mocked as much as it mocks accepted roles and behaviors. Almodóvar, one needs to remember, does not shy away from facile types of humor. He may resort, for instance, to regional accents, to Andalusian in particular, a dialect stereotypically associated with Spaniards who are funny just because of the way they talk. The relatively cheap source of laughter in *Pepi* is an effeminate queen called Roxy, a minor character in the film who nonetheless becomes one of the signature figures of queer visibility at the time. Played by Fabio de Miguel, a.k.a. Fanny MacNamara, Almodóvar's partner in crime during his brief musical career, Roxy spoofs the glam diva persona, queers the homely Avon Lady figure, and turns into a sexually forward queen, at once embarrassing and delighting a heterosexual audience through his advances to an equally embarrassed and laugh-repressing postman. In Almodóvar's second film, MacNamara plays a porno star named Patty Diphusa, who in the opening scene displays his brand of outrageous queenery in a patio bar. There he sniffs nail polish, smokes marijuana, and drinks from two tall glasses at the same time while repeating the exclamation "What an overdose!" All shrieks and forwardness, he then proceeds to hook up with Riza Niro (Imanol Arias), the gay son of the emperor of the fictitious Tirán. In his flaming gay performances, MacNamara is in fact practicing the kind of queen comedy that risks the most while eliciting a homophobic laugh, the one that leaves prejudices intact or indeed reaffirms them. As Andy Medhurst argues in his discussion of the English queen comedy tradition, in his several variants this subcultural icon can be seen "as a reactionary and damaging misrepresentation, reinforcing a view of male homosexuals as weak, shrieking, sexless ninnies, a caricature constructed of fluff and fuss, a misfit made up of 50 per cent failed man and 50 per cent failed woman."[21] In the context of the new, uncensored Spain, Roxy and Patty Diphusa make people laugh, but their comic power may be more a matter of empowering a heterosexual audience to find amusing what is so different from its normative idea of masculinity. In Brad Epps's words, "Fabio's own undoing [of sexual identities] is 'sad' in part because it is played for fun: as if the only figure who could be so violently disfigured and still remain 'comical' had to be hysterical, gay, and transvestite."[22]

On the other hand, Medhurst also offers the competing view of the effeminate queen in comedy, the one who "can be a cause for gay celebration, an index of defiance, an embodiment of survival, and a fabulous refusal to conform and behave."[23] This is the image most commonly accepted in the case of MacNamara's appearances in Almodóvar's first movies. And rightly so, since, in Marvin D'Lugo's very apt formulation, "the issue of gayness . . . has to be viewed within the broader circulation of a discourse that is specific to a local cultural context (Spanish gay culture as an intervention in the process of social demarginalization in the decade following Franco's death) as well as to a series of transnational themes, modulated through the subversive qualities of melodrama as an expressive mode."[24] I, too, would like to emphasize that celebration and defiance are very much part of MacNamara's act and persona as well as of Almodóvar's queer aesthetics in his first two movies. Yet I do not want to overlook either that such a defiant celebration cannot be said to be free from its own ambivalences, which in this case seem to hinge on the laughter they occasion. In addition, it should be noted that there were other ways to intervene in the process of the demarginalization of gays in Spain at the time, like the different gay liberation fronts throughout the Spanish state. Almodóvar's filmography will have space for other types of queens and queers, for men in drag, transvestites, and transgender people, but here, in what I am considering as the *Movida* movies, the effeminate queen is still a figure who, as the life of the party, seems to be one step away from becoming the butt of a joke.

If one insists on finding a manifesto of queer identity, however unarticulated or provisional at this stage of Almodóvar's career, *Laberinto* certainly becomes a more problematic text than *Pepi*. This is not because of the noted presence of another effeminate queen but because of some of its gay male figures or, in general, because of Almodóvar's treatment of heterosexual and homosexual relations in the film. Riza Niro, in particular, ends up having sex with the ex-nymphomaniac Sexilia (Cecilia Roth) in a plane, just like in the first install-ment of the popular soft-porn *Emmanuel* series, as one of them points out. A couple of scenes before, Riza confesses to Sexilia that before meeting her he "liked men," and Sexilia responds: "I also was a nymphomaniac before I met you." How seriously are we to take this dialogue? And, more pertinently, what is the movie saying about the nature of homosexuality while celebrating its presence in Spanish society in such a spectacular way? James Mandrell asks the question of seriousness in a more sweeping way when he wonders how seri-ously we are to take "the action and the conclusion" of the movie. His answer is "Probably not all that seriously. But probably more seriously than we would like to admit."[25] This after having analyzed the movie as seriously as any of the metaphorical films of Carlos Saura and after having stated that the film ulti-mately betrays Almodóvar's "professional latent heterosexuality."[26] In his own take on the question of seriousness, Brad Epps adds that "promiscuity and ho-mosexuality [in *Laberinto*] . . . are plotted as pathological and hence as problems to be overcome." And he continues: "Passion may be labyrinthine, but it ap-parently needs to be set straight. Whether or not the story of such straightening should itself be taken straight is, however, another question."[27] The measure of how straight he takes the film's straightening to be comes in the form of a very sophisticated and insightful analysis where virtually no psychological or cin-ematographic nuance is left unexamined. How expert readers of the director's oeuvre have negotiated this subject seems to validate my choice of the adjective "disorienting" in connection with the comic image of homosexuality in *Laberinto*.

There is no denying that a gay character is "cured" in the film and that his happy transition to monogamous heterosexuality runs suspiciously paral-lel to that of a nymphomaniac who leaves her sexual compulsion behind. It is also worth noting that the film presents both "conditions" as the effects of a childhood trauma in which the discourse of trauma itself seems to be at once deployed and ridiculed. This is an approach to the explanatory powers of the traumatic that is very explicit on the director's part. "I've always taken traumas as something of a joke," he has declared, "but they comprise a separate genre in film. In life you can't explain everything with traumas, but in comedy you can; they justify everything."[28] Following filmic conventions, two-thirds of the way into the film narrative a flashback scene lets the audience know that Sexilia's photophobia and sex addiction are the result of her father's neglect. Riza's homosexuality is in turn the outcome of Sexilia's tacit rejection. It all happened on a beach when they both were teenagers. After Sexilia's father disregards his daughter's plea for help (Toraya [Helga Liné], her stepmother, is trying to seduce Sexilia's friend Riza), she approaches a group of boys and accepts their proposal to play "husband and wife" with them. The nubile Sexilia in fact boldly agrees to be the wife of all of them right there and then. Riza, who has successfully fought back the advances of Toraya, finds Sexilia occupied in her game and, dejected, disappears behind some bushes with the only boy in the group not interested in playing husband to a girl.

I would say that in this flashback there is neither Freud nor Hitchcock but a parody of both in which the discourse of trauma seems deprived of any serious explanatory powers, either psychological or cinematic. This mock-traumatic moment notwithstanding, an audience schooled in both popular psychoanalysis and psychological thrillers still seems to be at pains to engage with this image of homosexuality in the face of such a trauma-cure relation. One solution has been to deem it as uncharacteristic in the director's filmography: this is a non-Almodovarian Almodóvar moment, so to speak. A more sophisticated take would consider the portrayal of this "cure" as "characteristic of the skepticism towards the idea of homosexuality as a discrete libidinal territory which recurs throughout Almodóvar's work."[29] This is a convincing attempt at neutralizing the problematic fate of this gay character by inserting his "cure" into a progressive Almodovarian discourse regarding sexuality, but only if one overlooks the fact that the idea of a cure for homosexuality seems a world removed from flexible, nonreductive ideas of what homosexual desire may be or entail. A safer attempt at Almodovarizing this moment is to invoke humor. What the director does here is to reproduce "in burlesque mode, topics of the old disciplinary model of homosexuality current under Franco."[30] Convincing enough again, except for the fact that the dialogue happens to be filmed as a very honest and tender conversation between the two lovers in the back of a taxicab. Even if the burlesque could be isolated in the scene, what would empower the audience to find the humorous treatment of homosexuality less troubling here than when authoritarian values are treated in the same burlesque, humorous manner?

Seriousness, then, is as piecemeal in the analysis of these movies as it is the redeeming or indicting value of their comedy. And that is, I insist, what needs to be taken into account. As with any other potentially solemn or social concern that can be traced in these two films, how seriously to take the sexual politics in either *Pepi* or *Laberinto* depends on how much this madcap type of humor either gets in the way or is overlooked. Screwball and incongruity may sabotage the seriousness of the themes treated and the figures represented, yet the discussion returns time and again to what Almodóvar is saying precisely about those themes and precisely through these means. It would be better, then, to accept that the films themselves are the ones that compel viewers to have it both ways. It would be much better indeed to work with the hypothesis that there is no way to separate the serious from the comic, that that is precisely the phenomenon with which we have to contend first and foremost. What I have called disorienting humor in this first Almodóvar film calls attention to the fact that, with regard to *La Movida* and the transition, laughing and understanding are subjected to similar dynamics. If the transition was not a joke, it surely had a great amount of laughing in it whose liberatory side effects were as ambiguous and as uncertain as many of the efforts to change values and attitudes and feelings. More crucially, as much as *La Movida* could be the land of "anything goes" or "nothing is sacred," this does not mean that it provides a safe haven for ultimately inconsequential statements about the state of the nation after Francoism. It is not enough to simply say that it was a moment of freedom after the death of the dictator. It was also a moment in which freedoms, in the plural, were at once enjoyed and tested. And, as I have tried to demonstrate here, comedy was one of the key factors in both that enjoyment and that examination. In any case, the sociocultural phenomenon and the sociopolitical process can and must be connected in more complex, meaningful ways.

Paul Julian Smith is the scholar who ties *Pepi* to the process of the transition rather than just to *La Movida* in a more decisive way. He goes so far as to read the film "as a *ruptura pactada*, a negotiated break with the past."[31] He is, of course, using the vocabulary of politics, the one that presents the Spanish transition as halfhearted and flawed. Yet the negotiation he refers to is actually a question of aesthetics and cultural frameworks. In Smith's view what tempers the break with the past is precisely the local: "In its celebration of earlier forms of hispanicity (the *maja*, the *zarzuela*), in its fond homage to international camp (Scarlett O'Hara, the Avon Lady) the film suggests that the modernity which it proclaims so shamelessly is inextricable from the dead forms which preceded it and which it claims, nonetheless, to have superseded."[32] The list of dead forms either weighing down modern euphorias or deeply lodged in the heart of them can be extended. It would contain also a popular Spanish music beat (*pasodoble*), the traditional Basque dish *bacalao al pil pil* that Pepi cooks for Bom, and even the final reference to boleros, the Latin music of melodrama and commonality to which Bom redirects her musical ambitions after her punk-rock adventure. Formally and aesthetically speaking, one more aspect of a culturally specific look may be taken into account in this negotiated break with the past where the concessions to modernity in the negotiation, it may seem, take the form of a local look.

I would like to argue that the laughter in these *Movida* films is also due to how they look as films: there is humor in the film aesthetics as much as there is humor in the situations and the dialogue. A significant part of this humor could be linked not to the technical imperfection of the film but to the meaning one can find in its imperfection. Due mainly to a lack of funding, technical imperfections may deserve many adjectives, a multiplicity that in turn conjures up either a noble or mundane domain. Camp, kitsch, and even punk are already rich concepts to describe cultural products in which a lack of quality or a deliberate contempt for technical sophistication could have humorous consequences.[33] Camp is an especially productive term to apply to Almodóvar's early films, and Alejandro Yarza's work is the book of reference in this regard.[34] A term used by less illustrious theorists and with much less circulation would be the Spanish adjective *cutre*, a word that, even though it can be rendered as "vulgar," "coarse," "shabby," or "tacky," I will use here in Spanish. Like *cursi*, *cutre* does not translate well and should be kept in its original language, just as we keep "camp" and "kitsch" in theirs. For a cultural phenomenon such as *La Movida*, in which the flamboyant and the glamorous have been invoked with such frequency, *Pepi* in particular does look *cutre*. The vulgarity is plainly visible, and I have spoken already of the strategic use Almodóvar makes of it. Likewise, the locations, for instance, are painfully gray and unglamorous. Flaky building walls and dirty streets with battered brick corners saturate the first sequences, and the regular housewife mannerisms and attire when Luci enters the scene are hard to miss. When the action takes place in "party" locations, the environment is equally crass and unappealing. The first frames dedicated to the "General Erections" setting show a cramped, homely kitchen as the interior location and then display a courtyard with stained walls, a blackened staircase, and a chipped window frame in which Bom perches herself in a pink leotard, green socks, and gray high-heeled shoes (see fig. 21). The colorful Almodóvar, the one who paints sets to match a character's dress, will come later. For the moment, and aside from Bom's and Pepi's gaudy wardrobe, a number of very humble (and *cutre*) painted lightbulbs will do (see fig. 22).

Almodóvar's brand of camp at this stage, then, may be operating with the

Figure 21. Perched in a window

Figure 22. Partying with Pepi, Lucy, and Bom

codes of the postmodern, as it was becoming fashionable to say back then and as it turned out to be later in the appreciations of the director's work, yet an integral part of his postmodernity is the presence of a coarse, homely, and crummy reality that the word *cutre* might reflect better than the word "camp." *Laberinto* would do away with the typical housewife figure and her homely aesthetics. It would also add more showy international references and a representation of the underground music scene of the 1980s in Madrid. Yet one of the underground musicians is shown selling costume jewelry door to door with his merchandise in a plastic bag, a SEAT 600 (a *seiscientos*) car is visually prominent in one key scene, and a doorkeeper dressed in a quilted robe defecates on herself when she is repeatedly prevented from going to the bathroom after taking a laxative. *La Movida*, in Almodóvar's very particular representation, definitely reserves a space for a look that, from camp to kitsch, may be labeled differently but could also be called *cutre*, and that term could yoke the local and the comic in a more precise way.

Whether camp or *cutre*, kitsch or punk, the presence of that local-inflected and puzzlingly serious comedy in Almodóvar's *Movida* films establishes the grounds for a dark humor that does not disappear in his next movies. The transition keeps on transitioning the country in pushes and jerks, and the movement it generates is about to deliver the victory of politicians on the left and to survive the authoritarian impulses of the military. Yet the existence of dark habits and nagging questions regarding what we have done to deserve our present is still there to be confronted with an unnerving smile.

Hysterically Serious

Dark Habits tells the story of Yolanda (Cristina Pascual), a cabaret singer whose boyfriend dies after using adulterated heroin she bought for him. Still in her glittering work dress, Yolanda hides from the police in a convent in which virtually every nun is in fact a redeemed sinner with a name as impious as Sister Manure (Marisa Paredes) or Sister Sewer Rat (Chus Lampreave). The mother superior (Julieta Serrano) is a lesbian who snorts cocaine and falls in love with the singer to whom she offers shelter. There is also a tiger on the premises, together with a chaplain (Manuel Zarco) who falls for one of the nuns (Lina Canalejas) and declares his love to her, fittingly, in the privacy of a confessional. The couple has been sewing fashionable outfits for the very boringly dressed virgin statues of Catholic iconography. One of the nuns, Sister Manure, consumes LSD, the drug of choice in the 1960s counterculture scene. Her acid trips are linked to a religious experience and to a higher level of perception.

Even after such a succinct synopsis of the plot, the film's irreverent use of Catholic rites and figures seems evident. Yet the efforts to isolate the Catholic Church as the film's object of satire — mainly on the grounds of its complicity with the dictatorial regime — do not fare well with what the images of this extraordinary nunnery actually offered their audience in the Spain of the early 1980s. When focusing on the irreverent nature of the images, a number of critics rightly emphasize that a very reactionary and militant understanding of the Catholic faith was one of the ideological pillars of Francoism. The paradigmatic analysis in this vein could be Mark Allison's classic introductory guide to the cinema of Pedro Almodóvar where the community of nuns is described as "a grotesque caricature of a religious order."[35] In my view, neither the grotesque nor the caricaturesque have a role in what *Dark Habits* does as a dark comedy. Nor would I subscribe to a contextualization of the movie that sees its relation with the sociopolitical milieu in the following way: "The convent's degeneration into excess and caricature is the result of the discrepancy between the social role of religion under Franco and its redundancy in the 'anything goes' culture of democratic Spain."[36] If we review the reactions to the film — including the immediate ones — the truth is that a sizable number of them did not privilege sacrilege among the film's possible intentions, as if the farcical in Almodóvar's films still remained a hindrance to political satire.[37] Some critical voices, including mine, have in turn argued that *Dark Habits* is not an anticlerical film, that Catholicism was never the target.[38] From among the many ways to uphold this stance while still keeping in focus the importance of religious topics and images in the film, one could choose Marvin D'Lugo's: Almodóvar's "interest is not in lampooning religious belief but in examining it as an expressive code."[39]

It would come as no surprise if I say that I am interested once more in the workings of dark humor and in how this movie relates both to the madcap pop productions that preceded it and to the new stage of the nation's transition that starts with the PSOE's victory at the polls. The disorienting value of the dark humor in *Pepi* and *Laberinto* seems to become now a more concrete and even disciplined engagement with serious concerns where the operative term is still "incongruity." In the previous two movies, seriousness was a possibility to factor in almost as an afterthought when evaluating the relative ease with which to laugh in the face of violence or sexual aggression. Seriousness now is a more central issue that affects both form and content in a film that is still comic and still dark. From crazy plots in which one could make out the presence of serious concerns, we have moved on to very serious stories that are told, in actress Julieta Serrano's words, "in ways that make the audience laugh."[40]

Redemption is the lead motif of *Dark Habits*, and the first, subtler redemption in the film is connected with aesthetics. Almodóvar's third feature starts with no comedic markers and ends in all seriousness, with a nun's chilling cry of heartbreak filmed in a dolly shot that makes the camera withdraw, in effect replicating the romantic abandonment she has just suffered. Comedy is not the main genre involved in the makeup of this film. Melodrama, the other genre of preference in Almodóvar's palette, needs to be accounted for if one is to gauge precisely how such a humorless genre mixes with a comedy that still touches on subjects like death, drug use, treason, and heartbreak.

Not coincidentally, the film also displays an array of technical choices that signal the presence of a savvier filmmaker. Let us call him a more serious one. For the first time, the director can move the camera; for the first time, he has the means to locate it either up high or at ground level. Dolly and traveling shots are now part of the director's arsenal in what becomes, in several senses, a less playful filmic endeavor. While *La Movida* films had hardly anything technically remarkable in them except flaws, *Dark Habits* opens with a succession of camera placements that clearly indicate the presence of a *metteur en scène* with a better budget. This new cinematographic seriousness becomes apparent from the very first sequence in the film. After an artsy title credit sequence shot made with

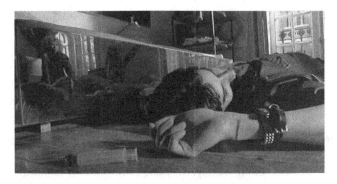

Figure 23. A junkie's death

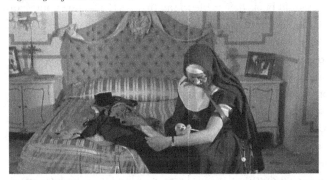

Figure 24. The junkie-nun

time-lapse technique, we meet Yolanda and her boyfriend inside the apartment they seem to share. Two shots, one with the camera at a very low angle in the living room and another from high above, filming Yolanda in the bathroom, announce a will to mark the sequence formally, to make it distinct. Yolanda's boyfriend will collapse while she is sitting on the toilet, and another low-angle camera will frame the lifeless body with the syringe frame-front and Yolanda's image reflected in a piece of furniture behind (see fig. 23). Drug use may very well be "a source of humor" in *Dark Habits*, although not here and not filmed in this way.[41] Furthermore, in the first image in which one can argue that drug use is played for laughs, formal considerations cannot but qualify where the sources of comedy are to be found in such a scene.

Soon after Yolanda enters the convent, the mother superior offers her some heroin and then goes on to inject it herself to assure her guest that the drug is in good condition (see fig. 24). A nun shooting up heroin: now that's comedy. I will resist the temptation to call such an image Buñuelian simply because of its possible anticlericalism. I will not call it surrealist either on account only of its shock value. Once again, I need to invoke seriousness in the appreciation of Almodóvar's comedy of the incongruous and the bizarre. For the process of shooting up the drug is offered in elegant jump dissolves, each one taking us to the next step in a procedure that begins to feel like a ritual. The music score possesses an ominous quality, Hitchcockian in spirit, although no parodic overtone appears to be at play. Finally, we have a stand-in for the audience in Yolanda, who does not seem to find what she sees either scandalous or amusing. Her two reaction shots, at the beginning and at the end of such a bizarre sight, show her mildly astounded at first and definitely accepting at the end. In an image shown like this, it is hard to distinguish the sacrilegious from the sacralizing. Put another way, it would be as defensible to say that such a scene denotes an indictment of the Catholic Church as it would be to say that it demonizes drug consumption or, for that matter, that it glamorizes it. In fact, the scene may have nothing to do with passing judgment on a social problem as grim as heroin consumption. It might engage, instead, with how that problem has been represented, framed, or, indeed, imagined. Almodóvar could be responding hence not to the drug problem at the time, which existed, but to its dramatization in a panicky public domain by the sensationalist media.

Heroin is the most lethal drug of *La Movida*, and the death that opens the film has already set a somber tone in relation to that drug that could no doubt be extended to the world outside the silver screen. Already in the late 1970s, heroin was indeed claiming its share of lives in Madrid. However, as the work of Juan Carlos Usó has shown, heroin addiction and its fatal consequences were a media epidemic before they became a real one.[42] Starting in the summer of 1978 in Spain, an alarmist press would popularize the image of heroin addicts, who were invariably associated with crime, self-destruction, and even the country's degeneration. That summer also saw a supposed public service campaign to fight drug addiction financed by an ad company. It consisted of large billboards in the form of an obituary with the name and the age of the deceased left blank ("fill in with your own," one could read in parentheses). At the bottom of the billboard the motto of the campaign, "drugs kill," was written in capital letters. The mythic leftist journal *Diario 16* applauded this gimmick at the time, while writer Eduardo Haro Ibars, closer himself to the drama of substance abuse, decried the campaign because of its melodramatic tone and lack of specificity in the admonition — neither hashish nor acid had caused a single death. He also denounced its bad taste and its connivance with the repressive powers of the police, which, in his view, were not only law enforcement officers on the street but also an army of "sociologists, psychiatrists and reporters."[43]

Heroin circulation in the Madrid of *La Movida* was a drug problem, but it was also a problem of representation, of narratives and images to produce and circulate. Four years later, *Dark Habits* moved that problem to the realm of popular culture by filming a very different heroin user in a very different mode. One could say that Almodóvar entered the fray belatedly and of course irreverently. Yet his irreverence ultimately has less to do with the Catholic Church than with the army Haro Ibars saw as another branch of the disciplinary powers. Maybe the image of a nun shooting up is at least as bizarre as the image of a heroine user who does not look shady, destitute, or doomed. In any case, the comedy here is not a "simple comedy of contrast" but a more complex and unsettling "comedy of merger and fusion."[44] The incongruity that fuels this comedy may result not so much from a shocking way of filming nuns as from a shocking way of filming junkies. Whatever the case, it is reasonable to conclude that at the core of this film's humor lie drug use, death, and addiction. There also lie women, ambiguously free women in the midst of a transitional period whose liberatory powers were starting to show some limitations.

If *Dark Habits* shows that freedom has come to the convent, the freedom it shows is certainly not an absolute one, since there are several constraints figured in the film. There is a hierarchy and there are economics in the convent. There are also dominant ideas regarding good taste and the ethics of representation, both reified in the mother superior's attempt at burning the popular novels Sister Sewer Rat has secretly written. Although some critics inevitably invoke the Inquisition at this point, religious faith does not drive book burning in the film; aesthetics and ethics do, since the books are based on the life of the redeemed sinners who have paraded through the convent. No inquisitor burned books because he objected to bad literature or to the exploitive practices of representation. If that convent is subject to become a national allegory, the resulting figure should be more complex than a degenerate space of outdated religiosity seasoned with the simplifications of "anything goes." In fact, the symbolic relation between the inside and the outside of this secluded community is ironically thematized in the film itself when Sister Sewer Rat tells her real sister that "times have changed and life is not the same," only to be told that "all that is just a nun's fantasy" and that everything "out there" is exactly as it was when she entered the convent.

As serious as any other commentary this film makes about the state of the country in a year in which *La Movida* was starting to turn mainstream, to conceive of *La Movida* as a "nun's fantasy" would be a fitting way to describe it as a hysterically funny moment in the history of a democratic Spain or as a hysterically serious moment, as I wrote earlier. In the discussions of the term that favor the semiotic rather than the medical, hysteria presents, very revealingly, problems of classification and signification, problems to be interjected also into the comic/serious dynamic. Brad Epps once more provides the meaningful link between hysteria and comedy in Almodóvar when he calls the former "an oddly adequate figure for Almodóvar's films, where comedy itself is open to dramatic revision."[45] Within the emotional excesses of the times (and of the critical discourses that revisit them), the excesses inside the convent are both relative and extreme, and they still translate the comedy of incongruity into an incongruous laughter that is fraught with inconsistencies and improprieties. The question to be posed yet again concerns the value and the meaning of all this joking with such serious matters and in such serious times.

(Almost) All Joking Aside

The most economical way to account for Almodóvar's distinctive filmmaking is to call it paradoxical. This is what the most complete collection of essays on the Spanish director to date does when its editors write the following: "Celebrated and denigrated by critics as serious and superficial, political and apolitical, moral and immoral, feminist and misogynist, experimental and sentimental, universal and provincial, Almodóvar has charted a path from the countercultural margins of his native Spain to an international mainstream which, while still consistent with the Institutional Mode of Representation as developed and criticized by Noel Burch, is not reducible to its dominant Hollywood modality."[46]

In the course of the previous pages, it has been my contention that comedy could be the key factor that sets up most of these dichotomies. For instance, to acknowledge or ignore the humorous treatment of some subject matters may determine if the film in question is thought of as moral or immoral. Humor, in fact, may serve as a regulating valve of sorts that works against the rigid borders that such a series of contradictions stakes out. On account of their disorienting humor, Almodóvar's movies in general, and these first three in particular, can appear moral or immoral, feminist or misogynist, political or apolitical, and, indeed, superficial or serious. Yet my main point has been that, in order to be true to the films themselves, one does not have to decide; deciding, in fact, either stacks the game or ruins it. The movies are thus moral *and* immoral, feminist *and* misogynist, political *and* apolitical. They are seriously superficial or superficially serious, which prompts the revealing suspicion that the relation between laughter and seriousness is not only a matter of the former qualifying or indeed *undoing* the latter. The comic in Almodóvar does not amount to a clear and uncomplicated process of irreverence. Dark humor, as I have been saying in different ways, does not separate the laughable from the serious, since the two modes seem to be connected by their mutual condition of possibility. Whether we are facing gallows humor or the more compromising dark laughter I have discussed in relation to the classic film comedies of the 1960s, there is no either/or proposition at work. And the crucial point to take into account after all this discussion of Almodóvar's dark humor is that it does not happen in the void: a laughter such as this takes place in the aftermath of a dictatorship and at the shaky threshold of a new democratic state. Thus located, "paradoxical" seems to be the appropriate term to describe the director's position too. In relation to *La Movida*, for instance, Epps and Kakoudaki use the terms "chronicler, leader, participant, critic, independent artist, or naysayer."[47] They also conclude: "It is only in hazy retrospect, then, that the *Movida* can be seen as absorbing Almodóvar or, better yet, that Almodóvar can be seen as absorbing the *Movida*."[48] Broadening the question, we may likewise ask if Almodóvar absorbed the transition or, better yet, if the transition absorbed Almodóvar's films at all. And my answer will return the discussion to the liberatory discourses of the nonneurotic production of desire mentioned at the beginning of this chapter.

In his first three feature films, there is not a single family under the rule of Oedipus. The "familial complex" does not articulate the social production of desire, nor does it rest on the repressions of the neurotic. Many critics have already noted that in *Pepi* the characters have virtually no family background. Repressed desires are hardly an issue when the latent violence of gender inequality in the household is turned into the space of masochistic bliss. In *Dark Habits* there is a dead father, the marquess, who is called a fascist by his widow. Even though the mere mention of a dead fascist father sets off every kind of metaphorical alarm, the symbolic or narrative weight of that father figure is not that significant. If anything, the degree of obviousness here, in some measure reminiscent of the one operating in the character of the right-wing policeman in *Pepi*, puts everything on the table. The unimportance of repressed desires seems to parallel the inconsequence of hidden meanings. Stating the obvious in this case seems tantamount to liberation from the allegorical readings that necessarily burdened so many of the so-called dissident films under Francoism. The dead fascist here is, then, a dead fascist, and his daughter, the redeemed sinner who occupied Yolanda's room before her, will have a son raised by monkeys, like Tarzan. Between the obviousness and the silliness, a serious allegorization of this subplot is, if not impossible, certainly pointless.

As for *Laberinto*, there are two fathers who sleep with their daughters. In one case, the father actually forces himself on his daughter, who, in turn, presents her situation to a friend (Sexilia) in the most factual, untraumatized way possible. With hardly any desire being the result of neurosis and hardly any lost object to speak about, this is a cinematic world in which laughing at that which is traumatic is neither cruel nor therapeutic. If we keep in mind the omnipresence of *desencanto* and melancholia in the narratives of Spanish transition, Almodóvar's first movies provide a space for the intervention of laughter into the serious business of making a transition, a laughter that ultimately questions not only how seriously to take that process but also how seriously to take oneself. Dark humor in this case also counters the narcissistic discourse of the neurotic, nostalgic, melancholic, disenchanted self. In that very precise way of using comedy, Pedro Almodóvar's role within *La Movida* and *La Movida*'s role within the transition can be thought of as intimating that it was all neither a success nor a failure but a deadly serious joke.

7

Back with a Vengeance

Laughing Darkly in Post-1992 Spain

hree decades after the golden era of the Spanish dark comedy in film,
with the dictator dead for more than fifteen years, dark humor returned
to Spanish cinema in a conspicuous, meaningful manner. It was the early 1990s,
and, however contested the legacies of its transitional years might be, Spain had
a monarch and a stable parliamentary democracy. The year to which critics like
Teresa Vilarós stretch the end of the country's transition, 1992, has just come
and gone.[1] This was the year in which Seville became the site of a universal
exhibition, Barcelona celebrated the Olympic Games, and Madrid was chosen
as the cultural capital of Europe. Five years later, Frank Gehry's Guggenheim
Museum in Bilbao was inaugurated. In the Spain of the 1990s, every collective display of nationhood — Spanish, Catalan, and Basque — seemed to aim at
presenting an image of newness, of the future, even of perfectibility to a global
audience.

Spanish cinema could not but join this national euphoria through several
means. Spanish production numbers jumped from forty-seven in 1990 to an
average of seventy throughout the decade. The share of viewing figures also
doubled for a Spanish cinema that, for the moment, seemed to have left behind
an exceptionalism grounded on historical traumas and fratricide narratives.
The so-called transnationalization of Spanish cinema moved steadily forward,
a phase that involved an array of changes, ranging from new conditions of

production and distribution to the internationalization of both Spanish actors and Spanish directors.

It is precisely at this time that a series of films go back to dark laughter as a means to engage with, or to intervene in, any smooth, unproblematic production of national images. It was at this time that Alex de la Iglesia launched his career as a feature film director with *Acción mutante* (*Mutant Action*, 1993) and followed it with the equally dark *El día de la bestia* (*The Day of the Beast*, 1995). In the same years, Juan José Bigas Lunas's *Ruedo Ibérico* (*Iberian Bullring*) trilogy got under way with *Jamón jamón* (*Ham Ham*, 1992) and continued with *Huevos de oro* (*Golden Eggs*, 1993) and *La teta y la luna* (*The Teat and the Moon*, 1994). In 1993 Almodóvar's very dark and controversial *Kika* premiered to the delight only of die-hard fans of the director. In 1995 Alejandro Amenábar's first movie, *Tesis* (*Thesis*), made a splash in Spanish film circles. One year earlier, another first movie, *Justino, un asesino de la tercera edad* (*Justino, a Senior Citizen Assassin*) (Luis Guridi and Santiago Aguilar, 1994), revisited the world and the iconography of bullfighting to offer the country its first retiree serial killer. Even the old master, Luis García Berlanga, directed *Todos a la cárcel* (*Everybody to Jail*, 1993), a movie scripted with his old partner in crime, Rafael Azcona. By the end of the decade, just one year after Gehry's spectacular and polarizing Guggenheim Museum was unveiled, Santiago Segura presented *Torrente, el brazo tonto de la ley* (*Torrente, the Stupid Arm of the Law*, 1998), a film reviled by some as the epitome of the lowest type of Spanish humor and hailed in the press as the national production that finally defeated Hollywood within the Spanish market.

Of course, not all these films make use of dark humor in the same way. In fact, I would not call most of them dark cinematographic comedies in the same way I have used that term in the previous chapters. However, there is no denying that they collectively signal a dark turning point in the production of national images in Spanish cinema. While other cultural critics have already taken upon themselves the task of questioning the institutional images and discourses that characterize the 1990s in Spain, I would like to incorporate into that questioning the doings and *undoings* of a dark humor that, in some cases, returned to the Spanish cultural landscape with a vengeance. While Francoist developmentalism was the milieu in which to study the classics of the Spanish dark film comedy, the question now is: What does post-1992 Spain have to offer as the geopolitical context that facilitates this meaningful resurfacing of dark laughter in Spain? Two of the earlier-mentioned films are particularly suitable in answering this question: *Acción mutante* and *Justino, un asesino de la tercera edad*. These are filmic texts whose ties to the classic dark comedies of the 1960s seem stronger precisely because the way they intervene in their milieu is also more comparable. Openness seems to be the official trope to be questioned once again, and once again dark humor appears as the chief weapon at the film-makers' disposal. However, this time dark laughter serves not only as a means to contest triumphalist discourses of openness and modernization but also as a concept to nuance the critical inquiry into this post-1992 Spain. Dark humor, and not the still-present *desencanto* or the equally ubiquitous melancholia, as we shall see, is once more the key to discriminating between the ethical and epistemological demands these films make on their audience.[2] Ultimately, dark humor becomes, yet again and at the same time, a matter of hermeneutics, of knowledge, and of rethinking, even reimagining the nation.

Spanishness, Dark Comedy, Science Fiction, and Horror

Director Alex de la Iglesia has called himself a mixer of genres, and that seems to be one of the main reasons to consider him as a "popular auteur."[3] His first feature-length film, *Acción mutante*, is indeed a hybrid in which science fiction is the main frame of reference but where there is also room for, at least, the caper film story, the western, and the slasher genre. The film tells the story of the members of a terrorist group who call themselves "mutants." Most of them are, in fact, people with disabilities, and their target is whatever represents beautiful, fit, obsessed-with-health individuals. They may attempt to kidnap a plastic surgeon one day and riddle a fitness class in progress with bullets the next. Their spaceship has been christened *Virgen del Carmen*, a very popular Spanish fishing boat name. The mining planet on which they have crashed by the end of the film is called Axturias, a pun on the name Asturias, the northern region in Spain known, among other things, for its mining industry.

In *Acción mutante*, then, science fiction, one of the film genres with less tradition in Spanish cinema, meets a very local and culturally specific sense of humor made more specific by the rough-and-ready look of most of the film's sci-fi paraphernalia. This is, beyond a doubt, science fiction "made in Spain," technical and thematic crudeness included. This is a film that purposely looks to place itself in what was at the time unmarked territory in Spanish cinema, yet it is rife with marks of Spanishness. This is, ultimately, an effort to *Spanishize* science fiction, and this is done in part as a response to what de la Iglesia perceived as the dominant practice in the Spanish cinema of his time. As he embarked on his first project, only three things seemed to be clear in the young director's mind: he did not wish to make the film version of a prestigious novel, he wanted to avoid the Spanish civil war and its aftermath, and he was not interested in childhood traumas.[4] Simply put, he did not want to do what Spanish film had been doing to stake out its cultural specificity for years.

This move away from the traumas of the recent past and this programmatic cannibalization of "un-Spanish" genres are also detectable in Luis Guridi and Santiago Aguilar's film *Justino*, even if such a Spanish occupation as bullfighting is an integral part of this 1990s film comedy. In fact, when they were asked to classify their movie, its two directors invented a curious, almost untranslatable film category. This black-and-white feature about a retired *puntillero* (the assistant to a bullfighter, who basically finishes off the bull) turned serial killer is, according to them, a *chascarrillo negro*, a "dark little joke."[5] Even if they spoke in jest, their creation of such a generic label clearly reveals their willingness to anchor their work in a national, even local specificity, together with a playful problematization of the very concept of film genre. A cross between an autochthonous dark comedy and an indie horror movie, *Justino* provokes generic considerations that are necessarily linked to questions — and questionings — of national cinema, which, in turn, raise issues of genre formation, cultural specificity, and viewer expectations. This series of issues also have a place in the analysis of de la Iglesia's hyperbolic and densely local reworking of popular genres in his first film.

Both Spanish productions of the early 1990s invite us to investigate how the concept of national cinema is strengthened or debunked by the use of "indigenous" and "foreign" film genres. Likewise, they both may prompt questions regarding what "Spanishness" may still mean as a notion reflected or enacted in the story about a life of serial killing after a career in bullfighting and in the outrageous narrative of a disabled and freakish group of very inept terrorists. A final question would address in more general terms what image of Spain these movies add to the constellation of "national images" being produced in a decade in which the adjective "transnational" would be so frequently invoked. The country was indeed at a cultural crossroads, looking simultaneously backward and forward, projecting triumphant images of transnational modernity, and yet unable to forgo a very distinct and problematic model of national genealogy that had 1492 as its ultimate referent. Caught between micro- and macrolevels of imaginable communities, the country was visibly searching for images to represent its alleged essence and ambitions to both international and intranational audiences. The nation's film production of this period echoes in general the same cultural and representational anxieties as the specific films analyzed here.

Enmeshed in a generic and national hybridity that references Almodóvar to Ridley Scott, suffused with both the desire to reach beyond the country's borders and the wish to invoke an all-too-local cultural background, *Acción mutante* crashed the ongoing party of display-centered modernity Spain had been throwing since the early 1980s.[6] The first part of this chapter will examine in detail the mutations that dark humor has undergone since the classic productions of the 1960s in this violent and extremely politically incorrect film.

Armed with the very Spanish *puntilla* (the special dagger used in a bullfight to ultimately kill the bull), Justino enters the same cultural landscape in a low-budget, genre-blending production to portray one of the first cinematographic serial killers in the country. The second part of this chapter will read closely the character and crimes of this assistant bullfighter to elucidate how his displaced usage of the *puntilla* adds blood, irony, and darkness to the representational anxieties of a Spain on the eve of the twenty-first century.

As I wrote in the first chapter, horror and science fiction movies, more than any other type of film, lend themselves to readings that reveal them as expressions of collective fears and the screening of moral concerns. This realization certainly applies to *Acción mutante* as (vernacular) sci-fi film and to *Justino* as (mock) horror movie. Collective anxieties and concerns about the moral degradation of a post-1992 Spain can be discerned in the tale of this group of mentally and physically handicapped terrorists as well as in this portrayal of an assistant bullfighter forced into early retirement.

Post-1992 Syndrome

Post-Franco Spanish cinema has been divided and "mapped" in different ways, but the most frequent periodization dates its real beginning to 1982, seven years after the dictator's death. As noted in the previous chapter, this was the year of the Partido Socialista Obrero Español (PSOE) victory in the general elections. A left-wing party whose leaders had a history of opposition to the old dictatorial regime, the PSOE remained in power until 1996, when a combination of economic and political scandals resulted in its defeat in favor of the much more conservative Partido Popular (PP). This "socialist Spain" can be subjected to further subdivisions, but it can be contemplated as a period in which there were very concrete institutional plans to overhaul the national film industry.

The PSOE's first victory in 1982 was followed by a new law for the national cinema industry, the so-called Miró law, named after the recently appointed *directora general de cinematografía*, Pilar Miró Romero. The law wanted to promote *good* films, which essentially meant films that could be viewed as cinema of quality. As Nuria Triana-Toribio aptly puts it, "Producers in particular wanted a cinema that could be successfully distributed in Europe, and that, in a manner similar to the NCE [*nuevo cine español*] of the 1960s, was in dialogue with other European national cinemas; only this time, now that Spain was a democratic country, it was an actual contender for the label of European cinema."[7] The same critic goes on to emphasize how the PSOE's official policy for the renovation of a national cinema in the 1980s sounded eerily similar to the Francoist rhetoric of the 1940s. The public relations spirit behind the renewed efforts to clean up Spain's image and to appeal to an international learned audience in doing so echoes the travails of the Franco regime at the dawn of the 1960s.[8] A reflection of greater consequence for the purposes of this chapter contemplates the effects the *ley Miró* had in suppressing a strand of filmmaking thought to be consubstantial with an alleged national cultural difference. Quoting Triana-Toribio once more, "Spanishness for some writers is 'gritty social realism' characterized by an 'ugliness' and 'awkwardness' that could not have surfaced in the 1950s and 1960s, due to censorship, but which is where authentic Spanishness resides."[9] If certain aesthetics of the ugly or the awkward is the condition of possibility of a Spanish national cultural specificity, then *Acción mutante* certainly qualifies as one of those excessive exercises of cultural distinctiveness. This line of argumentation clearly reinforces a vision of Spanish culture whose self-regard, so to speak, depends on an experience of modernity that rejects stylization or idealization. In the midst of the celebratory and display-centered modernity of the 1992 Barcelona Olympics and the Seville Expo of the same year, ugliness, at many levels, had a transgressive value. This aesthetics of the ugly, or predilection for "bad taste," is certainly in need of some contextualization.

As Marvin D'Lugo has argued, one can start by saying that Spanish cinema during the 1990s started to occupy a "liminal position."[10] Asserting itself as a European cinema and, at the same time, reaching across the Atlantic toward its cultural and linguistic area of affinity in Latin America, Spanish cinema was simultaneously searching for a "visual identity" and a viewing market. Subsidies from the different European cultural agencies and coproductions were part of this search.[11] D'Lugo frames his reflections on this moment in Spanish cinema with Fredric Jameson's expression "geopolitical aesthetics."[12] He also poses the question for which I would like to find an answer in the rest of this chapter. "What does [cinema] tell us about the nature of community," he asks, "as expressed in contemporary Spanish films and its value in the global system?"[13] Regional, national, and international audiences are entities to take into account when examining a national cinema in which different processes of transnationalization are at play. As suggested before, this is a question of geopolitical aesthetics that involves cultural discourses other than cinema.

Among the institutional events that took place in 1992, Seville's universal exhibition was the one that produced the most spectacular images of newness and of transnational excitement. A quick review of the explicit agenda of the event and of its unintended results may help to contextualize my discussion of the cinema of the early 1990s. Expo '92 was compulsively promoted not as a trade fair but as a cultural macroevent, and not only Spain but also the vast majority of the 109 participating countries had to confront the problem of creating and projecting a national image within the confined space of an exhibition building. As Penelope Harvey has shown compellingly, the tension between nation and state haunted many of the exhibitors' pavilions.[14] Likewise, the invitation that was made to the different countries to reflect on the last five hundred years of national history forced many of them to impossible essence-staging acts and complex identity-politics statements. Quite frequently, national stereotypes were simultaneously fought and invoked. The collection of "images" left by Expo '92 that attest to all those representational challenges and anxieties is truly impressive. Peru, for instance, had few references to its Inca past and decided to go even farther back in time to show the country's truly ancestral origins. Switzerland's pavilion greeted visitors with the sign "Switzerland does not exist," and it did not contain references to Swiss cheeses, banks, mountains, and precision; yet the gift shop at the exit undermined all these deconstructive good intentions by making Swiss chocolate, watches, and clocks readily available to the departing visitor.[15] Chile presented the world with arguably the most famous iceberg after the one that sunk the *Titanic*. This sizable mass of ice was taken from the Antarctic. It was sculpted, broken into pieces, and transported to the Chilean pavilion to be reassembled and exhibited for the duration of the fair. The intention was to show a technologically capable country also blessed with pristine wilderness and a poetic spirit.

Spain's impossible balancing act was to portray itself as a community un-problematically anchored in 1492, the year in which its ancestral Jewish community was forced to leave, the last Muslim kingdom was defeated, and the brutal imperialist undertaking in the Americas got under way. With that year as a historical reference, the country was to be "discovered" as a harmonious blend of autonomous regions and brand new Europeanness. With so many representational dues to be paid — with so many overlapping communities to be imagined — the national entity projected at the Expo was one of a country at the same time idealized and highly self-reflexive where cultural and socioeconomic optimism carried the day.

It was in this context of high representational stakes and bold statements on what a nation might be or look like that both *Acción mutante* and *Justino* made their respective "interventions." Let us start by evaluating how the former's mutant dark laughter contested those triumphalist national discourses of new images and new beginnings. In de la Iglesia's first feature, in fact, we can say that the entire country has been to the Expo, and all they got was a lousy T-shirt.

Axturias, My Beloved Country

It is a detail too pregnant with meaning to go unnoticed. Right after the crew of mutants in *Acción mutante* crashes into the planet Axturias, Ramón Yarritu (Antonio Resines), its leader, literally drags the kidnapped Patricia (Frédérique Feder) through a barren landscape. They finally encounter an all-male, sex-obsessed family of four. Two of them wear worn-out T-shirts on which one can easily spot Curro and Coby, the mascots for the 1992 Seville Expo and the 1992 Barcelona Olympics, respectively (see fig. 25).

In this futuristic dark and violent film comedy, set in 2012, these two pieces of clothing figure as cheap souvenirs to remember those two supposedly distant events that are so fresh, however, in the audience's minds. The Olympics and the Expo had just happened a year ago, and there they were on the screen, covered in filth and covering the unfit bodies of two crazy inhabitants of a made-up planet. In one of the crudest examples of the kind of low humor that peppers the film, the two T-shirt-wearing characters ejaculate as soon as they see Patricia. Apparently, the planet Axturias does not have any women. Merely the sight of one woman causes this bodily reaction precisely in the males who exhibit the icons of the country's latest attempt to display its ultracivilized side. One of them is played by Santiago Segura, soon to be famous as the character Torrente, a lazy, drunken, chauvinistic, sexist, racist, and homophobic former policeman. Whatever debt to a new image of the country and its different nationalities the momentous events of 1992 affirm, it surely comes undone by the crude moments, gross-outs, and political incorrectness that fill this movie. Even though Nuria Triana-Toribio does not consider the films of Alex de la Iglesia as fully belonging to the category she names "neo-vulgar Spanish film," there is an argument to be made regarding how much *Acción mutante* precedes the *Torrente* saga in its crudeness, in its provocative nature, and even in its playful exhibition of backwardness. If *Acción mutante* is arguably the first successful science fiction film in Spanish cinema, it certainly owes its success as much to the various uglinesses and deformities it flaunts as it does to the localism of its references.

The other obvious moment of historical self-reflexivity takes place early in the film, and it can be related to the point just made. It is the scene in which what has been called the "celebratory phase of Spanish postmodernity" is symbolically obliterated.[16] This is the period that would coincide with the political

Figure 25. Worn souvenirs from the
Expo and the Olympics

transition, *La Movida*, and the first film productions of Pedro Almodóvar studied in the previous chapter. During a wedding reception sequence, characters
dressed in extravagant outfits are massacred in what could be described as an
orgy of blood and tackiness. Among the actors, two of Almodóvar's early muses,
Rossy de Palma and Bibi Andersen, play small roles. Almodóvar was the producer of de la Iglesia's first film, and the young director realized how nervous
he was having his backer on the set the day of the shooting. Twenty years after
the movie's premiere, in an interview for the online magazine *Tudeocio*, de la
Iglesia described the times in which the movie was made as characterized by
"modernity," the "films of Pedro Almodóvar," and an "explosion of design."
He claims to have gone after all that with the intention to smash (*machacar*) it
all, vindicating along the way all that was dirty and "fun and that goes against a
clarity of ideas."[17] We have already seen what the 1980s in Spain and especially
in Madrid may have looked like, and I have definitely tempered the image of
fireworks and flamboyancy *La Movida* may have presented. But the fact remains
that in 1985 a magazine such as *Rolling Stone* could speak of a "new Spain,"
describe what the capital of the country was experiencing as a "coming out
party," and even compare the Spanish city to "San Francisco in the Sixties."[18]
    De la Iglesia's film, then, attempts to hit two targets at the same time: the
country's official euphoria of 1992 and the mythology of the first cultural phenomenon of democratic Spain. As we have seen, the latter has been often considered as the ephemeral outpouring of the *niños de papa* (spoiled brats) and
"beautiful people," the groups so emphatically despised in the film by Ramón
Yarritu himself. The collateral damage is also twofold: the kind of national,
trauma-oriented cinematography of quality supported by the *ley Miró* and the
country's most recent attempts at a commercial cinema that could vie with Hollywood's box-office success. Let us see how all these targets are simultaneously
hit in the actual narrative of the film.
    When one of the conjoined brothers in the terrorist band gets killed, his
still-attached sibling carries him around the desert until a hermit finds them,
takes them to his cave, and stuffs the dead side of the pair. Upon seeing his dead,

Figure 26. "He looks like a dummy"

mummified brother, the by now inconsolable survivor can only say between sobs, "He looks like a dummy" (see fig. 26). He certainly does, and, in pointing it out, the character is basically voicing the thoughts of the audience. Those thoughts should also trigger a reflection on the part of critics regarding how bad *Acción mutante* looks at times. Put differently, this is not Hollywood grade-A science fiction, to be sure; and it is not so because neither the budget nor the technical and industrial resources are in place. In interviews at the time, the director and members of the movie's cast and crew repeatedly praised each other for what they accomplished in spite of the lack of money and tradition. The special effects team had to be brought in from France. Production problems had to be solved by inventiveness and ingenuity. If one cannot compete in technical prowess with the powers that be in global cinema, one can certainly outwit them. One can even flaunt one's flaws as a badge of honor and, yes, of distinctiveness. Now, we have seen technical shortcomings being linked to cultural specificity or identity politics in cinema before. It was in the 1960s that Glauber Rocha in Brazil, Fernando Solanas and Octavio Getino in Argentina, and Julio García Espinosa in Cuba spoke of an aesthetics of hunger (1965), the possibility of a third cinema (1969), and the advantages of an imperfect cinema (1969), respectively. I do not presume to equate this early film of Alex de la Iglesia with these very politically committed calls for a dissident filmmaking outside Hollywood's parameters. Yet the imperfections, together with the flaunted artificiality of both plot and props, surely deserve a reading that may find in them cultural relevance and not just a scarcity of funds. The same goes for all that genre mixing and blending in the film. There must be more than a fierce disposition to entertain behind this film genre roller coaster. And maybe the first cause for reflection would be precisely that, when watching *Acción mutante*, we witness a vertiginous succession of generic formulas and references rather than the ontological stability of a hybrid. If genre impurity can be a sophisticated way to renew specific film genres — like, say, grafting in gardening — from a taxonomic point of view, there is something much more transgressive in virtually lumping film genres and visual references at the pace this movie does.

Ultimately, this multigeneric thrust could be to a national cinema what antiessentialism is to identity politics.

The roller coaster genre is another circumstance that can be read as a willingness to not get pinned down or fixated. To quote Valentina Vitali and Paul Willemen, if "genre and nation are intrinsically and complexly linked," then a film that embarks on a genre that has no tradition in its film history and that, moreover, jumps from one to another in rapid succession takes aim at the very concept of the nation as an entity to be represented in stable terms.[19] Ironically, this is done with a number of very local, very untranslatable references that go from the imitation of regional accents to the already noted references to the here and now of 1992 and its aftermath. On the other hand, if "genre's ability to construct and contain meaning for an audience is very similar to how national discourses interpellate a citizenry," then *Acción mutante* interpellates a citizenry of freaks, really, of noticeably abnormal or unusual subjects.[20]

Finally, all this technical and generic discussion, which, after all, is but a discussion of both looks and outward impressions, has to be linked to the unseriousness of the project. I noted in the introduction to this book that the debates on Spanishness in film deep down had been debates on excess: excess of representation, excess of locality that may or may not be understood beyond the nation's borders. The excess in this case also concerns the darkness of the film's humor.

A Dark Comedy of Many Deaths: Violence, Morality, and Complicity

The darkness of laughing at that which is not good reaches new heights in movies like *Acción mutante*. First, there is the question of using disability for laughs. The disabled individuals of *El cochecito* have no doubt come a long way. The main humorous premise of de la Iglesia's movie is, of course, to endow a group of handicapped people with agency, and with a violent one at that. There is no easy compassion to be elicited from the audience in connection with this group of differently challenged individuals. Yet how much the movie uses disability itself as a laughingstock may compromise the anti-beautiful people message of the story. How seriously one takes the parable is a matter of careful examination, as is the question of morality in general when judging what such a violent and often offensive film holds as its main target. If disability is the concept ambiguously broached here, then women are treated miserably without a doubt. One of the iconic images of the film is the stapled lips of Patricia as she is held for ransom in the *Virgen del Carmen*. She is going to be slapped, dropped to the ground, dragged by the hair, and gang-raped. Violence against women in this movie is filmed for laughs, as is violence in general, which leads to a familiar question in this book: How seriously are we to take violence and its depiction? Or, rather, how meaningful or meaningless is violence when it is instilled in this type of excessive, comic, irreverent narrative? Violence and death have been seen so far as points of inflexion in the dark comedies of the 1960s, and they played their part in the analysis of Pedro Almodóvar's *Movida* films. From the very first scene, *Acción mutante* shows that violence is what sets the tone and not what changes it.

An extreme close-up of a man shouting is the film's first image after the credits stop rolling. He is immediately gagged. When the camera dollies back, we can see him being restrained by four figures in black, while two others stand in the background. Also in the background is a dead woman lying on a heart-shaped waterbed. She is naked from the waist up, her face covered with a pillow that has a bullet hole in it. A stream of water from the punctured bed has been forming a pool of blood and water around the body. The decoration of the room is certainly minimalist, with tall, bare, white walls and a huge Christ-on-the-cross picture of a very muscular man, supposedly the victim of the attempted kidnapping. The gagging and the décor bring to mind the break-in scene in Stanley Kubrick's *A Clockwork Orange* (1971). What follows is a clownish dialogue between the kidnappers regarding the condition of the victim, his death by asphyxiation, and his uselessness as a corpse. The band of intruders exits the room to the iconic theme music of the TV series *Mission: Impossible*. The last one is a handicapped person using a futuristic floating vehicle instead of a wheelchair. There are so many references in this brief opening scene that it is virtually impossible to anticipate what kind of movie we are about to see and, more importantly, what kind of position as spectators we are supposed to assume. How to assess the purpose of this violence is equivalent to the task of evaluating if things are said jokingly. The problem is compounded by the coexistence of different degrees and kinds of violence.

In a strategy developed fully in his second film, *El día de la bestia*, this graphic yet caricaturesque violence either follows or coexists with the presence of a violence that feels less cartoonlike, even if it is also displayed in excess. In the case of *Acción mutante*, right after the opening scene there are images of oversized policemen beating up a defenseless demonstrator who holds a board sign with the word "peace" on it. Caricature also has the virtue of making flaws more visible, of putting on the table what may not be properly perceived anymore. Is this brief and hyperbolic scene of police brutality a representation of violence that aims at a serious social problem? Is the gratuitous slapping of Patricia an equally gratuitous use of violence against women? The questions could multiply in the face of so many violent acts in this movie with the potential to be tied to so many ethical questions. Binarisms are always reassuringly clarifying, so let us use the one frequently invoked when discussing violence in film. Is *Acción mutante* aestheticizing violence, or is it making it a subject for serious reflection? This dilemma corresponds to the conceptualization of a "strong" or "weak" violence in film as theorized by Devin McKinney. For McKinney, *strong* violence has a legitimate place in film since it has to do with content, with pointing out a social problem. *Weak* violence is, in turn, a violence confined to style, to form, to a banalization of the serious concern out in the world to which the film refers.[21] Of course, this dichotomy gets blurred the moment other considerations are taken into account. For instance, how do *Acción mutante*'s very noticeable imperfections and its evident artificiality affect the reading and the evaluating of the violence represented? Is all the referentiality to other films a way to situate the narrative of the film in a moral place beyond good and evil? To emphasize the role of dark humor in the film seems to me to be the key to a fruitful elucidation of the film's ethics of violence.

Film violence, or the fascination with the witnessing of violence, became, in fact, a common trend in the early 1990s both in Spain and abroad. In Spain the post-1992 landscape showed an increasing preoccupation with crime but also with how the media treated the problem. The private TV channel Telecinco, launched in 1990, became the epitome of sensationalist media coverage, where shock value and titillation, or *morbo*, are the main values. Both Pedro Almodóvar's *Kika* (1993) and Alejandro Amenábar's *Tesis* (1996) addressed this phenomenon, albeit very differently. Before making it a more integral part of his second feature film, de la Iglesia included this rise of crime-obsessed media in *Acción mutante* too. A TV crew is present at the bar where Patricia's father (Fernando Guillén) is supposed to deliver the ransom for his daughter. This moment of social satire is inserted in the middle of a deliriously crazy ending in which a shooting rampage becomes a bloodbath of artifice. The sequence starts with a westernlike bar brawl that refers more to the so-called spaghetti westerns of the mid-1990s that were filmed mostly in the south of Spain. It ends with a chorus of miners rising from the dead, singing a habanera-like tune as the movie credits roll. The self-reflexiveness on steroids that culminates this final sequence pushes the film to a symbolic dead end, so to speak. There is no way to turn but to the revelation of the film as film, as artifice: at the end, it has all been a big joke. The question is, of course: Whom are we kidding? *Acción mutante* may be clearly mocking Hollywood apocalyptic action movies, yet the multiple local, even generational, references, together with the showiness of its make-do science fiction look, take us to the interesting area of cultural self-deprecation. The dark laughter of the 1960s is indeed a distant echo here. Yet the interplay with dark humor, the concept of Spanishness, and the question of ethics remain in this cultural intervention in the supposedly new Spain of the early 1990s. Another rough-looking, genre-mixing, typical Spanish movie adds to the analysis of these renewed uses of dark humor in Spanish film. In this case the governing foreign genre to brand as "made in Spain" is none other than the serial killer movie.

Justino's Family Resemblances and Cultural Interventions

As we saw in the previous chapters, Spanish cinematic dark comedies had their heyday in the early 1960s. Death figured prominently in each of the four films analyzed, as did old age and laughter. Death, old age, and laughter play a significant part in the making of *Justino*. The differences between those movies and *Justino* can be easily discerned, of course. Yet the familiarity, the "resemblances," are equally noticeable in images that conjure up *El cochecito*, for instance, and in situations where characters are forced to prove their consent with, or flaunt their defiance toward, the moral order surrounding them. I have being arguing all along that the characters featured in those classic dark comedies are morally ambiguous while they are simultaneously compliant and rebellious; that their key actions, in their excess, change the field of choice in which they occur; and that their needs, the object of their desires, redefine the very idea of necessity within a given socioeconomic environment. Justino's killings could be placed in this interpretive framework. However, what is worth emphasizing in the case of this particular dark comedy is that, in recapturing the spirit of those dark comedies of the 1960s, *Justino* explores the possibility of going as local as possible in the Spanish cinematic and cultural scene of the 1990s, much as *Acción mutante* does.

First, there is the question again of how the film looks from a technical point of view. *Justino* was first filmed in 16 mm and transferred later to a 35 mm format. The grainy look of the images and the barely audible dialogue between two nonprofessional actors earmark these images from the beginning: this is a low-budget, independent film. *Justino*'s "rough look" (in the majority of the acting, the overall quality of the images, the improvised feeling of some of the shooting locations) may display a very humble oppositional aesthetics. After all, *Justino* is to be seen as we have seen *Acción mutante*: in stark contrast with the lavish commercial productions that surround it, productions such as *Todos los hombres son iguales* (*All Men Are the Same*) (Manuel Gómez Pereira, 1994), and the Spanish blockbuster of the year, *La pasión turca* (*The Turkish Passion*) (Vicente Aranda, 1994), for instance. The most viewed Spanish films of the year, however different in subject matter and tone, epitomize the attempts of the Spanish industry to be commercially successful mainly through high technical quality, conventional narratives, and the star power of a very recognizable cast, the exact opposite of La cuadrilla's film.

Judging its oppositional nature in broader terms, *Justino* confronts the country's official representations of itself in the early 1990s as a smooth-running organism that has finally managed to become a successful fusion of tradition and innovation, of local specificities and global inclinations. Against the background of this idealized state-sanctioned spectacle, *Justino*'s grainy images of *almohadilleros* (cushion vendors), *puntilleros*, other bullfighters' assistants, and retirees' residential homes function as a strategic, low-budget return to an underworld of archaic cultural forms. *Justino* is, in fact, the first member of a trilogy that its directors labeled "España por la puerta de atrás" (Spain through the back door).[22] The name was inspired precisely by a scene in *Justino* in which the main character exits the bullring through the back door in clear contrast with what a triumphant matador does (*salir por la puerta grande*, or "to exit through the main door") and in clear contrast with the triumphant institutional images of the nation-state promoted in Seville two years earlier. Bearing in mind the representational strategies deployed by both the national film industry and the nation's official images of itself in the early 1990s, we can embark on a close reading of *Justino* as an ironic staging of Spanishness and a deliberate "going local" and "looking rough" in the midst of all the refined global and transnational image projection. Yet, in this case, the close reading requires beginning with an analysis of how this visual text *sounds* and not with how it *looks*.

A Serial Killer *Made in Spain*

The first scene of *Justino*, a scene inserted in the middle of the movie's opening credits, sets the tone, literally, for the rest of the moving images that are to follow. In this first scene, the musical score alternates between a threatening tune and a festive, semifolkloric melody. The former is a clear reference to horror films; the latter is reminiscent of the soundtrack that accompanied *El cochecito*, *Plácido*, or *El verdugo*. The soundtrack in a dark comedy may become one of the most significant resources to widen the breach between the narrative's subject matter and its tone. In the classical Spanish dark comedies mentioned previously, the audience has to wait until more somber aspects of the plot appear in the film to truly perceive the extent to which the soundtrack contributes to the rift between the images and the sound. In *Justino* this mismatch can be heard from the very beginning. Furthermore, the horror soundtrack is heard over the opening credits, and the carnivalesque, vaguely folkloric music starts the instant an axe begins chopping the horns of a recently defeated bull. When Justino launches his criminal career, the image/sound clash will also be underlined in a very particular way. Indeed, each use of the *puntilla* to kill actual people and not bulls is punctuated by an ironic sound effect, a musical underlining that makes the killings less horrific and turns each murder into less of a slaying. Later in the movie, a *pasodoble* will add more local flavor to the soundtrack. On the other hand, a whole sequence in which Justino struggles to dispose of his neighbor's body will be scored by a jazzy, Mancini-like theme that pulls the musical references of this film toward a more cosmopolitan sound and even to a different decade. There are also two festive tunes. One is "música de fiesta finlandesa" (Finnish party music), as the directors call it; the other enlivens the celebration of Sansoncito's retirement. Regarding the former, the directors spoke of their intention to make it sound like "the kind of music in one of those tapes you have in your car."[23] These are melodies that decontextualize the story as much as the *pasodoble* anchored it as national folklore. This movie wants to be heard in a very particular way: it sounds either very local, or it has the sound of a caricatured elsewhere. The killings it shows, in turn, are "softened" by a sound effect that belies their horror.

So the tone — or, rather, the dissonances — have been set. From the opening scene onward we will not only hear but also witness the making of a Spanish serial killer. And Spanish he is. The cultural specificity of this serial killer is, of course, determined by his profession or, to be precise, by the continuation of a profession from which he had been forced to retire prematurely. This killer kills as if he were performing the last *suerte* or "stage" of the so-called *fiesta nacional*. At this point what a *puntillero* does during a bullfight is, in fact, a mercy killing. The bull is dying but not yet dead, and this assistant bullfighter, without any glamour or drama, puts the bull out of its misery. Justino does a minilecture on how to perform such a *suerte*. It is not an art, he reminds his group of friends, and, when done properly, there is not even that much blood.

The ironic Spanishness of this serial killer is, therefore, established through ironic references not to the glamorous aspects of the world of bullfighting but to the lower ranks of that world. Other movies have borrowed from the bloody *fiesta nacional* to interrogate the role of stereotypical images and clichés in both local and foreign perceptions of a Spanish national cultural identity. The aforementioned Almodóvar's *Matador* (1986) and Bigas Lunas's *Jamón jamón* (1992) are, of course, the first ones that come to mind. Regarding the former, since it features two serial killers and hence a possible resemblance to what this movie concerns itself with, it bears repeating that Justino is not that high in the power pyramid of bullfighting. In fact, these days a *puntillero* does not belong to any team at the service of a bullfighter, as he once did. A *puntillero* works for and in a particular bullring; he is that extremely specialized worker tied to a very concrete facility, to a bullring, that cleans up the mess left by the most prestigious matador precisely when he cannot be true to his name. Class considerations are present in *Justino* right from the outset, and they have to be taken into account when the killing starts and when motives are to be elucidated.

Why people kill others, kill themselves, or even wish that somebody else was dead are integral components of the darkness, the moral ambiguity, and the "politics of death" differently invoked in *El verdugo*, *El cochecito*, *Viridiana*, and *El extraño viaje*. Why this early-retired *puntillero* kills, and kills repeatedly, brings something new to this family of cinematic Spanish killers and death wishers. It brings, first and foremost, a degree of excess that results in a figure that has to be read in light of those who populate the serial killer subgenre of horror, a subgenre, as previously indicated, with virtually no tradition in Spanish cinema.[24]

A serial killer film is a matter of numbers. It is also a matter of motives. Numbers and motives make serial killer movies horror stories where the monsters may walk among us and look like us yet be involved in the production of some sort of deadly mathematical sublime. Such movies, then, are as much about monstrosity as about normalcy; even identification — in the concrete way the term is used within the medium of the moving image — may play a part in how this type of movie influences the spectator. Or, in other words, cinematic serial killers have been provoking more than just repulsion or horror in their audiences.

In a genealogical model of genre criticism, Fritz Lang's *M* (1931) would be the first serial killer movie. In the next decade Charlie Chaplin would abandon his charming tramp persona to become the widower serial killer Monsieur Verdoux. Both films turn their criminal protagonists into subjects to be loathed on account of their crimes yet pitied and, to some extent, understood in view of their circumstances. Emotions and judgments are equally mobilized when they are not brought to a deadlock. Arguably, what made audiences empathize with Peter Lorre's character in *M* is an editing that turns him into the hunted individual and, above all, a final scene in which the killer of innocent little girls claims he cannot help his murderous inclinations. The pathological is invoked as the source of monstrosity. The possibility exists that his hideous crimes are the direct outcome of sickness, not evil.

Chaplin's movie offers, together with the a priori liability of its leading actor—even if the tramp persona is not on the screen—a cynical rationale for a series of murders that, according to the main character, pale in comparison with the much more serious and massively serial wartime killing. His criminal profits are small change when compared with those of the weapons industry. That both movies end in a courtroom seems to highlight the demands for a verdict they make on their audience.

Justino presents us with another ambiguous killer, with a likable one at least, a fact that complicates passing judgment on his murderous acts. What I have called before—in connection with Pepe Isbert's characters in *El cochecito* as well as in *El verdugo*—an investigation of the "ethics of empathy" is very much present in the way this movie introduces its Spanish serial killer. In leading spectators to disapprove at one level (intellectually? morally?) and condone at another (emotionally? symbolically?) the character's actions, the potential viewers of these movies are themselves confronted with their own moral dilemmas. In consonance, precisely, with what a dark comedy is supposed to do (to problematize the moment of and occasion for laughter), these Spanish dark comedies make it problematic to manage efficiently any kind of moral compass. This is done in a variety of ways.

First, there is what I would call a "redeeming montage" or "redeeming editing," a way of putting scenes together so the spectator is forced to identify and even empathize with characters who, for all we know, do not deserve either our feelings of identification or our empathy. When Justino struggles to hide Doña Pura's body from his friends, the possibility of the criminal being caught is filmed as Hitchcock filmed some of his villains in times of trouble and as Lang filmed some of the most memorable scenes of *M*. In those scenes, the possibility of the criminal being caught feels more like a moment of danger than an occasion for justice. In Justino's first killings, the redeeming qualities of the killer appear also in images of macabre tenderness, in moments of absurd postcrime warmth toward his victims. Justino covers his son's slain body as if he were putting him to bed one last time and places a pillow beneath his daughter-in-law's head to make her eternal rest more comfortable. These are more than humorous oddities, and they are not the only ones that complicate the visual description of our serial killer. Very early in *Justino* the main character helps a handicapped person in a vehicle whose primitiveness refers back to the less affluent members of Don Anselmo's physically challenged friends in *El cochecito* (see fig. 27). What Justino does with the invalid by pushing him in the wrong direction, despite the man's repeated protests, amounts to another visual description of this character's moral fiber: his actions, his motives, his now-kind-now-murderous intentions are equally unclear. The number of times

Figure 27. Pushing in the wrong direction

in which we see his face partially shadowed could point to nothing more symbolic than the final visual clue to this man's ambiguous moral grounds and to his problematic likability.

Ultimately, the likeability of this killer is inversely proportional to how unlikable the characters around him are. The directors surround the murderer with unpleasant (when they are not despicable) individuals who range from an abusive boss to negligent family members. "Social rage" explains, if not condones, the crimes, if only at a symbolic level. Yet as the film progresses, Justino's victims do not seem to deserve, not even symbolically, their deaths. What drives Justino to kill is not as easy to discern as it may appear. A roster of his victims does not clarify or consolidate his motives.

Our serial *puntillero* kills his son and his daughter-in-law first. Then he murders a woman on a subway platform while she is being mugged by teenagers. Doña Pura, his annoying neighbor, becomes Justino's third victim. The list continues with a one-armed drunk who insults him and his friend, two policemen who laugh at his confession, and all the residents of a nursing home. Justino kills family members for living space and possibly to extract revenge for the way he has been treated. He kills an unknown woman for money, a neighbor so that a party he is throwing can continue, and a handicapped person plus two police officers out of either pride or spite. The final mass killing is also for money, but this time behind the financial need there is a very humble dream: the possibility of retiring to the touristic city of Benidorm with his friend, which involves, in fact, the possibility of making Sansoncito's dreams come true rather than Justino's own. Justino starts killing to have a room of his own and ends up annihilating a group of old people to make a friend happy.

Early retirement under very unfavorable conditions seems to be the first recognizable cause of emotional distress for Justino in the film. It is one of the measures aimed at lessening the effects of one of the worst recessions in the European Union during the 1990s. By 1993 Spain's honeymoon with Europe was over. The other transition, the economic one, the one that allowed the Spanish economy to enter the European Common Market in 1986 and remain competitive, has officially ended. The country is now exposed to the full force of EU competition. Reduced investment, falling production, and public deficit ensue. By the beginning of the 1990s, Spain had the oldest population in the EU, while the country's unemployment rate remained one of the highest in the Continent. However, finances and morals are two sides of the same coin in this national picture, just as they are in *Justino*. The 1990s saw the infamous Torras-KIO and Banesto bankruptcies (1993 and 1994, respectively) and the downfall of "star" bankers such as Mario Conde and "maverick" financiers such as Javier de la Rosa. The so-called *cultura del pelotazo* (a culture of political corruption and abuse of power for financial gain) was in full swing.

Taken as a whole, this economic, demographic, and moral context reframes Justino's killing. His actions can be said, then, to express not only rebellion against but also communion with the spirit of his times. If in the first two murders the murderer seems to have lost his mind and in the next four he appears either impulsive or desperate, then the mass killing in the nursing home is done with premeditation and for a rather calculated financial gain. In fact, this last killing partakes of a certain "modest proposal" logic, however unaware the killer is of his Swiftean ways. What is there to do with so many elderly people living under such sad retirees' life conditions? Justino just kills them all, takes their savings, and consolidates those savings to create a truly satisfying retirement plan for himself and his friend Sansoncito. The absence of remorse and the business-like attitude of the killer match the moral climate of a period in Spain during which a banker nicknamed "the shark" (Mario Conde) seemed to be a model of social success. The dark comedies of the 1960s had not only Francoism but also the new Opus-affiliated technocrats taking the country to modern capitalism, forcing Spain either to contend with or respond to it. They reflected an economic reform that forced many Spaniards to emigrate in order to help in creating an "economic" miracle that also involved the boom of the national tourist industry. These movies took account of an economic openness that did not match the climate of cultural and political repression suffocating the country. These movies had individuals struggling in a social order in which the repressing forces were getting blurrier and the acts of true rebellion more problematic.

Justino, in turn, depicts a Spain of bust after the boom of the 1980s, a Spain that seems determined to make a splash in the world's concert of nations. The country had an established and stable, yet still somewhat dark and threatening, democracy in which the sources of social evil were harder to pinpoint and their perverse ideology misrecognized as finances. *Justino* shows a Spain struggling

Figure 28. The Osborne bull and the road to Benidorm

economically because of its new *apertura*, its opening, first to a European and world economy for which it was not entirely ready and second to an international audience whose perception of the country's past and present had to be at once contested and confirmed. In the early 1960s, whatever image the Spain of the regime's star politician and minister of information and tourism Manuel Fraga Iribarne wanted to sell to the international community, *El verdugo* was sure to discredit it by bringing its reluctant and clumsy executioner to the touristy island of Mallorca to carry out a brutal death penalty. In the early 1990s, whatever triumphant images of transnationalism the Spanish film industry and Spanish national institutions were bent on producing, *Justino* took care to question them through its underworld of taurine figures, its scavenger-produced look, and its hard-to-translate *chascarrillos*. How to look Spanish, for whom or for what, matching whose preconceptions and revealing which hidden anxieties in the process remain questions at the core of what this series of movies has to offer as either serious or ironic screenings of Spanishness. In that respect, the cinematic family *Justino* belongs to is the Spanish dark comedies of the early 1960s, but its close cousins are the already-analyzed *Acción mutante* and *El día de la bestia*, Bigas Lunas's *Ruedo Ibérico* series, with *Jamón jamón* as the first installment, and even Santiago Segura's blockbuster *Torrente* (1998). As in these other excessive, dark, national-icon-fixated films, in *Justino* there is a deliberate performance of Spanishness that mixes a tad of Hollywood-inspired generic allusions with a heavy dose of local references, local humor, and national clichés for global consumption. *Justino* carries this throughout, all the way to its final scene.

The final shot of the movie shows a bus on its way to Benidorm with the sign of a massive black silhouetted bull in semi-profile, the symbol of the Osborne sherry company, on the horizon (see fig. 28). More than the retirees' paradise Sansoncito champions, Benidorm represents the epitome of urban planning atrocities and cheap tourism wonderland, where fish and chips and happy hours have altered the coastline and its culture forever. The black Osborne bull silhouette is visual shorthand for a national stereotype that has been fully embraced. Still standing by popular demand after the passing of the law that banned this kind of commercial advertisement on Spanish motorways, it displays the image others expect to see associated with Spain. A real bull was butchered in the opening images of the film, which is, of course, the unseen fate of the animal after it has been so visibly fought with and killed. The stereotypical, two-dimensional Osborne bull points one last time to a mocking Spanish imaginary that is there for others to see, that is produced for the passing onlooker, and that offers an ironic display of Spanishness after a gruesome one has been acknowledged. Whether the joke is on us or on them, it is hard to tell, just as difficult as telling the difference between what really represents "us" and who constitutes the "them" we are representing. *Justino*, as an independent Spanish dark comedy about a retiree serial killer who comes from the lowly provinces of bullfighting, plants itself firmly in that representational interregnum to keep us wondering, simply, whom we are kidding.

Afterlaughter

Whom are we kidding? What are we laughing about? In whose company? At whose expense? And what insights are we gaining about ourselves and the world in the process? Read in the light of each other, *El cochecito*, *El verdugo*, *Viridiana*, and *El extraño viaje* articulated the grounds for a visual reflection on the ethics of dark laughter and, furthermore, on the processes by which laughing translates into knowledge. The deaths that interrupt comedy are there to force a pause, to turn comic discharge into recognition, perhaps self-recognition. The realities of the 1960s in Spain — realities of modernization, of commodification, of life under dictatorship — are also there to be *intervened* in rather than reflected upon. The *imagining* community has been formed (and interpellated) shot after shot. The end result is a constellation of images reframing modernity, telling us how the task of modernizing the local and the different may look on-screen.

Almodóvar comes along when the dictatorship is over, and he proceeds to add disorientation to a comedy film practice in which questions of timing and propriety were paramount. His transitional laughter kept dark humor as the vital ethical tool to examine the unstable place the laughing subject had in the serious process of changing a country.

The 1990s brought about their own version of the business of laughing at that which is not good. Along the way, they injected laughter and darkness into the discussions of national cinema and of the national overall. Visuality and cultural specificity were still the concepts conflated or condensed in the medium of the moving image at a moment in which the country began to readdress openness and commit fully to international display. Self-fashioning and performance, ways to look and occasions to be seen, the meanings of movement and consumption, the modalities of complicity, the structure of perversions, and the dislocations of desire — all these questions have returned in post-1992 Spain, as has a laughter that means, above all, self-questioning. This is visual anthropology within fiction film; this is the expression of a visual ontology that asserted itself as the country hurriedly entered commodity capitalism in the early 1960s, made a limited but meaningful cameo in the years of the transition, and resurfaced in the 1990s to help in the imagining of a community still tangled with its Spanishness in the midst of a variety of representational demands.

An afterword will not make the arguments this book has offered any more forceful, nor will it reveal in a brighter light its possible insights on Spanish film and modern culture. Resorting to Stanley Cavell one final time and, through him, to Wittgenstein, I could say that I have tried to use the latter's notion of criteria in my film genre research program. Hence I did not "start out with a known kind of object" to study, but I hope I ended up "knowing a kind of object."[1] I have called that object *Spanish dark cinematic comedy* or, simply, *dark laughter*. Serious as an aftershock or deceptively slight as an afterthought, the afterlaughter in this study resonates louder with the delayed realization that filming the nation in this case is mostly a question of laugh and death.

Notes

Chapter 1. Familiar Questions

1. Borges, *Other Inquisitions*, 104.

2. See Lakoff, *Women, Fire and Dangerous Things*, 5–153. "Gradience" is a term taken directly from his work on categories.

3. See Tudor, *Theories of Film*. For a complete study of the concept of film genre and its historical and theoretical vicissitudes, see Altman, *Film/Genre*.

4. Quoted in Cavell, *Pursuits of Happiness*, 32.

5. Ibid., 29, italics in the original.

6. Jameson, *Signatures of the Visible*, 101, italics in the original.

7. Grant, *Film Genre Reader*, xv.

8. Ibid.

9. For a discussion of film genre as ritual, see Cawelti, *The Six-Gun Mystique*; and Schatz, *Hollywood Genres*. For a contestation of such a view, see Neale, *Genre and Hollywood*.

10. English, *Comic Transactions*, 9.

11. Tudor, *Theories of Film*, 149.

12. Gledhill, "Rethinking Genre," 221.

13. Vitali and Willemen, *Theorizing National Cinema*, 5.

14. Ibid., 16.

15. Anderson, *Imagined Communities*, 6.

16. Ibid., 24–25.

17. Ibid., 4.

18. The same term in Spanish (*españolidad*) has negative connotations, since it is the term of preference for nationalist calls to create a Spanish (i.e., Francoist) cinema. However, even the discussion of a so-called *españolidad cinematográfica* in the 1940s, so susceptible to ideological simplifications, presents nuances that show that not every voice in the rigid cultural landscape at the time prescribed the same things for the creation of a true national cinema. On this, see Nieto Ferrando, *Cine en papel*, 79–141.

19. Medhurst, *A Popular Joke*, 25.

20. Gilroy, *Small Acts*, 72.

21. Camporesi, *Para grandes y chicos*, 37, my translation. Unless otherwise noted, all translations from scholarly texts originally in Spanish are mine. I have also rendered into English the dialogues from the films.

22. Ibid.

23. Eugenio Montes, quoted in ibid., 50.

24. Ibid., 21–22.

25. Cavell, *The World Viewed*, 85.

26. See Castle, *Masquerade and Civilization*.

27. See Noyes, "La Maja Vestida."

28. Ibid., 214. For a general discussion of Spain's exoticism within the European imaginary, see Torrecilla, *España exótica*. Torrecilla's valuable research does not focus on the visual, although it begins with the eighteenth-century tension between the foreign (French) and the autochthonous (*lo plebeyo*). His main interest is to investigate the process by which a gypsified Andalusia functions as a metonymy for the Spanish nation as a whole. *Carmen* is, of course, a major figure in his reflections, a figure he also studies in its more contemporary versions, like Saura's. See Torrecilla, "La modernización."

29. Graham and Labanyi, *Spanish Cultural Studies*, 14.

30. García Canclini, *Hybrid Cultures*, 3.

31. Appadurai, *Modernity at Large*, 3, my italics.

32. Chakrabarty, *Provincializing Europe*, 84.

33. Woods Peiró, *White Gypsies*, 15.

34. De Riquer i Permayer, "Social and Economic Change," 259.

35. Crary, *Techniques*, 10.

36. Ibid.

37. Torreiro, "¿Una dictadura liberal?," 295.

38. For a thorough review of the different accounts of the NCE since its beginning, see Faulkner, *A Cinema of Contradiction*.

39. Kovács, *Screening Modernism*, 82.

40. See Pérez Rubio and Hernández Ruiz, *Escritos sobre cine español*, 96–103.

41. Tubau, *Hollywood en Argüelles*.

42. Marsh, *Popular Spanish Film*, 16–17.

43. Quoted by Nieto Ferrando, *Cine en papel*, 230.

44. Zunzunegui, *Los felices sesenta*, 161–85. The term "grotesque tragedy" makes reference to the way Carlos Arniches, the most famous *sainete* writer of the twentieth century, described some of his plays.

45. Lyon, *The Theatre of Valle-Inclán*, 106.

46. All quotes are from Valle-Inclán, *Luces de Bohemia*.

47. "The most beautiful images in a concave mirror are absurd," says Max Extrella. Later on, Don Latino, his main interlocutor in this scene and throughout the play, says that he has fun with those images, to which Max replies that he too has fun with them. See Valle-Inclán, *Luces de Bohemia*, act 12.

48. Hopewell, *Out of the Past*, 59.

49. Kinder, *Blood Cinema*, 39; Cerdán, "España, fin de milenio," 241.
50. Breton and Polizzotti, *Anthology*, xiv.
51. Critchley, *On Humour*, 71.
52. Leach, *British Film*, 144.
53. Ibid.
54. Marsh, *Popular Spanish Film*, 12.
55. Ibid.
56. Medhurst, *A Popular Joke*, 14.
57. Beckett, *Watt*, 48.
58. Critchley, *On Humour*, 50.
59. Crofts, "Reconceptualizing National Cinema/s," 56.
60. Ibid.

Chapter 2. Movement and Paralysis, Dissidence and Identity

1. San Miguel and Erice, "Rafael Azcona," 7.
2. Kinder, *Blood Cinema*, 112.
3. Bauman, *Consuming Life*, 28, italics in the original.
4. Frye, *Anatomy of Criticism*, 43.
5. Ibid., 177.
6. Ibid., 169.
7. Wittgenstein, *Philosophical Investigations*, 197.
8. Rafael Azcona, author of the film script, also encouraged the comparison when he complained: "Why keep on discussing Don Anselmo's *cochecito* and not his son's, a 600, if I remember correctly" (Sánchez, *Otra vuelta*, 208).
9. The first SEAT 600 came out of the factories in 1957. In the early 1960s there was still a two-year waiting period to get one after its purchase.
10. In the famous reorganization of Franco's administration that took place in 1957, Laureano López Rodó embodied the regime's new technocratic spirit. In 1965 Fernández de la Mora published his thesis on the sunset of ideologies, that is, of course, a euphemism to announce the more wishful than real end of a political opposition to the regime.
11. See Marsh, *Popular Spanish Film*, chap. 6.
12. Cavell, *Themes out of School*, 174.
13. Deleuze, *Cinema 1*, 23.
14. Frye, *Anatomy of Criticism*, 179.
15. Cavell, *Pursuits of Happiness*, 54.
16. Ibid., 56.
17. Žižek, *Enjoy Your Symptom*, 105. Kierkegaard is the reference in this case. For a discussion of this type of act from a Lacanian perspective, see also Žižek, *The Ticklish Subject*, 360–77.
18. It is worthwhile to remember that the print of the movie approved for national

exhibition contained an extra scene in which Don Anselmo calls his family on the phone to warn them about what he has done.

Chapter 3. Complicity Dissected

1. The structure of expanding circles in which I place both movies makes me look at them side by side and delay the analysis of *Viridiana*, chronologically the film that would follow *El cochecito*.

2. Cañeque and Grau, *¡Bienvenido, Mr. Berlanga!*, 52.

3. Perales, *Luis García Berlanga*, 250–51.

4. Cañeque and Grau, *¡Bienvenido, Mr. Berlanga!*, 60.

5. Gómez Rufo, *Berlanga: Confidencias*, 298.

6. Hopewell, *Out of the Past*, 62.

7. Losilla, "La llamada," 54.

8. Marsh, *Popular Spanish Film*, 126.

9. Benet, "La última voluntad," 44.

10. Martín, *La gramática*, 147.

11. According to a letter by the minister of information and tourism, the brains behind the defamation campaign that he sees in the movie is Ricardo Muñoz Suay, the film's producer. The letter can be read in its entirety in Gubern, *La censura*, 217–23; and in Gómez Rufo, *Berlanga: Confidencias*, 326–37.

12. Quoted in Higginbotham, *Spanish Film under Franco*, 52.

13. Quoted in Gómez Rufo, *Berlanga: Confidencias*, 31.

14. Quoted in Franco, *Bienvenido, Mister Cagada*, 210.

15. Quintana, "Falsa luna de miel," 76–77.

16. Gómez Rufo, *Berlanga contra el poder*, 298.

17. Benet, "La última voluntad," 48.

18. Sánchez-Biosca, "Un realismo," 89.

19. Cañeque y Grau, *¡Bienvenido, Mr. Berlanga!*, 51.

20. Marsh, *Popular Spanish Film*, 127.

21. Both statements appear in *Cahiers du cinéma*, Moullet's in March 1959 (Hillier, *Cahiers du Cinéma*, 148), and Godard's in July of the same year (ibid., 62). In the same venue, Nicholas Ray also declared the following: "The way I treat the camera [is] making it look for the truth by letting it play for me, like an actor" (ibid., 123). Berlanga's camera may or may not be considered an actor in *El verdugo*, but it is indeed a camera with an ethical drive, so to speak, searching for some frame of reference amidst a morally confusing situation.

22. Among the most suggestive reading of the scene (sometimes referred to just as a single shot), I would single out Vicente Sánchez-Biosca's ("Un realismo," 85–87). This critic considers these moving images as representative of Berlanga's ethical stance and realism. See also the article dedicated in its entirety to the scene by Berthier, "Arret sur image."

23. In this case, what can be seen or what can be shown is conditioned by extratextual factors. The movie suffered fourteen cuts by the censor that made it four minutes shorter than the director wanted it. It goes without saying that filming an execution was a real impossibility and not an aesthetic option. There was no way for the camera to follow the group of men into the execution chamber. However, I am analyzing here the cinematographic text we have, not the one we could have had.

24. See Benet, "La última voluntad."

25. Hopewell, *Out of the Past*, 62.

26. The director himself seems to be bothered by the talk of a "Berlanga long take." A number of his comments on his technical choices show a deliberate effort to not take himself seriously as an auteur. Declarations like "I never look through the visor" or references to convenience and laziness when asked about his predilection for the sequence shot are frequent in his interviews.

27. Rothman, *Hitchcock: The Murderous Gaze*, 131.

28. Bordwell, *On the History*, 59.

29. Seguin, "Le plan pluriel," 139.

30. Llinás, "*El verdugo*: Algunos aspectos," 328.

31. Seguin, "Le plan pluriel," 138.

32. See Passolini, *Heretical Empiricism*, 167–86. While the mechanisms I occupy myself with here are not exactly the ones the Italian director described, the concept of semisubjectivity itself has been inspired by Passolini's reflections.

33. Browne, "The Spectator-in-the-Text," 199.

34. See, for instance, Carr and Fusi, *España, de la dictadura*, 98. The regime's initial ambivalence toward immigration as a social phenomenon affected *El verdugo* too. The occasions during which the subject of leaving for Germany is brought up were censored.

35. Crumbaugh, *Destination Dictatorship*, 2.

36. MacCandell, *The Tourist*, 40.

37. Ibid.

38. Esteve Secall and Fuentes García, *Economía*, 104.

39. Gubern, *La censura*, 218.

40. See Ríos Carratalá, *Lo sainetesco*.

41. Fernán-Gómez, *El tiempo amarillo*, 68.

Chapter 4. Don Jaime's Laughter

1. This particular one is Alejandro's. Buñuel spoke of other foundational ideas for the movie, most notably a childhood fantasy in which he would drug the queen of Spain and lie in bed with her. See Pérez Turrent and de la Colina, *Luis Buñuel*, 137.

2. Conley, "Viridiana Coca Cola," 51.

3. "In the majority of instances the pathological character in a perversion is found to lie not in the content of the new sexual aim but in its relation to the normal" (Freud, *Three Essays*, 27).

4. Sandro is interested in "Buñuel's perverse stance as a filmmaker, his wish to turn spectators away from the ideological assumptions about the true and the natural and to force them out of uncritical viewing habits" (Sandro, *Diversions of Pleasure*, 152).

5. Feher-Gurewich, "A Lacanian Approach," 192.

6. Pérez Turrent and de la Colina, *Luis Buñuel*, 138–39.

7. That restrained laughter may have other meanings or serve other purposes. Buñuel himself suggests another interpretation of Don Jaime's smile: "He may be laughing at himself. . . . Don Jaime smiles because he, in turn, thinks something like this: What a ridiculous old man I am, what sort of stupid things [*tonterías*] have I done" (Pérez Turrent and de la Colina, *Luis Buñuel*, 142). He also explains that a reaction like that in the face of Fernando Rey makes his subsequent suicide more shocking.

8. Russell, "Buñuel," 45.

9. Evans, *The Films of Luis Buñuel*, 27.

10. López Villegas and Buñuel, *Escritos*, 199.

11. Russell, "Buñuel," 45.

12. Stam, *Subversive Pleasures*, 102.

13. Ibid., 103.

14. Bazin, *The Cinema of Cruelty*, 58.

15. James Prakash Younger, quoted in Russell, "Buñuel," 50.

16. Ibid.

17. Gunning, "Response to Pie," 121.

18. Russell, "Buñuel," 53. In fact, she extends this to the second part of the movie: "as is the seriousness with which *Viridiana* takes herself and her religious calling" (ibid.).

19. In *Viridiana* the figurations of voyeurism are obvious, and virtually every commentator on the film has duly taken them into account. Ramona looks through a keyhole, Rita spies on Viridiana on two occasions. In one of them the young girl functions as the subjective view from where we observe Don Jaime kissing his niece and pressing his face against her breast.

20. See Mulvey, "Visual Pleasure"; and Mulvey, "Afterthoughts."

21. Butler, Laclau, and Žižek, *Contingency*, 117.

22. Aranda, *Luis Buñuel*, 245.

23. Fuentes, *Buñuel*; Sánchez-Biosca, *Viridiana*, 12.

24. Stam, *Subversive Pleasures*, 103.

25. There are other reasons to question the carnivalesque nature of the scene, most notably, the recognition that the beggars keep on acting, talking, and behaving like beggars. In a very naturalistic way, they do what they cannot not do: they let their instincts and desires run amok. There is no "world upside down" theme here, beyond the fact that these members of the lower class are in the place they do not belong: the master's home, eating the master's food with the master's silverware, drinking the master's wine, and listening to the master's music.

26. Stam, *Subversive Pleasures*, 93–94.

27. Bakhtin, *Rabelais*, 11–12.

28. Ibid., 12.

29. Durgnat, *The Crazy Mirror*, 79.

30. An outraged article on the movie in *L'Osservatore Romano*, the official newspaper of the Vatican, caused alarm back home, and the Franco regime quickly proceeded to strip the movie of its Spanish nationality and to fire the national director of cinematography.

31. Russell, "Buñuel," 54.

32. Conley, "Viridiana Coca Cola," 54.

33. Ibid., 52.

34. Ibid., 58.

35. Deleuze, *Cinema 1*, 125.

36. Ibid., 128.

37. Ibid., 130.

38. Ibid., 127.

39. O'Connor, *The Adorno Reader*, 171.

40. Sandro, *Diversions of Pleasure*, 153.

Chapter 5. Modernizing Desire

1. Marsh, *Popular Spanish Film*, 135.

2. The future (and last) prime minister of Francoist Spain, and his predilection for these types of small-town settings, is supposed to have been behind the initiative. He apparently liked *historias de pueblo* (small-town narratives). Curiously enough, Arias Navarro was Madrid's mayor at the time.

3. Steele, *The Corset*, 1.

4. Ibid.

5. Mira Nouselles, *The Cinema of Spain*, 120.

6. Haug, *Critique of Commodity Aesthetics*, 8.

7. Valis, *The Culture of Cursilería*, 15.

8. Ibid., 4, 16.

9. Ibid., 5.

10. Ibid., 19.

11. Marsh, *Popular Spanish Film*, 172.

12. Kracauer, *Theory of Film*, 98–99.

13. Mira Nouselles, *The Cinema of Spain*, 126.

14. Zunzunegui, *Paisajes de la forma*, 38.

15. Marsh, *Popular Spanish Film*, 177.

16. Truffaut, *Hitchcock*, 19.

17. See Deleuze, *Cinema 1*.

18. Orr, *Hitchcock*, 54.

19. Rothman, *Hitchcock*, 1.

20. Ibid., 180.

21. Gunning, "Hitchcock," 17.
22. Rothman, *Hitchcock*, 320.
23. Miller, "Hitchcock's Hidden Pleasures," 16.
24. Rhomer and Chabrol, *Hitchcock*.
25. Wood, *Hitchcock's Films*, 5.
26. Orr, *Hitchcock*, 55.
27. O'Neill, "The Comedy of Entropy."
28. See Žižek, *Looking Awry*, 125–40.
29. Torreiro, "¿Una dictadura liberal?," 318.
30. Hopewell, *Out of the Past*, 44.
31. Ibid., 44–45.

Chapter 6. Almodóvar Interlude

1. Deleuze and Guattari, *Anti-Oedipus*, 23.
2. Epps and Kakoudaki, "Approaching Almodóvar," 6.
3. For a text paradigmatic of the first approach, see Triana-Toribio, "A Punk Called Pedro." For an approach that emphasizes the presence of Almodóvar's "core themes" in a film like *Pepi*, see Acevedo-Muñoz, *Pedro Almodóvar*.
4. Prego, *Así se hizo la transición*; Morán, *El precio*.
5. Tussell, *La transición española*; Medina, *Exorcismos*.
6. Moreiras Menor, *Cultura herida*; Labanyi, "Memory and Modernity"; Vilarós, *El mono del desencanto*.
7. Labrador Méndez, *Letras arrebatadas*, 64.
8. Egea, "El desencanto."
9. Marí, "La Movida como debate," 129.
10. See Pérez-Sánchez, *Queer Transitions*.
11. Stapell, "Just a Teardrop," 369.
12. Song and Nichols, "¿El futuro ya estuvo aquí?," 106.
13. "[The] rejection of any political and transcendental involvement [*compromiso*]" follows from the conditions of "a disenchanted youth in the face of political and social problems, with a bleak professional [*laboral*] future" (Escudero, "Rosa Montero," 148–49).
14. The Spanish director has expressed his admiration for, and recognized his creative debt toward, some of the directors whose classic films I have examined in the previous chapters: Berlanga, Ferreri, and Fernán-Gómez. Almodóvar describes *El extraño viaje* with particular enthusiasm. See D'Lugo, *Pedro Almodóvar*.
15. Critchley, *On Humour*, 74.
16. Ibid., 74–75.
17. All of these artists deserve focused attention in order to determine the type of humor I take as representative of the youth subculture in the Spanish of *La Movida*.

For example, the graphic artist Ceesepe is the author of the underground *El día que muera Bombita* (1983), a film that centers on a bullfighter. Las Costus and Ouka Leele, along with some of their paintings and photographs, also appear in Almodóvar's *Movida* movies.

18. Smith, *Desire Unlimited*, 1.

19. For a very revealing overview of the three "theories" of humor, see Critchley, *On Humour*, 1–22. Together with the incongruity theory, he reviews the so-called superiority and relief theories.

20. Vidal, *El cine de Pedro Almodóvar*, 19.

21. Medhurst, *A Popular Joke*, 87.

22. Epps, "Figuring Hysteria," 108.

23. Medhurst, *A Popular Joke*, 87.

24. D'Lugo, *Pedro Almodóvar*, 6.

25. Mandrell, "Sense and Sensibility," 51.

26. Ibid., 45.

27. Epps, "Blind Shots," 324.

28. Vidal, *El cine de Pedro Almodóvar*, 59.

29. Smith, *Desire Unlimited*, 28.

30. Ibid.

31. Ibid., 17.

32. Ibid.

33. For a discussion of an "aesthetics of bad taste" that would encompass the first four movies by the director, see Acevedo-Muñoz, *Pedro Almodóvar*.

34. Yarza, *Un caníbal en Madrid*, links camp to the subversion of the old regime's signs and values. For the impact and distinctiveness of camp in Spanish culture, see Garlinger and Song, "Camp: What's Spain."

35. Allison, *A Spanish Labyrinth*, 31.

36. Ibid.

37. For an insightful reflection on farce and on Almodóvar's comedy in general, see Medhurst, "Heart of Farce."

38. Vidal, *El cine de Pedro Almodóvar*, 62.

39. D'Lugo, *Pedro Almodóvar*, 32.

40. Vidal, *El cine de Pedro Almodóvar*, 98.

41. Epps and Kakoudaki, "Approaching Almodóvar," 9.

42. Usó, *Drogas y cultura*.

43. Haro Ibars, "La droga mata," 7–10.

44. Smith, *Desire Unlimited*, 39.

45. Epps, "Figuring Hysteria," 99.

46. Epps and Kakoudaki, "Approaching Almodóvar," 1.

47. Ibid., 7.

48. Ibid., 8.

Chapter 7. Back with a Vengeance

1. Vilarós, *El mono del desencanto*, 3.

2. The melancholic view is Cristina Moreiras Menor's, and the invocation of the epochal disenchantment belongs to Peter Buse, Nuria Triana-Toribio, and Andy Willis. The former speaks of a national "loss of an object" in post-1992 Spain, in effect equating the loss apparently experienced after Franco's death. See Moreiras Menor, *Cultura herida*, 188. The latter trio of authors finish their analysis of *Acción mutante* by describing the film as "steeped in the *desencanto*," hence going back in time, as if it were 1976 all over again. See Buse, Triana-Toribio, and Willis, *The Cinema of Álex de la Iglesia*, 51.

3. Buse, Triana-Toribio, and Willis, *The Cinema of Álex de la Iglesia*, 4.

4. Ordóñez, *La bestia anda suelta*, 100.

5. Even though the most logical translation is "little joke," a *chascarrillo* is not really a joke, a *chiste*, in Spanish. The *Diccionario de la Real Academia* defines the term as an "anécdota ligera y picante" (light and racy anecdote) and as a "cuentecillo agudo o frase de sentido equívoco y gracioso" (witty short story or phrase with an equivocal and funny meaning). Neither an "anecdote" nor a "short story" or "phrase," *Justino*, in fact, cannot be described with this hard-to-translate term. The term, rather than describing the movie, brands it, makes it "local" or, again, slightly untranslatable.

6. Buse, Triana-Toribio, and Willis, *The Cinema of Álex de la Iglesia*, 34.

7. Triana-Toribio, *Spanish National Cinema*, 113–14.

8. Ibid., 117.

9. Ibid., 132.

10. D'Lugo, "The Geopolitical Aesthetics."

11. See also Besas, "Financial Structure"; and Rimbau, "La 'década socialista.'"

12. D'Lugo, "The Geopolitical Aesthetics," 78.

13. Ibid.

14. See Harvey, *Hybrids of Modernity*.

15. Ibid., 93.

16. Moreiras Menor, *Cultura herida*, 273.

17. "El orígen de mi cine es Tudela."

18. Spitz, "The New Spain," 34.

19. Vitali and Willemen, *Theorizing National Cinema*, 16.

20. Ibid.

21. See McKinney, "Violence."

22. The other two movies are *Matías, juez de línea* (1996) and *Atilano, presidente* (1998). They were both received very unfavorably by the critics. Before *Justino*, between 1980 and 1990, the tandem Luis Guridi and Santiago Aguilar "perpetrated" (as they put it) thirty shorts in super-8 and super-6 in a 35 mm format.

23. All quotes from the directors are from their commentary in the DVD edition of the movie.

24. The aforementioned *Matador* is the story of two serial killers. *El bosque del lobo* (*The Wolf's Forest*) (Pedro Olea, 1970) could be the only other forerunner for *Justino*. The serial killer movie, in its "modern" tradition, has in fact been recognized as an "American genre" (i.e., from the United States). Films as different as *Henry, Portrait of a Serial Killer* (John McNaughton, 1986) and *The Silence of the Lambs* (Jonathan Demme, 1991) constitute part of this "national" corpus of serial killers. For an excellent introduction on the topic, although restricted to serial killers driven by sexual impulses, see Cettl, *Serial Killer Cinema*. For a more comprehensive study of the serial killer figure focused on US cultural production, see Simpson, *Psycho Paths*.

Afterlaughter

1. Cavell, *The Claim of Reason*, 16.

Bibliography

Acevedo-Muñoz, Ernesto R. *Pedro Almodóvar*. London: British Film Institute, 2007.

Allison, Mark. *A Spanish Labyrinth: The Films of Pedro Almodóvar*. London: I. B. Tauris, 2001.

Altman, Rick. *Film/Genre*. London: BFI Publishing, 1999.

Anderson, Benedict. *Imagined Communities: Reflections on the Origin and Spread of Nationalism*. Rev. and extended ed. London: Verso, 1991.

Appadurai, Arjun. *Modernity at Large: Cultural Dimensions of Globalization*. Minneapolis: University of Minnesota Press, 1996.

Aranda, Francisco. *Luis Buñuel: Biografía crítica*. Barcelona: Lumen, 1969.

Bakhtin, M. M. [Mikhail Mikhailovich]. *Rabelais and His World*. Bloomington: Indiana University Press, 1984.

Bauman, Zygmunt. *Consuming Life*. Cambridge: Polity Press, 2007.

Bazin, André. *The Cinema of Cruelty: From Buñuel to Hitchcock*. New York: Seaver Books, 1982.

Beauvoir, Simone de. *La Vieillesse*. Paris: Gallimard, 1970.

Beckett, Samuel. *Watt*. Paris: Olympia Press, 1953.

Benet, Vicente José. "La última voluntad del verdugo." In *"El verdugo"—"Le Bourreau" de Luis García Berlanga: En homage à Ricardo Muñoz Suay*, edited by Annie Bussière-Perrin and Vicente Sánchez-Biosca, 41–50. Co-textes 36. Montpellier: Centre d'études et de recherches sociocritiques, 1997.

Berthier, Nancy. "Arret sur image (autour d'un plan d'Elverdugo)." In *"El verdugo"— "Le Bourreau" de Luis García Berlanga: En homage à Ricardo Muñoz Suay*, edited by Annie Bussière-Perrin and Vicente Sánchez-Biosca, 99–116. Co-textes 36. Montpellier: Centre d'études et de recherches sociocritiques, 1997.

Besas, Peter. "Financial Structure." In *Refiguring Spain: Cinema, Media, Representation*, edited by Marsha Kinder, 241–59. Durham, NC: Duke University Press, 1997.

Bordwell, David. *On the History of Film Style*. Cambridge, MA: Harvard University Press, 1997.

Borges, Jorge Luis. *Other Inquisitions, 1937–1952*. Translated by Ruth L. C. Simms. Austin: University of Texas Press, 1984.

Breton, André, and Mark Polizzotti. *Anthology of Black Humor*. San Francisco: Monroe, 1997.

Browne, Nick. "The Spectator-in-the-Text: The Rhetoric of *Stagecoach*." In *Film Theory and Criticism: Introductory Readings*, edited by Leo Braudy and Marshall Cohen, 148–63. New York: Oxford University Press, 1999.

Buse, Peter, Nuria Triana-Toribio, and Andy Willis. *The Cinema of Álex de la Iglesia*. Manchester: Manchester University Press, 2007.

Bussière-Perrin, Annie, and Vicente Sánchez-Biosca, eds. *"El verdugo"—"Le Bourreau" de Luis García Berlanga: En homage à Ricardo Muñoz Suay*. Co-textes 36. Montpellier: Centre d'études et de recherches sociocritiques, 1997.

Butler, Judith, Ernesto Laclau, and Slavoj Žižek. *Contingency, Hegemony, Universality: Contemporary Dialogues on the Left*. New York: Verso, 2000.

Camporesi, Valeria. *Para grandes y chicos: Un cine para los españoles, 1940–1990*. Madrid: Turfan, 1994.

Cañeque, Carlos, and Maite Grau. *¡Bienvenido, Mr. Berlanga!* Barcelona: Destino, 1993.

Carr, Raymond, and Juan Pablo Fusi. *España, de la dictadura a la democracia*. Barcelona: Plantea, 1979.

Castle, Terry. *Masquerade and Civilization: The Carnivalesque in Eighteenth-Century English Culture and Fiction*. Stanford, CA: Stanford University Press, 1986.

Cavell, Stanley. *The Claim of Reason: Wittgenstein, Skepticism, Morality and Tragedy*. Oxford: Oxford University Press, 1982.

———. *Pursuits of Happiness: The Hollywood Comedy of Remarriage*. Cambridge, MA: Harvard University Press, 1981.

———. *Themes out of School: Effects and Causes*. San Francisco: North Point Press, 1984.

———. *The World Viewed: Reflections on the Ontology of Film*. Cambridge, MA: Harvard University Press, 1979.

Cawelti, John. *The Six-Gun Mystique*. Bowling Green: Popular Press, 1985.

Cerdán, Josetxo. "España, fin de milenio: Sobre *El día de la bestia* (Álex de la Iglesia, 1995)." In *La historia a través del cine: Transición y consolidación democrática en España*, edited by Rafael Ruzafa, 235–56. Bilbao: Servicio editorial de la Universidad del País Vasco, 2004.

Cettl, Robert. *Serial Killer Cinema: An Analytical Filmography with an Introduction*. Jefferson, NC: McFarland, 2003.

Chakrabarty, Dispesh. *Provincializing Europe: Postcolonial Thought and Historical Difference*. Princeton, NJ: Princeton University Press, 2007.

Conley, Tom. "Viridiana Coca Cola." In *Burning Darkness: A Half Century of Spanish Cinema*, edited by Joan Ramon Resina and Andrés Lema-Hincapié, 43–60. Albany: State University of New York Press, 2008.

Crary, Jonathan. *Techniques of the Observer: On Vision and Modernity in the Nineteenth Century*. Cambridge, MA: MIT Press, 1990.

Critchley, Simon. *On Humour*. London: Routledge, 2002.

Crofts, Stephen. "Reconceptualizing National Cinema/s." In *Film and Nationalism*, edited by Alan Williams, 25–51. New Brunswick, NJ: Rutgers University Press, 2002.

Crumbaugh, Justin. *Destination Dictatorship: The Spectacle of Spain's Tourist Boom and the Reinvention of Difference.* Albany: State University of New York Press, 2009.

Deleuze, Gilles. *Cinema 1: The Movement-Image.* Minneapolis: University of Minnesota Press, 1986.

Deleuze, Gilles, and Félix Guattari. *Anti-Oedipus: Capitalism and Schizophrenia.* Minneapolis: University of Minnesota Press, 1983.

De Riquer i Permayer, Borja. "Social and Economic Change in a Climate of Political Immobilism." In *Spanish Cultural Studies: An Introduction; The Struggle for Modernity*, edited by Helen Graham and Jo Labanyi, 259–71. Oxford: Oxford University Press, 1995.

D'Lugo, Marvin. "The Geopolitical Aesthetic in Recent Spanish Films." *Post Script: Essays in Film and the Humanities* 21.2 (2002): 78–89.

———. *Pedro Almodóvar.* Urbana: University of Illinois Press, 2006.

Durgnat, Raymond. *The Crazy Mirror: Hollywood Comedy and the American Image.* New York: Dell, 1972.

Egea, Juan F. "El desencanto: La mirada del padre y las lecturas de la transición." *Symposium* 58.2 (2004): 79–92.

"El orígen de mi cine es Tudela: Entrevista a Alex de la Iglesia." *Tudeocio*, November 29, 2011. http://www.tudeocio.com/index.php/cultura/cine/151-alex.html.

English, James. *Comic Transactions: Literature, Humor, and the Politics of Community in Twentieth-Century Britain.* Ithaca, NY: Cornell University Press, 1994.

Epps, Brad. "Blind Shots and Backward Glances: Reviewing *Matador* and *Labyrinth of Passion*." In *All about Almodóvar: A Passion for Cinema*, edited by Brad Epps and Despina Kakoudaki, 295–338. Minneapolis: University of Minnesota Press, 2009.

———. "Figuring Hysteria: Disorder and Desire in Three Films of Pedro Almodóvar." In *Post-Franco, Postmodern: The Films of Pedro Almodóvar*, edited by Kathleen M. Vernon and Barbara B. Morris, 99–124. Westport, CT: Greenwood Press, 1995.

Epps, Brad, and Despina Kakoudaki, eds. *All about Almodóvar: A Passion for Cinema.* Minneapolis: University of Minnesota Press, 2009.

———. "Approaching Almodóvar." In *All about Almodóvar: A Passion for Cinema*, edited by Brad Epps and Despina Kakoudaki, 1–34. Minneapolis: University of Minnesota Press, 2009.

Escudero, Javier. "Rosa Montero y Pedro Almodóvar: Miseria y estilización de la Movida Madrileña." *Arizona Journal of Hispanic Cultural Studies* 2 (1998): 147–61.

Esteve Secall, Rafael, and Rafael Fuentes García. *Economía, historia e instituciones del turismo en España.* Madrid: Pirámide, 2000.

Evans, Peter William. *The Films of Luis Buñuel: Subjectivity and Desire.* Oxford: Oxford University Press, 1995.

Faulkner, Sally. *A Cinema of Contradiction: Spanish Film in the 1960s.* Edinburgh: Edinburgh University Press, 2006.

Feher-Gurewich, Judith. "A Lacanian Approach to the Logic of Perversion." In *The

Cambridge Companion to Lacan, edited by Jean-Michel Rabaté, 191–207. Cambridge: Cambridge University Press, 2003.

Fernán-Gómez, Fernando. *El tiempo amarillo: Memorias*. Madrid: Debate, 1990.

Franco, Jess. *Bienvenido, Mister Cagada: Memorias caóticas de Luis García Berlanga*. Madrid: Aguilar, 2005.

Freud, Sigmund. *Three Essays on the Theory of Sexuality*. Edited by James Strachey. New York: Basic Books, 1975.

Frye, Northrop. *Anatomy of Criticism: Four Essays*. Princeton, NJ: Princeton University Press, 1957.

Fuentes, Víctor. *Buñuel: Cine y literatura*. Barcelona: Salvat, 1989.

García Canclini, Néstor. *Hybrid Cultures: Strategies for Entering and Leaving Modernity*. Minneapolis: University of Minnesota Press, 1989.

Garlinger, Patrick Paul, and Rosi H. Song. "Camp: What's Spain to Do with It?" *Journal of Spanish Cultural Studies* 5.1 (2004): 3–11.

Gilroy, Paul. *Small Acts: Thoughts on the Politics of Black Cultures*. London: Serpent's Tail, 1993.

Gledhill, Christine. "Rethinking Genre." In *Reinventing Film Studies*, edited by Linda Williams and Christine Gledhill, 221–43. London: Arnold, 2000.

Gómez Rufo, Antonio. *Berlanga: Confidencias de un cineasta*. Madrid: Ediciones JC, 2000.

———. *Berlanga contra el poder y la gloria*. Madrid: Ediciones Temas de Hoy, 1990.

Graham, Helen, and Jo Labanyi, eds. *Spanish Cultural Studies: An Introduction; The Struggle for Modernity*. Oxford: Oxford University Press, 1995.

Grant, Barry Keith, ed. *Film Genre Reader*. Austin: University of Texas Press, 1986.

Gubern, Román. *La censura: Función política y ordenamiento jurídico bajo el franquismo (1936–1975)*. Barcelona: Península, 1981.

Gunning, Tom. "Hitchcock and the Picture in the Frame." *New England Review* 28.3 (2007): 14–31.

———. "Response to Pie and Chase." In *Classical Hollywood Comedy*, edited by Kristine Brunovska Karnick and Henry Jenkins, 120–22. London: Routledge, 1995.

Haro Ibars, Eduardo. "La droga mata." *Ozono* 6.37 (1978): 7–10.

Harvey, Penelope. *Hybrids of Modernity: Anthropology, the Nation State and the Universal Exhibition*. London: Routledge, 1996.

Haug, Wolfgang Fritz. *Critique of Commodity Aesthetics*. Minneapolis: University of Minnesota Press, 1986.

Higginbotham, Virginia. *Spanish Film under Franco*. Austin: University of Texas Press, 1988.

Hillier, Jim, ed. *Cahiers du Cinéma: The 1950s; Neo-Realism, Hollywood, New Wave*. Cambridge, MA: Harvard University Press, 1985.

Hopewell, John. *Out of the Past: Spanish Cinema after Franco*. London: BFI Books, 1986.

Jameson, Fredric. *Signatures of the Visible*. London: Routledge, 1990.

Kinder, Marsha. *Blood Cinema: The Reconstruction of National Identity in Spain*. Berkeley: University of California Press, 1993.

Kovács, András Bálint. *Screening Modernism: European Art Cinema, 1950–1980.* Chicago: University of Chicago Press, 2007.

Kracauer, Siegfried. *Theory of Film: The Redemption of Physical Reality.* Princeton, NJ: Princeton University Press, 1997.

Labanyi, Jo. "Memory and Modernity in Democratic Spain: The Difficulty of Coming to Terms with the Spanish Civil War." *Poetics Today* 28.1 (Spring 2007): 89–116.

Labrador Méndez, Germán. *Letras arrebatadas: Poesía y química en la Transición española.* Madrid: Devenir Ensayo, 2009.

Lakoff, George. *Women, Fire, and Dangerous Things.* Chicago: University of Chicago Press, 1990.

Leach, Jim. *British Film.* Cambridge: Cambridge University Press, 2004.

Llinás, Franscesc. "*El verdugo*: Algunos aspectos sobre la puesta en escena berlanguiana." In *Berlanga*, edited by Julio Pérez Perucha, 32–51. Valencia: Ayuntamiento de Valencia, 1981.

López Villegas, Manuel, and Luis Buñuel. *Escritos de Luis Buñuel.* Madrid: Editorial Páginas de Espuma, 2000.

Losilla, Carlos. "La llamada del relato." In *"El verdugo"—"Le Bourreau" de Luis García Berlanga: En homage à Ricardo Muñoz Suay*, edited by Annie Bussière-Perrin and Vicente Sánchez-Biosca, 99–116. Co-textes 36. Montpellier: Centre d'études et de recherches sociocritiques, 1997.

Lyon, John. *The Theatre of Valle-Inclán.* Cambridge: Cambridge University Press, 1983.

MacCandell, Dean. *The Tourist: A New Theory of the Leisure Class.* Berkeley: University of California Press, 1999.

Mandrell, James. "Sense and Sensibility: Or Latent Heterosexuality and *Labyrinth of Passions*." In *Post-Franco, Postmodern: The Films of Pedro Almodóvar*, edited by Kathleen M. Vernon and Barbara B. Morris, 41–57. Westport, CT: Greenwood Press, 1995.

Marí, Jorge. "La Movida como debate." *Arizona Journal of Hispanic Cultural Studies* 13 (2009): 127–41.

Marsh, Steven. *Popular Spanish Film under Franco: Comedy and the Weakening of the State.* New York: Palgrave Macmillan, 2006.

Martín, Annabel. *La gramática de la felicidad: Relecturas franquistas y posmodernas del melodrama.* Madrid: Ediciones Libertarias, 2005.

Martín-Santos, Luis. *Tiempo de silencio.* Barcelona: Editorial Seix Barral, 1981.

McKinney, Devin. "Violence: The Strong and the Weak." *Film Quarterly* 46.4 (Summer 1993): 16–22.

Medhurst, Andy. "Heart of Farce: Almodóvar's Comic Complexities." In *All about Almodóvar: A Passion for Cinema*, edited by Brad Epps and Despina Kakoudaki, 118–38. Minneapolis: University of Minnesota Press, 2009.

————. *A Popular Joke: Popular Comedy and English Cultural Identities.* London: Routledge, 2007.

Medina, Alberto. *Exorcismos de la memoria: Poéticas y políticas de la melancolía en la España de la transición.* Madrid: Ediciones Libertarias, 2001.

Miller, D. A. "Hitchcock's Hidden Pleasures." *Critical Inquiry* 37 (Autumn 2010): 106–30.

Mira Nouselles, Alberto. *The Cinema of Spain and Portugal*. London: Wallflower, 2005.

Morán, Gregorio. *El precio de la transición*. Barcelona: Planeta, 1991.

Moreiras Menor, Cristina. *Cultura herida: Literatura y cine en la España democrática*. Madrid: Ediciones Libertarias, 2002.

Mulvey, Laura. "Afterthoughts on 'Visual Pleasure and Narrative Cinema' Inspired by King Vidor's *Duel in the Sun* (1946)." In *Feminist Film Theory: A Reader*, edited by Sue Thornham, 122–30. New York: New York University Press, 1999.

———. "Visual Pleasure and Narrative Cinema." In *Feminisms: An Anthology of Literary Theory and Criticism*, edited by Robyn R. Warhol and Diane Price Herndl, 438–48. New Brunswick, NJ: Rutgers University Press, 1997.

Neale, Steve. *Genre and Hollywood*. London: Routledge, 2000.

Nieto Ferrando, Jorge. *Cine en papel: Cultura y crítica cinematográfica en España, 1939–1962*. Valencia: Generalitat Valenciana, Instituto Valencià de Cinematografia Ricardo Muñoz Suay, 2009.

Noyes, Dorothy. "*La Maja Vestida*: Dress as Resistance to Enlightenment in Late-18th-Century Madrid." *Journal of American Folklore* 111.440 (1998): 197–217.

O'Connor, Brian, ed. *The Adorno Reader*. Oxford: Blackwell, 2000.

O'Neill, Patrick. "The Comedy of Entropy: The Contexts of Black Humour." *Canadian Review of Comparative Literature* 10.2 (June 1983): 145–66.

Ordóñez, Marcos. *La bestia anda suelta: ¡Álex de la Iglesia lo cuenta todo!* Barcelona: Glénat, 1997.

Orr, John. *Hitchcock and Twentieth-Century Cinema*. New York: Wallflower, 2005.

Passolini, Pier Paolo. *Heretical Empiricism*. Edited by Louise K. Barnett. Bloomington: Indiana University Press, 1988.

Perales, Francisco. *Luis García Berlanga*. Madrid: Cátedra, 1997.

Pérez Rubio, Pablo, and Javier Hernández Ruiz. *Escritos sobre cine español: Tradición y géneros populares*. Zaragoza: Institución Fernando el Católico, 2011.

Pérez-Sánchez, Gema. *Queer Transitions in Contemporary Spanish Culture: From Franco to La Movida*. New York: State University of New York Press, 2007.

Pérez Turrent, Tomás, and José de la Colina. *Luis Buñuel: Prohibido asomarse al interior*. Mexico City: Planeta, 1986.

Prego, Victoria. *Así se hizo la transición*. Barcelona: Plaza & Janés Editores, 1995.

Quintana, Ángel. "Falsa luna de miel en Mallorca o el espejismo de la modernidad en el cine español." In *"El verdugo"—"Le Bourreau" de Luis García Berlanga: En homage à Ricardo Muñoz Suay*, edited by Annie Bussière-Perrin and Vicente Sánchez-Biosca, 67–78. Co-textes 36. Montpellier: Centre d'études et de recherches sociocritiques, 1997.

Rhomer, Eric, and Claude Chabrol. *Hitchcock*. Paris: Éditions Universitaires, 1957.

Rimbau, Esteve. "La 'década socialista' (1982–1992)." In *Historia del cine español*, edited by Román Gubern et al., 399–447. Madrid: Cátedra, 2009.

Ríos Carratalá, Juan A. *Lo sainetesco en el cine español*. Alicante: Universidad de Alicante, 1997.

Rothman, William. *Hitchcock: The Murderous Gaze.* Cambridge, MA: Harvard University Press, 1982.

Russell, Dominique. "Buñuel: The Gag, the Auteur." *Canadian Journal of Film Studies/ Revue canadienne d'études cinématographiques* 18.2 (2009): 45–65.

Sánchez, Bernardo, ed. *Otra vuelta en el cochecito.* Logroño: Ayuntamiento de Logroño, 1991.

Sánchez-Biosca, Vicente. "Un realismo a la española: *El Verdugo* entre humor negro y modernidad." In *"El verdugo"—"Le Bourreau" de Luis García Berlanga: En homage à Ricardo Muñoz Suay,* edited by Annie Bussière-Perrin and Vicente Sánchez-Biosca, 79–90. Co-textes 36. Montpellier: Centre d'études et de recherches sociocritiques, 1997.

———. *Viridiana: Estudio crítico.* Madrid: Paidós, 1999.

Sandro, Paul. *Diversions of Pleasure: Luis Buñuel and the Crises of Desire.* Columbus: Ohio State University Press, 1987.

San Miguel, Santiago, and Víctor Erice. "Rafael Azcona: Iniciador de una nueva corriente cinematográfica." *Nuestro cine* 4 (1962): 3–7.

Sastre, Alfonso. *Anatomía del realismo.* Barcelona: Editorial Seix Barral, 1965.

Schatz, Thomas. *Hollywood Genres: Formulas, Filmmaking, and the Studio System.* New York: Random House, 1981.

Seguin, Jean-Claude. "Le plan pluriel dans *El Verdugo.*" In *"El verdugo"—"Le Bourreau" de Luis García Berlanga: En homage à Ricardo Muñoz Suay,* edited by Annie Bussière-Perrin and Vicente Sánchez-Biosca, 99–116. Co-textes 36. Montpellier: Centre d'études et de recherches sociocritiques, 1997.

Simpson, Philip L. *Psycho Paths: Tracking the Serial Killer through Contemporary American Film and Fiction.* Carbondale: Southern Illinois University Press, 2000.

Smith, Paul Julian. *Desire Unlimited: The Cinema of Pedro Almodóvar.* London: Verso, 2000.

Song, Rosi, and William Nichols. "¿El futuro ya estuvo aquí?" *Arizona Journal of Hispanic Cultural Studies* 13 (2009): 105–11.

Spitz, Bob. "The New Spain." *Rolling Stone,* June 6, 1985, 33–34.

Stam, Robert. *Subversive Pleasures: Bakhtin, Cultural Criticism, and Film.* Baltimore, MD: Johns Hopkins University Press, 1989.

Stapell, Hamilton. "Just a Teardrop in the Rain? The Movida Madrileña and Democratic Identity Formation in the Capital, 1979–1986." *Bulletin of Spanish Studies* 86.3 (2009): 345–69.

Steele, Valerie. *The Corset: A Cultural History.* New Haven, CT: Yale University Press, 2001.

Torrecilla, Jesús. *España exótica: La formación de la imagen española moderna.* Boulder: Society of Spanish and Spanish-American Studies, 2004.

———. "La modernización de la imagen exótica de España en *Carmen,* de Saura." *Anales de la literatura española contemporánea* 26.1 (2001): 337–56.

Torreiro, Casimiro. "¿Una dictadura liberal? (1962–1969)." In *Historia del cine español,* edited by Román Gubern et al., 295–340. Madrid: Cátedra, 2009.

Triana-Toribio, Nuria. "A Punk Called Pedro: La Movida in the Films of Pedro Almodóvar." In *Contemporary Spanish Cultural Studies*, edited by Jordan Barry and Rikki Morgan-Tamosunas, 274–82. London: Arnold, 2000.

———. *Spanish National Cinema.* London: Routledge, 2003.

Truffaut, François. *Hitchcock.* Rev. ed. New York: Simon & Schuster, 1984.

Tubau, Iván. *Hollywood en Argüelles: Cine americano y crítica española.* Barcelona: Publicacions i Edicions de la Universitat de Barcelona, 1984.

Tudor, Andrew. *Theories of Film.* New York: Viking, 1974.

Tussell, Javier. *La transición española: La recuperación de las libertades.* Madrid: Historia 16, 1997.

Usó, Juan Carlos. *Drogas y cultura de masas (España 1855–1995).* Madrid: Taurus, 1996.

Valis, Noël Maureen. *The Culture of Cursilería: Bad Taste, Kitsch, and Class in Modern Spain.* Durham, NC: Duke University Press, 2002.

Valle-Inclán, Ramón María del. *Luces de Bohemia.* Madrid: Espasa-Calpe, 1979.

Veblen, Thorstein. *The Theory of the Leisure Class.* 1899. Rpr., Durham, NC: Duke University Press, 2012.

Vidal, Nuria. *El cine de Pedro Almodóvar.* Barcelona: Destino, 1988.

Vilarós, Teresa. *El mono del desencanto: Una crítica cultural de la transición española (1973–1993).* Madrid: Siglo XXI, 1998.

Vitali, Valentina, and Paul Willemen. *Theorizing National Cinema.* London: British Film Institute, 2006.

Wittgenstein, Ludwig. *Philosophical Investigations.* Translated by G. E. M. Anscombe. New York: Prentice-Hall, 1958.

Wood, Robin. *Hitchcock's Films.* Rev. ed. New York: Columbia University Press, 2002.

Woods Peiró, Eva. *White Gypsies: Race and Stardom in Spanish Musical Films.* Minneapolis: University of Minnesota Press, 2012.

Yarza, Alejandro. *Un caníbal en Madrid: La sensibilidad camp y el reciclaje de la historia en el cine de Pedro Almodóvar.* Madrid: Libertarias, 1999.

Žižek, Slavoj. *Enjoy Your Symptom! Jacques Lacan in Hollywood and Out.* London: Routledge, 2001.

———. *Looking Awry: An Introduction to Jacques Lacan through Popular Culture.* Cambridge, MA: MIT Press, 1992.

———. *The Ticklish Subject.* London: Verso, 1999.

Zunzunegui, Santos. *Los felices sesenta: Aventuras y desventuras del cine español, 1959–1971.* Barcelona: Paidós, 2005.

———. *Paisajes de la forma.* Madrid: Cátedra, 1994.

Index